PAYMENT SYSTEMS AND PRODUCTIVITY

PAYMENT SYSTEMS AND PRODUCTIVITY

Angela M. Bowey and Richard Thorpe
with Phil Hellier

Foreword by A. W. J. Thomson

Macmillan Education

ISBN 978-1-349-18108-7   ISBN 978-1-349-18106-3 (eBook)
DOI 10.1007/978-1-349-18106-3

© Angela M. Bowey and Richard Thorpe 1986
Softcover reprint of the hardcover 1st edition 1986

All rights reserved. For information, write:
St. Martin's Press, Inc., 175 Fifth Avenue, New York, NY 10010
Printed in Great Britain
Published in the United Kingdom by The Macmillan Press Ltd.
First published in the United States of America in 1986.

ISBN 978-0-312-59925-6

Library of Congress Cataloging in Publication Data.
Bowey, Angela.
Payment systems and productivity.
Bibliography: p.
Includes index.
1. Wage payment systems. 2. Wages and labor
productivity. 3. Incentives in industry. I. Thorpe,
Richard, 1951–   . II. Hellier, Phil. III. Title.
HD4926.B72   1985   658.3'225   85–8360
ISBN 978-0-312-59925-6

Contents

Foreword by A. W. J. Thomson   vii
List of Tables   ix
List of Figures   xi
List of Appendices   xiii
Acknowledgements   xv

Preface

1	INTRODUCTION	1
2	PAYMENT SYSTEMS AND PERFORMANCE IMPROVEMENT	5
3	PRODUCTIVITY MEASUREMENT	36
4	PAYMENT SCHEME DECISION CHOICES	66
5	PAYMENT SCHEME PERFORMANCE	91
6	PAYMENT SCHEME PROCESSES	149
7	DEGENERATION OF PAYMENT SYSTEMS	215
8	CONCLUSIONS	254

APPENDICES   262
References   301
Subject Index   310
Name Index   313

Foreword

Pay as an issue is rarely far from the national consciousness. It is the issue over which many of our social conflicts are fought, our class divisions recognised, our personal self-esteem gratified or diminished. Yet almost all of the national consciousness of pay relates to its level, usually in comparison with other people or groups. Little public attention is given to the operation of payments systems. This is seen as the realm of the technical specialist, concerned with wage administration, work study or job evaluation, not in themselves functions which are redolent of grand principles or passions. Yet in terms of the provision of job satisfaction, of productivity, of the elements of motivation at work, pay systems are probably at least as important as the level of pay, and they assuredly do generate a great deal of low level conflict. It is therefore highly desirable for the importance of payment systems to be identified and researched, and books such as the present can add much more to our knowledge of the real operation of industry than the frequent pontification in print about the fairness or otherwise of a particular group's comparative pay.

The fact is that payment systems are a much maligned and underestimated subject of analysis. The reason for this is not only that it is not an outwardly exciting area of analysis, but also because it is a very complex one, and indeed it is an area which can all too easily suffer from superficiality. The tragedy of too many proponents of particular payment systems is that they claim too much for their particular system in terms of motivation, productivity enhancement and felt fairness so that they encourage a shift from over-enthusiasm to cynicism when all does not go well. It is certainly the case that pay systems often do produce side effects which tend to become more important as time goes on, so that there is a growth in the number of appeals or the amount of manipulation or the cost. Indeed there is a pervasive view amongst personnel managers that there is a built-in decay factor in payments systems and that they need replacing after perhaps five years. The result is resigned acceptance of a cyclical change, with an eye kept open for the next fashion in payments systems. The problem with this approach is that it tends to detach the payments system from the broader goals and operations of the organisation and exacerbate the problem of decay. It is not surprising to learn from a recent European-wide survey of employees' views of their company's management that British managements score least well in the areas of pay and communications.

It may be impossible to avoid these problems of decay and renewal but one important step in doing so is to achieve a better understanding of the nature of payments systems. This is why books such as this one by Angela Bowey and Richard Thorpe are to be greatly welcomed. They have a wealth of experience of investigating pay issues over many years and recently carried out a very substantial project which is used to learn lessons of how pay systems should be conceived, introduced and operated. They emphasise that the way in which this process is carried out is as important as the substantive dimensions of the system, that time spent in reconnaissance is time well spent, that the system should be integrated into organisational policy rather than being taken off the peg and that consultation and communications are the key to acceptability. Equally practically, they examine the effectiveness of different types of scheme, take up the often vexed issue of productivity measurement, and discuss the process of system design. This is the most comprehensive book of its kind and it deserves a wide readership.

A. W. J. Thomson
Dean
Scottish Business School

List of Tables

2.1	Percentage of employees in Britain receiving incentive payments	6
2.2	Types of incentive bonus schemes in the UK, 1968–77	25
2.3	Calculating added value	26
2.4	Simple example of an added value bonus scheme scheme calculation	28
2.5	Added value bonus scheme calculation	29
2.6	A simple example of a Scanlon plan	30
2.7	Aspects of the effort–reward bargain	34
3.1	Uses of productivity measurement at the level of the firm	38
3.2	Alternative perspectives and appropriate measures for productivity/performance	54
4.1	Senior managers' priorities for organisation success and payment scheme objectives	80
4.2	Most common interviewee perceptions of payment scheme objectives	81
4.3	Questionnaire responses indicating each payment scheme objective	84
4.4	Payment scheme objectives as indicated by men and women in joint white collar or blue collar payment schemes	86
4.5	Blue and white collar employees' and supervisors' job satisfaction requirements	87
5.1	Summary of dates of negotiation and implementation of the schemes in the survey	93
5.2	Comparison of objectives and achievements: a management evaluation	101
5.3	Priorities for organisation success compared with the improvements achieved by payment schemes (From management questionnaire responses)	103
5.4	Anticipated reductions in manpower: questionnaire responses (Bowey, 1980)	104
5.5	Organisations that experience labour force changes as a result of the payment scheme (Bowey, 1980)	105
5.6	Selected performance variables	109
5.7	Composite performance indices (questionnaire and interview responses)	110
5.8	Correlation coefficients between selected scheme effects and selected features of the schemes	112
5.9	Payment scheme classification based on inherent motivational assumptions	114
5.10	Payment scheme classification based on mechanics of operation	115

List of Tables

5.11	Correlation coefficients between four types of schemes and selected independent performance variables	116
5.12	Correlation coefficients between four types of scheme and composite performance indices	118
5.13	Payment scheme classification based on cluster analysis	120
5.14	Correlation coefficients between six cluster types and composite performance indices	121
5.15	Effects of contextual variables upon scheme type performance correlation coefficients	124
5.16	5th order partial correlation coefficients for type of payment scheme with performance variables	130
5.17	Variables which measure features of the organisation and its situation	132
5.18	Correlation coefficients between selected contextual features and selected independent performance variables	134
5.19	Associations between consultation and performance factors	138
5.20	Correlation coefficients between composite implementation indices and composite performance indices	140
5.21	Effects of contextual factors upon scheme implementation–performance correlation coefficients	141
6.1	Questions asked to determine the effect new schemes had on the way work is organised	161
6.2	Coalbridge Engineering Ltd: payment schemes, 1975–80	176
6.3	Coal output per year, 1970–76	195
6.4	Face incentive option	199
6.5	Output and bonus at Hillend Colliery	204
7.1	Stages of payment scheme effectiveness	216
7.2	Aspects of degeneration of payment systems in 6 organisations	226
7.3	Annual averages for bonus payments from old and new incentive schemes at Coalbridge	227
7.4	Coalbridge Engineering: shortfalls in target production hours – new product line	231
7.5	Group financial performance over 5 years	233

List of Figures

2.1	Types of financial incentive payment scheme	7
2.2	Actual recorded frequency of different effort scores	12
2.3	Motivation patterns of senior executives	18
2.4	Dimensions of participation	21
2.5	Pay norms and wage increases, 1965–82	24
2.6	Areas of activity which could contribute to improved performance	32
3.1	How manufacturing time is made up	41
3.2	Gold's hierarchy of performance ratios	44
3.3	Stages of organisational development	52
4.1	Determinist or positivist contingency theory	67
4.2	Simple model of motivation action by organisation members	68
4.3	Contingency model based on action theory	68
4.4	Positivist or deterministic model of contingency theory applied to payment systems	70
4.5	Normative model of contingency theory applied to payment systems	71
4.6	Key influences on payment system design	72
4.7	Alternative methods of assessing organisation performance	73
4.8	A normative contingency model of payment scheme design and implementation	79
5.1	Model of processes and factors influencing the outcome of a new incentive scheme	94
5.2	The analysis of payment scheme design as it affects performance	108
5.3	The analysis of contextual effects upon specific design–performance relationships	123
5.4	The analysis of context–performance relationships	132
5.5	The general analysis of context, implementation and performance relationships	139
6.1	Significant factors of incentive payment scheme success	149
6.2	The impact of contextual, design and implementation factors upon payment scheme performance	151
6.3	Normative contingency theory related to payment systems	152
6.4	The role of consultation in relation to objectives	154
6.5	Management bonus scheme perception	163
6.6	Employee bonus scheme perception	166
6.7	Model of the supervisor's dilemma	184
6.8	Modification and interpretation of policy in the main subsidiary company	187
6.9	The dynamics of payment scheme implementation	191

List of Figures

7.1	The degeneration process	22
7.2	Normal distribution of performance; no evidence of cross-booking	22
7.3	Performance skewed towards easy jobs; no evidence of cross-booking	22
7.4	Possible shape showing evidence of cross-booking	22
7.5	Coalbridge Engineering: comparison between times set by rate fixers (A), times claimed by employees (B), times eventually agreed after dispute (C), times achieved by the workforce after agreement (D) and times achieved during the period of dispute (E)	23
7.6	Coalbridge Engineering: earnings levels for skilled manual workers for 40 hours compared to pay norms in force at the time	23
7.7	Coalbridge Engineering: wage movements for three groups of employees, 1975–77	23
7.8	Government Engineering Workshop: average performance	23
7.9	Government Engineering Workshop: comparisons of total productive hours, standard hours of work produced and the time spent on measured work	23
7.10	Government Engineering Workshop: total man hours spent on measured work as a percentage of total productive hours (direct workers only)	24
7.11	Longshore Dock Company: performance figures	24
7.12	Domestic Appliance Ltd: performance figures	24
7.13	Hillend Colliery–national data: incentive pay per man-shift and overall output per man-shift	24
7.14	Latex Fabricators: value and volume of output per month, compared to the average performance (based on work measurement data)	24

List of Appendices

I	Details of the Study Reported in Chapters 4 and 5	262
II	Questionnaire on Incentives as Distributed to Employees and Senior Management	266
III	Construction of Composite Performance Indices	282
IV	Construction of Payment Scheme Implementation Indices	287
V	Sample Pages of Diaries	290
VI	Coalbridge Engineering: Calculation of Proposed Company Performance Related Payment Scheme	297

Acknowledgements

This book is based on research undertaken at the Pay and Rewards Research Centre, Strathclyde University and made possible by the funding of the Department of Employment, the Social Science Research Council (now the Economic and Social Research Council) and the University of Strathclyde, and the cooperation of over a thousand managers, shop stewards and shop floor employees who all gave their valuable time to answer questions and pass on their experiences.

Although the book is not solely concerned with that research project particular thanks should go to the other members of the research team who joined the project for various periods of time. Their contribution in both encouragement and ideas has to varying degrees been reflected in the text. Geoff Nichols was in charge of one of the diary studies and did much to pilot this technique for use later in the project; Fanny Mitchell undertook much of the essential administrative work as well as overseeing one in-depth study; David Gosnold was involved in the coding of data for the computer for its subsequent analysis; and Lawson Savery who joined the research during the data analysis stage assisted us with the retrieval and analysis of data.

During the research phase of the study we were fortunate in being joined at various times by researchers who gave us the benefit of their specialist knowledge. Bob Ferris, Head of the Department of Applied Economics at Footscray Institute of Technology, Australia, worked with us when the project was just beginning and made a substantial contribution to the research design and to the development of the questionnaires; Mark Franklin, Lecturer in the Department of Politics, Strathclyde University, advised us on the methods of data analysis and acted as consultant on problems of data management at various times during the project; Maggie Jordon, from the Survey Research Unit, Strathclyde University, contributed to the computer data analysis in the later stages of the project.

The project also received valuable assistance from many others from the patient content analysis coders – Marie Gosnold, Jane Bowey, and Christine Reid – to the whole generation of typists who saw the material develop: Fiona Avery, Jo Moyes, Irene Allison, Betty Mac-Farlane, Marriane Campbell and Ruth Hellier. Christine Reid from the Strathclyde Business School's Business Information Centre also provided us with a superb information service during both the research and the writing of this book.

Between the publication of our research report and the completion of this book the bulk of the secretarial and administrative work has fallen to May Leggate, to whom we are most grateful for her patience and continuing enthusiasm. We also thank Herbert Thorpe for his assistance in reading the proofs.

1 Introduction

Productivity has concerned managers, administrators and governments for many years and understandably so when one considers the wide differences in productive performance between individuals, companies and nations.

There have been many ways in which managers have sought to influence the productivity of their employees which include wage payment systems, efforts to reduce worker fatigue, improvements in human relations, changes in management style, better job design and job enrichment, participation and autonomous working groups. In spite of all the new techniques and theories, the incentive-based wage payment system continues to be widely used.

This book is written for managers, students of management, trade unionists and academics teaching in the field of motivation and reward who wish to better their understanding of the ways in which incentive payment systems influence employee and management behaviour and affect the productivity and performance of an organisation. Our hope is that this will lead to better decisions being taken about when and how such schemes should be introduced and how they should be designed and implemented.

The material is based on many years of research and advisory work on pay and productivity undertaken by ourselves and our colleagues, and in particular on a study of 63 organisations which introduced incentive payment schemes in the late 1970s at a time when many UK organisations were attempting to improve productivity by self-financing productivity schemes. Further work since that study has involved putting into practice the results and verifying the usefulness of the approach advocated.

There have been a number of studies of wage payment systems and their results are incorporated into our approach. Some of these have either been studies of existing schemes and others of the transition period during the introduction of a new scheme. The Strathclyde University study of 63 companies involved comparing a large number of schemes, all introduced at approximately the same time and studying the resultant processes of change in behaviour. The emphasis was placed on how the type of scheme adopted and the methods of design and implementation affected the success of the scheme over a period of time.

Previous studies (Roy, 1952; Mayo, 1949; Lupton, 1963) have provided a great deal of insight into some of the behaviour patterns which explain the failure of an incentive payment system to motivate higher performance. They have also provided important insights into the problems of people at work which can be caused by an inappropriate payment system. Many managers have seen an incentive payment scheme in operation where the employees concerned were working at very high performances and they believe that they will obtain the same benefits if they introduce such a scheme. Many managers still believe that so long as an incentive scheme is designed, maintained and 'operated' correctly, higher performances will follow automatically. They usually concede, however, that the benefits will last for a certain (unspecified) period before the system begins to 'decay'.

There has been little evidence available until now to disprove or support these beliefs. There existed a body of knowledge relating to the design of payment systems to suit a particular set of circumstances (Lupton and Gower, 1969; Lupton and Bowey, 1974), but there was still a gap in our knowledge about just what effects even an 'appropriate' scheme had on an organisation's performance both in the short term and the long term and what factors governed the measurable changes in productivity. This resulted in managers at local level and governments at national level making decisions when they were uncertain about the outcome.

This book endeavours to fill this gap. By using empirical research collected from a large number of British companies over a number of years, it examines the value of the previous contingency approach and casts new light on the importance of payment scheme design and implementation. It considers the value of participatory practices, giving original case evidence for their use. And for the first time, it provides a framework in which productivity measurement criteria can be examined and sets out the little understood processes of scheme degeneration and decay.

In Chapter 2 the main theories of motivation and payment are explained and reviewed. This is placed in the context of the many ways governments have sought to use pay to control and influence employees. This chapter cautions managers on a simplistic approach to effort and reward and gives research evidence of how incentive schemes designed to increase productivity can in some circumstances lead to the opposite result.

Chapter 3 tackles the important question of how to measure performance and productivity. It brings together a wide range of different approaches and highlights their advantages and shortcomings, assisting the manager to select an approach to measuring performance which is best suited to his particular organisation. It is useless to attempt to introduce an incentive payment system without linking it to appropriate and adequate measures of performance, and for this reason we recommended that payment system design starts with the measurement of productivity.

Chapter 4 deals with the decision choices faced by managers in the process of designing a payment system. It considers the importance of linking the objective of the payment system to the priority issues which it is important for the organisation to improve, and then tackles the difficult problem of converting objectives into an appropriate payment scheme design. It also considers ways of taking account of the employees for whom the scheme is intended, and the contingent factors in the organisation and its environment which may affect the outcome.

Chapter 5 considers the results of the major survey of payment systems results conducted at Strathclyde University and shows why some newly introduced schemes were successful and others were less so. On the whole the improvements in productivity achieved by these schemes were disappointing. A key factor in the degree of success was the manner in which the scheme had been designed and implemented. Careful attention is given in Chapter 5. to the importance of characteristics of the organisation and its environment (such as size, technology, market, etc.) as mediating factors between the type of payment scheme and the end results.

Chapter 6 sets out our interpretation of the results described in Chapter 5. It identifies the processes that are related to successful payment scheme performance and highlights the benefits to organisations of a participatory approach to payment scheme design. It links extensive consultation to measures of performance that are relevant to a company's priorities for success, to contingent, contextual and social variables and to the stimulation of trust, understanding and commitment amongst the workforce. These findings are reinforced by a detailed examination of three 'in-depth' case studies to illustrate how the process of involvement is associated with the success of an incentive scheme. The chapter ends with an account of one organisation which put into practice the approach we strongly recommend, and then describes the results they achieved.

Chapter 7 explains the little understood processes by which payment systems decay over time (that is the degeneration of the ratio of employees financial reward to measured performance/productivity). Detailed case examples are given of the ways in which different types of schemes performed over a three year period and these illustrate the types of dynamic processes which can occur. New insights are offered concerning scheme 'creep', degeneration and decay and the causes of these processes. Appropriate actions for responding to such situations are proposed.

Finally Chapter 8 summarises the main points made in the book and presents some useful guidelines for the practising manager on the application of today's state-of-the-art knowledge of payment system design and implementation.

2 Payment Systems and Performance Improvement

This chapter considers major theories about payment systems, employee motivation, and productivity found in the literature over the past 50 years and shows how these have evolved towards the current position and to the approach advocated in this book.

It may be useful, first of all, to consider the extent to which payment by results or incentive payment systems have been used in Britain. Table 2.1 shows the percentages of manual and non-manual workers to whom such schemes applied over the past 45 years. As can be seen, there was a gradual increase in the popularity of incentive schemes for men throughout this period, but the slight downward trend in the early 1970s was arrested in 1978, with increased interest in such schemes resulting largely from an incomes policy introduced by the Labour government of the day. This point will be considered again later. For female employees the trend was one of continual decline, except for a renewal of interest since 1977.

The picture in the United States was one of even greater decline in the coverage of incentives, to only about 30% of all US employees in the 1970s (McCormick, 1977).

PAYMENT SYSTEM DEVELOPMENTS

Going back to management practices and theories before 1940, we find that the predominant theory about employee motivation was the classical management approach, that since employees came to work to earn money, they would work better if they were given more money for better work. Incentive payment schemes were devised to reward extra work with extra pay, and great interest was shown in devising the best

TABLE 2.1 Percentage of employees in Britain receiving incentive payments

	1938	47	51	61		74	75	76	77	78	79	80	81	82	83
All industries and services															
Men	18	24	28	30	manual	41	41	38	37	42	44	42	44	45	47
	46	39	44	41	non-manual	8	7	8	7	11	13	12	18	17	19
Women					manual	34	31	31	30	32	34	32	32	32	34
	46	39	44	41	non-manual	3	3	3	4	6	8	7	12	13	14
Manufacturing industries only															
Non-manual men						8	9	9	8	15	18	20	23	20	22
Non-manual women						4	6	5	5	12	14	15	17	16	17

SOURCE *Ministry of Labour Gazette, and New Earnings Surveys, and McCormick (1977)*

way to relate the two. Various schemes were developed and introduced which produced a basic hourly rate of pay for rates of working up to some standard level, plus additional premium or bonus payments for faster rates of working, with 'gearing' of various kinds in the relation between bonus pay and rate of working. That is to say, in many of these schemes the relationship between pay and effort was geared away from a straight proportional relation, as illustrated in Figure 2.1.

With this theory that money provided the motivation to work, employers did not doubt that their workmen were doing their best to work as hard as they could. But they still observed differences in the productivity of different workers and of different factories, and concluded that some workers must be impeded in their efforts to work hard by factors beyond their control. The most likely factor was fatigue.

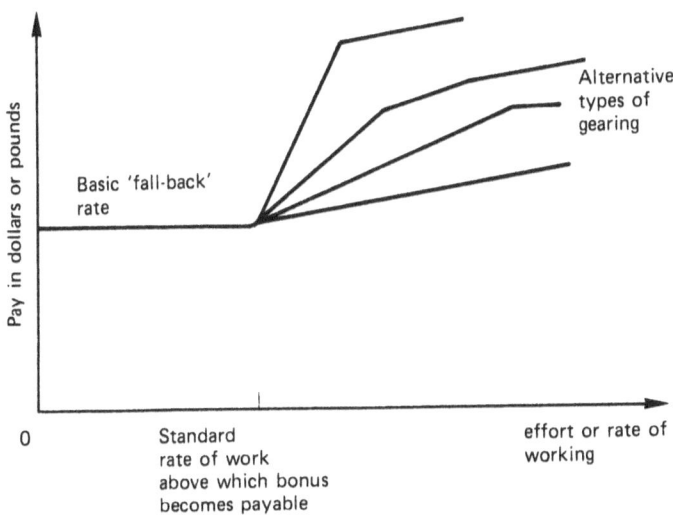

FIGURE 2.1 *Types of financial incentive payment scheme*

Interest then focused on ways of improving productivity by reducing the causes of worker fatigue. Studies were made of the effects of giving more frequent rest pauses, varying the temperature, the humidity, the lighting intensity, providing free meals, and so on.

Early studies in the 1920s indicated that they were on the right track. Elton Mayo and his colleagues from Harvard studied a Philadelphia textile mill where the company introduced more frequent rest periods, gave free meals and shortened the working day. The predominantly female labour force responded by improving their rates of working; and when the company took away the meals, the breaks, and returned to the former situation, they fell back to working to their former pace.

Mayo and his colleagues then set up a major series of studies at the Hawthorne works of the Western Electric Company to test scientifically what effect fatigue-inducing factors had on productivity, and to study worker behaviour in detail. The studies went on for almost ten years, and subsequently became so famous as to be part of the folk-lore of management, giving such terms as 'The Hawthorne Effect' to managers' day-to-day language (Landsberger, 1958). Their main finding was that relationships between people had a far greater effect on performance on the job than any of the fatigue-inducing factors they tested; and also a far greater effect than the financial incentives built into the company's payment system. In some of the experiments the working environment was changed drastically to assess how this influenced productivity (such as when the lighting was changed by small stages, being increased to a very high intensity and subsequently reduced to that of a moonlit night) and the productivity of the employees rose steadily through all the changes, due to the effect on morale of the new relationships established within the groups and between the researchers and the group (the Hawthorne Effect).

These results, and other evidence about employee behaviour in response to incentive bonus schemes (Roy, in Lupton 1972) led managers to reject current ways of improving productivity and turn to 'Human Relations' as the answer to the question 'How do I motivate my employees to work well?'.

Thousands of managers and supervisors were sent on training courses to learn the skills of being nice to their employees. During this period (the 1940s and 1950s) managers still believed that there could be *one* answer to the problem, and sought simple panaceas to guide their actions. Even today the great majority of managers in Britain, the United States, and other developed countries hold a belief that there is one best way to motivate employees to work well (whether they believe that one way is through financial incentives, good working environments, good human relations, enriched jobs, participation, or one of several other factors).

The theory of Human Relations Management held that conflict in the work situation was the cause of poor performance. To improve productivity a manager should concentrate on smoothing out all conflicts and establishing sound friendly relationships between himself and his staff and between the staff themselves. In some situations this works well; but not always. It would be futile for a manager to seek to improve productivity by asking about the wife and children of an employee whose colleagues had just been made redundant.

Many managers were led to make mistaken decisions on the basis of this theory about relationships. For example, in 1973, a manager of a small UK garment factory built a wall between two departments to reduce the arguments between their employees, only to find that productivity dropped rather than improved, because the conflict had been about the slow pace of work in one department which held up the efforts of the next department to make bonus earnings.

By the 1960s there was considerable confusion about the value of incentive bonus schemes and Human Relations Management, and a number of studies were conducted which indicated that the same management practice could be a resounding success in one organisation and a miserable failure in another.

For a time the proponents of each technique blamed the ineptness of application for these failures. Work study techniques with associated incentive bonus schemes would always work if they were put in 'properly', it was claimed. Human Relations would always work if done the 'proper' way. Again this is a standpoint still held by many managers today. But when faced with the evidence that improvements in productivity can be obtained with one technique in one situation and a different technique in another situation where the first technique did not work, it became clear that there could be no single panacea for motivating employees.

Joan Woodward (1958) was one of the first researchers to produce this kind of evidence, when she found that the most successful firms from each type of technology (small batch, mass production or continuous process) conformed closely to the average type of structure for that technology in terms of levels in the hierarchy, spans of control, ratio of industrial workers to staff etc. This work suggested that a company which wished to make itself successful should seek to match its structure to that which is appropriate to its technology.

Burns and Stalker (1961) made similar discoveries from their studies of textile mills and electronics factories in Britain at about the same time. They found that firms in the electronics industry operating with one kind of management system (characterised by loosely defined responsibilities and relationships, free communications and cooperation across hierarchical and divisional boundaries, which they termed

'Organic') were more successful than those operating with the alternative type of management system, which they termed 'Mechanistic' (characterised by clearly defined duties, responsibilities and authority, specified chains of command and structured channels of communication). And yet in the textile industry the reverse was true; the 'Mechanistic' firms were more successful than the 'Organic' firms. The major difference between textiles and electronics which Burns and Stalker identified as the reason for these results, was the higher rate of change and degree of uncertainty in the electronics industry and its market than there was for textiles. This rapid change and uncertainty was handled better by an organisation with a flexible structure, capable of learning and adapting in response to information and knowledge arising at any point within the organisation. Whereas in textiles this kind of 'Organic' system only resulted in time being wasted on unnecessary communications and conflict.

Just as the work of Woodward and Burns and Stalker showed that the principles of designing organisations for high effectiveness varied with the nature of the industry, its technology and environment, so the search for the key to high productivity reached the conclusion that factors which produced high productivity in one situation could be different from those contributing to high productivity in another.

One of the clearest demonstrations of this was in a television components factory in the North West of England, where Millward and Legge were asked to help the management to understand why some of the young ladies they employed responded well to the incentive bonus scheme and seemed to be highly motivated by it; whilst others working alongside them showed no interest in it at all. They found that when these young ladies first left school and started work, they took their unopened pay packets to their 'mum', who gave the daughter a fixed sum for her pocket money. This gesture was expected from the daughter until she reached the age of about eighteen, when it was agreed that she could open her own pay packet and give her 'mum' a fixed sum for board and lodgings. These younger girls at the factory consequently had little interest in the bonus system because they did not benefit from it; their mothers kept the variable part of their pay. When this arrangement changed and they kept the variable part themseves they became more concerned about earning more (Millward, 1968).

In this case, an identical pay system and identical work produced different effects on productivity in the two groups, due to the influence of another factor, the relationships within their families. Similar findings to this, showing different factors leading to high productivity and different factors affecting the way a motivator influenced productivity, led to a 'contingency' approach being taken to the design of wage payment systems. How could one design a payment system which would produce the desired result in a particular case?

The Wage Payment Systems Research Team led by Tom Lupton at Manchester conducted a series of studies of payment systems in operation to learn about the factors which could influence the way a pay system worked. This work led to guidelines being proposed for the design of wage systems, which took account of the state of some 29 factors in the organisation and in its environment, known to have an influence on wage system effectiveness (Lupton and Bowey, 1974). Earlier studies which had produced very negative findings concerning the effects of wage incentives on productivity were found to relate only to certain circumstances where this kind of scheme was not appropriate.

Donald Roy's study in the 1940s, for example, had revealed that a payment by results system could actually lead to holding down of productivity on the part of employees (Lupton, 1972). In the steelworks where Roy worked as an operator/observer, the employees were paid a bonus based on the time saved from the time allowed for a job, and the more time saved the higher the bonus. The time allowed for each job was set by work study officers who studied each task and then estimated how long an average worker working at normal pace would take to complete it. Since work study is not a precise science, we would expect that sometimes this estimate would be generous and allow too much time, and sometimes 'tight' and not allow enough. Assuming that the employees were working at the same pace throughout the week (and during a week they would work on a large number of batches of work, each batch having a time allowed) we could draw a graph of the frequency with which different rates of effort were recorded, and would expect this to peak roughly at the standard effort point, and tail away on each side of this maximum. But the recorded frequencies were nothing like this, as is shown in Figure 2.2. (not to scale).

The reason for this strange distribution was that on all the jobs which had been 'tightly' rated it was difficult for the employee to earn a worthwhile bonus. However, he was paid a 'full back rate' of 85 cents an hour irrespective of how slowly he worked whenever he failed to achieve the standard effort point. So on these jobs the employees saved their energy and worked slowly, hence the jobs to the left of the standard effort point were pushed down and appeared as the lower peak of jobs in Figure 2.2. The jobs which had loose rates and were easy to complete in the allowed time, were completed at great speed; and Roy found that after six months on the job he could easily earn bonus figures (and work at effort rates) more than 300 per cent above the base rate. But these high performances were never reported to management. The machine shop operators believed that if they told the company

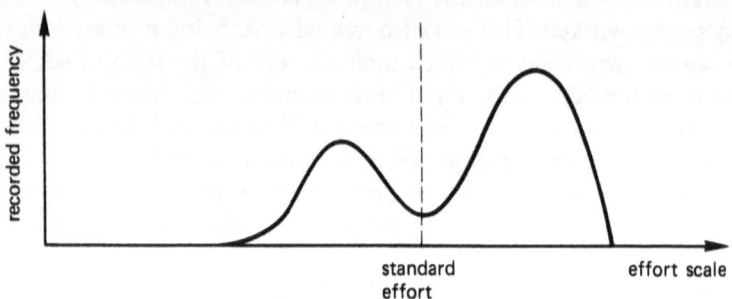

FIGURE 2.2   *Actual recorded frequency of different effort scores (not to scale)*

they had made a bonus of 45 cents or above, the work study officer would be on the shop floor the next day to reorganise the work so that the jobs or tasks concerned had changed and had to be re-timed (so as to correct the 'loose' rate). This may or may not have been true (the company denied that it would do this); but because they believed it, the employees kept their bonus earnings to a maximum of 44 cents per hour on any job. This meant that they had saved a great deal of time on the easy jobs, but only recorded a small proportion of it against those jobs. The rest of the saved time they allocated to other jobs, to raise them into the bonus-earning bracket, or wasted in an assortment of ways (cleaning up; tea breaks; chatting etc). Roy found that managing to waste all his surplus time whilst appearing to be working was one of the most difficult parts of his job. This finding was borne out in British studies of work in industry, for example by Jason Ditton (Ditton, 1979) in his study of a bakery; and by Richard Thorpe in his participant observation study of an engineering works (Thorpe, 1980). Thorpe reported that the most difficult part of the work he had to do was 'learning how to skive'. If these are the results of incentive payment schemes designed to motivate hard work and improved performance, there is something seriously wrong with the principles of those designs.

In the steelworks where Roy worked the bonus scheme which had been designed to raise productivity was causing employees to keep their output low on the 'tight' jobs because there was little possibility of earning bonus on them; and on the easy jobs, whilst they were working fast, the benefits of the time saved were not converted into higher productivity; they were allocated to other jobs or simply wasted.

In the engineering industry in Britain and the United States this kind of incentive scheme is still very common and the same problems can be found time after time. But because payment by results causes low productivity in one situation it is a mistake to believe it will always do so. There are situations where payment by results can bring about an increase in productivity. The following list shows the conditions necessary for PBR (payment by results) to produce a positive effect on productivity.

Requirements for Successful Payment by Results

1   Employees keen to earn higher pay.
2   Costs of production sensitive to increased employee effort.
3   Increased effort would produce measurable results.
4   Employee has a significant amount of control over results.
5   No problems of maintaining standards (e.g. quality and material usage).
6   Variations in output are tolerable.
7   Workflow hold-ups are rare and not prolonged.
8   Changes in task, product or method are infrequent.
9   Parity claims are not a severe problem.
10 Pay disputes are not a severe problem.
11 Short cycle repetitive work.
12 Particularly suited to a situation of very low productivity where incentives have not been used before (effect, however, may only be temporary unless the other conditions are met).

Where conditions 1 to 11 are not fulfilled there are an assortment of different problems which can arise. Many of these have been pointed out before (Bowey, 1976).

The following list points to just some of the problems that can arise when a payment system goes wrong. This may occur because it was the wrong kind of payment system for that situation; or because the way in which the company went about designing, introducing and operating it was not adequate.

Problems Which Can Arise with Payments by Results

1 *Social factors*. These can outweigh the effect of the incentive by causing or reinforcing behaviour patterns which give rise to low productivity.
2 *Tight and loose rates*. These can lead to cross-booking of time between tasks (to increase bonus) and restriction of output (to hide loose rates).
3 *Waiting allowances*. Paying average or near-average bonus for waiting time can lead to cross booking of time between bonus-earning and waiting time, e.g.

actual: worked 5 hours, waited 2 hours
falsely recorded as: worked 4 hours, waited 1 hour

Claiming to have completed 5 hours work in 4 hours means higher bonus rate for the full day. Such allowances can cause employees to welcome machine breakdowns; or even to cause them. And the organisation is also paying premium rates for time wasted when management shortcomings have caused delays.
4 *Lieu bonus*. A compensating bonus (paid, for example, during a teething period with new technology) can lead to cross-booking time between unmeasured work and bonus-earning measured work. Also, sometimes work itself is transferred from the 'unmeasured' machine and claimed as bonus-earning output from another machine.

Both of these can lead to deliberately slow output from new technology, to prolong teething period; and resistance to raising new machinery to full (bonus-earning) capacity.
5 *Rate drift*. Times allowed for jobs tend to become slack over time when changes in task, product or method require frequent setting of new rates, especially where there is a powerful workforce or union, or where the management use this as a way of smoothing industrial relations.
6 *Short cuts*. Employees find new methods of achieving high bonus, for instance putting two products through a machine together; or wrapping adhesive tape round a pulley wheel to increase diameter and so speed up machine. Sometimes this benefits both company and the employee. But sometimes safety is disregarded; or the machine breaks down more frequently; or disparities occur between workers; often managers resent these practices.
7 *False cost information*. If prices are based on labour cost data

taken from the bonus earnings sheets, they will be over or under estimated to the extent that time has been cross-booked by employees. This can very serious, resulting in products selling well which are under priced and vice versa, so lowering profit margins.

8 *Poor maintenance of scheme.* If the initial management effort is not maintained, an increasing proportion of tasks may become 'unmeasured' with a consequent increase in problems mentioned above.

9 *Resistance to change.* Perceived benefits of the bonus scheme may cause employees to resist change.

10 *Work scheduling control.* Supervisors may lose control of work scheduling either because employees pressurise them or in order to achieve industrial harmony by allowing the constraints deriving from the bonus scheme to dictate work allocation and scheduling.

For each kind of payment system, the Manchester team set out to produce information for determining when a situation was suited to the introduction of such a scheme. This 'contingency approach' was consistent with the work being done in other fields of management at the time, by Feidler on managerial style (Feidler and Chemers, 1974); by Morris and Burgoyne on management development (Morris and Burgoyne, 1973); by Lawrence and Lorsch on organisation design (Lawrence and Lorsch, 1967); by Vroom and Yetton on leadership (Vroom and Yetton, 1973) and others. Each of these researchers was examining the links between alternative management practices (in each specialist field), relevant characteristics of the organisation and its environment, and the resulting effects on organisational performance. Their findings were of special interest to managers wishing to choose the most suitable and effective management techniques for the particular contingent characteristics of their own organisation and its situation.

The study reported in Chapter 4 was designed on the basis of the contingency theory model of payment systems. It was hoped that it would produce evidence of the links between appropriate type of pay system, suitable situation, and resulting improvement in performance. As expected, the findings gave very little support for the view that the type of payment system has a major effect on the results achieved. All kinds of payment systems succeeded and failed in different organisations in our study. There were some objectives which some types of scheme tended to contribute towards better than others, however.

One of the major findings of the study is that payment systems do not fall neatly into categories to which labels can be applied. They vary in a multitude of ways. This gives an additional level of complication to the process of designing a suitable payment system.

Surprisingly, the study produced little evidence to support a contingency model of payment system results. The effect of the types of payment schemes were not increased to a significant extent when our sample was reanalysed holding various aspects of organisation and environment constant. This suggests that at least for this sample during the period 1977–80 it was not true that the most effective systems were the ones most suited to the contingencies of the organisation and its environment, if the traditional view is taken of what the appropriate contingencies are (size, technology, market, industry, rate of change, etc.).

This dramatic finding, from the point of view of prevailing theories of management, is consistent with Child's theory, that strategic decision-makers intervene between the management practice and the organisational context, to prevent any natural gravitation of organisations towards the most appropriate practice for their situation. Our findings go further than 'strategic contingencies' (Child 1972) and indicate that the major factor which explained the degree of success of these schemes was the amount of time and effort expended by the management first in the planning and design of the scheme, secondly in consulting and taking account of the views of managers, supervisors, employees and their representatives, and thirdly in the processes of implementation and close observation of its results. These points are considered in detail in Chapters 3 and 4.

Although all the above developments in payment systems were based on underlying theories of the motivation to work, these have not always been made explicit. Other methods of motivating high performance have also been developed, based on different theories of motivation. When considering the design of a payment system it is important to be aware of the limitations of pay and consider the alternatives which have been developed, such as job enrichment and participation. As enthusiasm for incentive payment systems waned in some sectors in the 1950s and 1960s, so these alternative approaches became more prominent.

ALTERNATIVE MOTIVATION PRACTICES

A major problem of considering money as a motivator for high productivity arises because money fulfils several different purposes in an organisation. By focusing on designing an incentive scheme one can upset the balance of other systems, such as the skill and responsiblity hierarchy; the recruitment and retention situation; willingness to work overtime; calculations of prices for products or services; recognition of powerful bargaining groups; desirability of promotion; traditional differentials; reward for age or length of service; compensation for working conditions; recognition of merit; attempts to control inflation. Money is used as an indicator as well as an influencing factor for all these, and should not be thought of simply as a motivator. Some types of incentive system upset these other arrangements that are measured in money a great deal. Perhaps the long term future of pay is to separate out these several purposes, decide which are the most important, and not use money for the others.

Over the past 25 years a great deal of attention has been given to job enrichment and participation as two ways of motivating employees to high productivity. Herzberg has suggested that money is never in fact a motivator, but only a 'hygiene factor' which can de-motivate people if it is not adequate; enriching their jobs, he believes is the way to motivate. The main shortcoming of this suggestion is that it proposes a panacea, and it is simply not true that the same solution will work in all situations where human motivation is concerned. There are differences between people working in the same organisation, even doing the same jobs; and dramatic differences between different organisations, different careers or jobs, and different geographical areas. Herzberg has based his work on Maslow's theory that people's needs are arranged in a hierarchy, with basic physiological needs at the bottom and achievement and self-fulfilment at the top. He concludes that in 'developed' societies the basic needs are satisfied, and since satisfied needs cannot serve as motivators, job enrichment is the answer for all. Evidence of quite different motivation patterns was found by Goldthorpe (1968) among Coventry car-assembly workers and by White (1973) amongst different kinds of management specialists. Goldthorpe's car workers preferred their repetitive, boring jobs which paid high wages to the much more interesting jobs for lower pay available to them nearby. And White's managers showed a variety of interests and fell into distinct groups.

Figure 2.3 shows the different types of motivation pattern, and the percentages and types of managers who belonged in each group, from White's sample of 2246 executives.

Some previous studies suggested that in the right circumstances

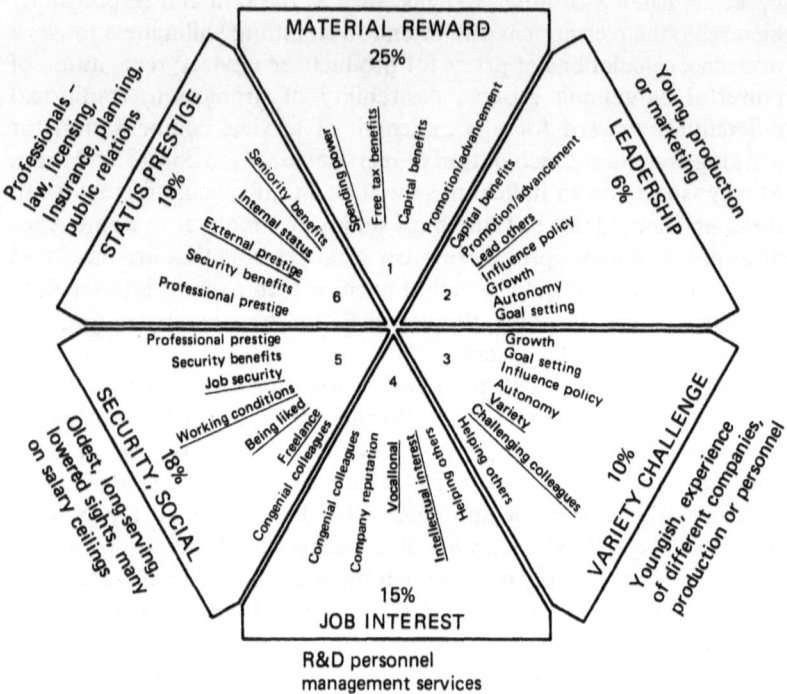

Note Items underlined are the dominant discriminatory variables.
SOURCE Michael White, 'Motivating Managers Financially', IPM, 1973.
FIGURE 2.3 *Motivation patterns of senior executives*

enriched jobs *can* provide employees with increased interest in performing better. Our own findings, discussed in Chapter 5, show a marked split between blue collar and white collar employees. The blue collar employees expressed more interest in opportunities for overtime, etc. whilst the white collar employees were far more interested in rewards such as opportunities to learn and develop new skills, being recognised for a job well done, etc. However, the top priorities of both groups were for regular increases in pay and job security. It would appear from this that job enrichment will be more appropriate to white collar jobs than blue collar; although work experiences and expectations clearly need to be taken into account.

Job enrichment has thus become one of the major alternatives to incentive payment schemes for seeking to motivate better work performance. However, there are a number of different ways of enriching jobs. Job rotation is probably the simplest. This is a system which allows (or programmes) employees to change jobs periodically during the day. If some of the jobs to be done produce strain when continued for long periods, this kind of changing around can be effective in reducing the strain generally, which can improve productivity directly, or indirectly by improving industrial relations. It can also work well if the employees welcome the chance to learn the other jobs because they think this will improve their promotion or job security prospects. But there is a danger that management may impose their own judgement of the desirability of rotating between jobs on workers who do not wish to move. If they see no advantages in moving about, the employees may resent having to learn new tasks, or resent the break in the rhythm of working; or resent the effect which moving has on their social relations (e.g. opportunities to chat etc.) in the work group.

Job enlargement is a different kind of job enrichment where the tasks done by the employee are increased to include more activities, usually with the aim of allowing the employee some satisfaction in completing a job, rather than only a part of it. For example, young ladies assembling radios at Philips in Eindhoven had their job enlarged from repetitively fitting the same parts on each radio, to putting together a complete radio. There are some situations where employees do derive greater satisfaction from completing a job, especially if the work requires some discretion or creativity in its performance. But Philips' young ladies were not happy with their newly-enriched jobs, and many of them left. They disliked the additional concentration required by the new jobs, and were apparently happier performing repetitive tasks which left their minds free for thinking and talking. This again highlights the danger of making assumptions about what will enrich someone else's job. There is even a sense in which a manager designing enrichment into a job denudes that job of autonomy. Given an opportunity, most people can think of ways to improve their own jobs; they do not necessarily appreciate someone else's ideas of an improvement.

When job enrichment involves a degree of self-direction in the new jobs, it is usually termed 'vertical' job enrichment. Some responsibilities which were formerly the duties or prerogatives of management and supervision are incorporated into the employee's job (for instance quality inspection; work allocation within a group; work scheduling). This kind of job enrichment is often popular with the recipients. The most common problem with it is not failure of the employees to respond, it is resentment generated among first line managers/supervisors, whose jobs have been denuded by the enrichment. It is for this reason that any programme of vertical job enrichment should start with examining management jobs, to ensure that *they* are rewarding before looking at enrichment of shop floor jobs.

An important point to bear in mind is that reward systems are very often tied to existing work arrangements. If the jobs are changed it is desirable to assess how the new jobs will affect incentive schemes, overtime arrangements, job evaluation systems, promotion procedures, and merit and appraisal procedures, and where necessary design new systems to meet the new situation. Some of the most successful changes in payment system have been those which were part of a programme of complementary changes introduced by the management.

Vertical job enrichment has features in common with some kinds of participation; both involve employees in decision-making which was formerly a management activity. But whereas job enrichment is usually introduced as a means of improving either efficiency or industrial relations, participation is advocated for a wide range of reasons, such as that it is believed:

(a) that increased participation will satisfy employee needs or demands and enable management to implement its policies more smoothly, meeting less resistance, and will consequently lead to improved efficiency;

or (b) that increased participation will enable the organisation to make fuller use of the expertise, knowledge and contribution which each employee can offer to make the system more effective in adapting and improving;

or (c) that increased participation will allow differing points of view to be expressed and decisions made which achieve a compromise between the interests of different groups; thus avoiding conflict at later stages, when it would be more disruptive;

or (d) that increased participation will allow employees more influence over their own working situation and will improve both the quality of their working lives and their satisfaction in doing their jobs, and although it may or may not lead to improvements in their performance, it is an important objective in its own right;

or (e) that increased participation will allow employees their rightful share of influence and control in the organisation.

In the mid-1970s many managers believed that participation would bring increased efficiency and productivity. To some extent the popularity of added value schemes and other company-wide schemes in the late 1970s was associated with the view that they were one step towards greater involvement of the individual employees in the affairs of the whole organisation.

The most promising indication that participation can lead to increased productivity comes from research into self-directing work groups and similar examples of this kind of participation. The evidence lies in the success of the Shell Oil Company's introduction of self-directing work groups (Hill, 1972) and a study by Marchington (1977) of a factory which introduced participative decision-making coupled with a company-wide bonus scheme based on added-value calculations. In each of these cases the participation was introduced as part of a wider package of changes designed to increase commitment to the organisation and to improve efficiency and productivity.

The enthusiasm for participation waned considerably when it was realised that the British government did not intend to implement the findings of the Bullock Report (Department of Trade, 1977) which had advocated a legal requirement for participation. To some extent this has distracted attention from the potential advantages of participation. Figure 2.4 shows the two key dimensions of participation, namely its intensity (ranging from merely 'informing' to handing over complete control to a co-operative) and its content (ranging from aspects of the working environment up to policy decisions). This demonstrates the very wide variety in types of participation which are possible. We still have a great deal to learn about the value and the results of different kinds of participation. Unfortunately, as a management practice,

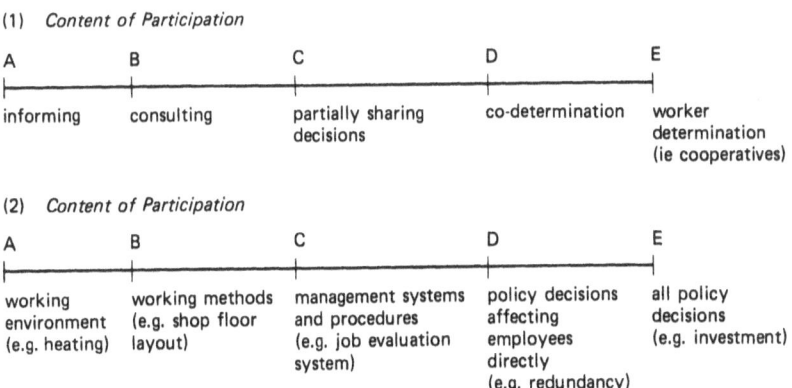

FIGURE 2.4 *Dimensions of participation*

participation suffers from the ideological connotations attached to it because of what some people see as its threat to managerial prerogatives and the natural order of control.

As suggested above, there had been a gradual swing away from incentive payment systems in Britain (even more so in the US) until the late 1970s. Job enrichment and participation were amongst the alternative methods of motivating which had become prominent. But since the late 70s there has been a return to incentive schemes, albeit of a different type, largely influenced by an incomes policy which encouraged 'self-financing productivity schemes'.

MORE RECENT PAYMENT SYSTEM DEVELOPMENTS

Incomes Policies

Table 2.1 (p. 0), showed changes in the use of incentive schemes in Britain over the past 50 years. Their gradual decline seems to have been reversed in the mid-1980s. A Labour Government came into power in the UK in 1974 and introduced various stages of incomes policy in an attempt to control inflation. In 1975 the limit of £6 per head per week increase in pay was introduced, but only for employees earning up to £8500 per annum. For those with higher earnings there was to be no increase that year. In 1976 there was a 5% pay limit with a £2.50 minimum and a £4.00 maximum increase per week per head. 1977 was the year of the 'social contract', with a 10% maximum increase in a company's wage bill, but extra payments above this level were to be allowed if they arose as a result of a self-financing productivity scheme. This Stage 3 incomes policy came into effect in August 1977, and from 1977 to 1979, when it ended, there was a considerable growth in the coverage of incentive schemes.

The decline in incentive schemes prior to 1977 reflected a mood of dissatisfaction with such schemes as a means of controlling and motivating employees to work better. The prevailing and fashionable management philosophies at that time favoured job enrichment, group working, and participation as means of encouraging better performance from employees. The effect of the Stage 3 Incomes Policy was temporarily to reverse this trend. Initially, this was resisted by many managers and it was not until mid-1978 that it was possible to detect in seminars with managers that the majority opinion had swung in favour of the view that productivity could be improved only by incentive payment systems.

The responses of management to the four years of incomes policy under the Labour Government have been described in Bowey and Thorpe (1980). Figure 2.5 shows in diagram form the various stages of incomes policy since 1965, and the average actual annual increases in earnings during each period.

In several parts of the public sector, plans had been underway for many months prior to 1977 to introduce incentive payment schemes for manual workers. These plans had, in many cases, been held up because previous rounds of incomes policy had prevented their introduction. Most of these public sector schemes at least had a long gestation and preparation period, and only a few of the public sector groups to whom incentives were applied during this period had hastily drawn up schemes which had been rushed in to 'get around incomes policy'.

In the private sector the picture was different, especially in manufacturing industries where there had been a steady decline in the use of incentives. In the first few months of the Labour Government's Stage 3 Incomes Policy at the end of 1977, many schemes were put together hastily and rushed in as a means of raising pay with little thought for the suitability of the scheme. In this context, it should be noted that all but five of the 63 organisations in the study reported in Chapter 4 had negotiated or introduced their incentive scheme during the period when Stage 3 of the Labour Government's Incomes Policy was in operation. In companies where the market was buoyant and company performance was improving, these schemes appear to have done no harm. But in the greater number of cases sales were declining and cost control was a vital element in company performance. In many of these cases the incentive schemes did not produce productivity improvements.

Another outcome of this period of incomes policy was a change in the nature of the schemes introduced. The new ones tended to be simple to introduce (because of the pressure for a scheme with a short lead time) and small as a percentage of total pay (because they were seen as a form of additional pay increase, and pay increases were in the order of 10% at the time).

One of the simplest types of incentive scheme to introduce is one based on company performance, as it does not require any complex procedures for measuring individual effort or output. An additional reason for the growth of this type of scheme was that all levels of staff could be included; and if incomes policies were to limit pay increases to 10% plus productivity pay, all staff had to be included in some kind of

24 *Payment Systems and Productivity*

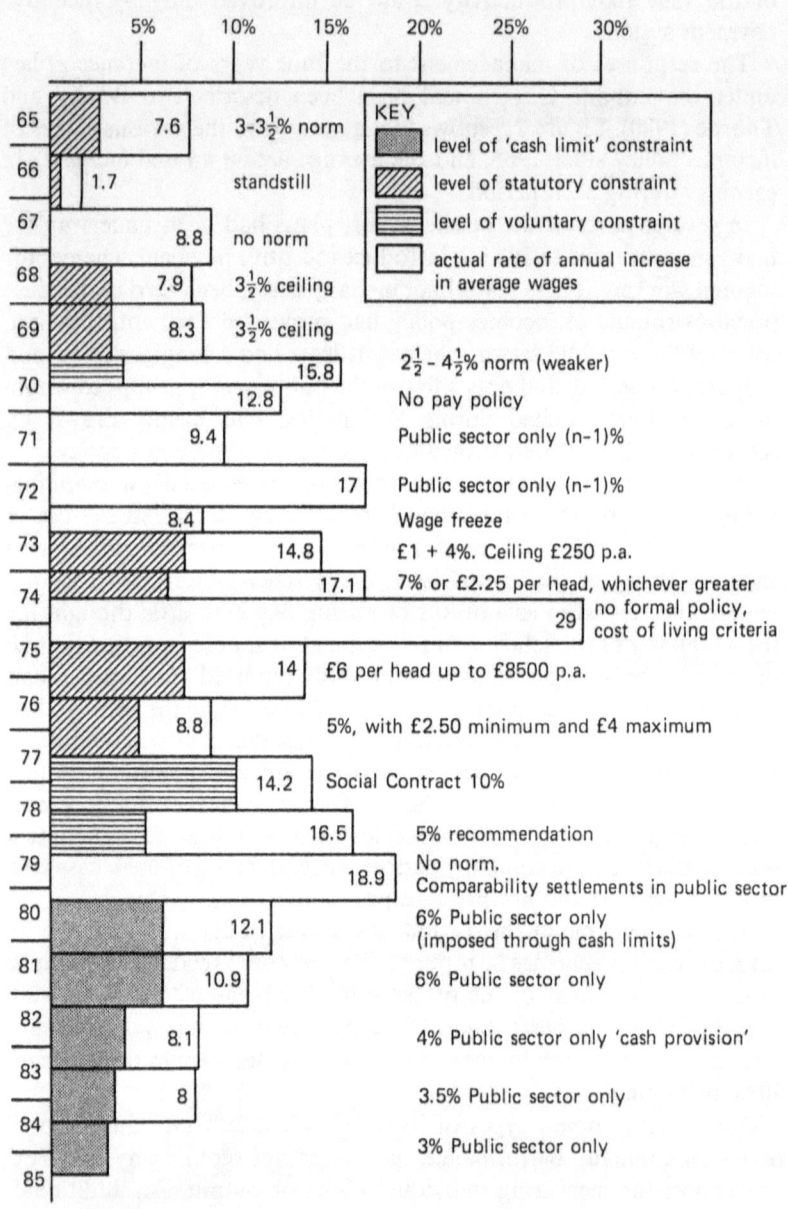

FIGURE 2.5 *Pay norms and wage increases, 1965–82*

scheme unless their pay differential over their subordinates was to be eroded by the productivity pay earned by the latter.

Collective bonus schemes can take a number of forms, and the next section discusses the ones which became popular in the UK in the late 1970s.

Collective Bonus Schemes

There was an increase in the use of collective bonus schemes in the late 1970s. This followed an apparent decline in the previous decade, as shown in Table 2.2. In the study reported in Chapter 4, a fifth of the schemes introduced were collective payment schemes based on company or plant performance, as opposed to only 7% of schemes in the wider working population. The 1977 New Earnings Survey showed that 2% of all employed manual men were being paid by company or plant-wide incentives, 12% by group incentives, and 14% by individual incentives. The proportion receiving company or plant-wide incentives increased from 2% in 1977 to an estimated 20% of all new schemes being introduced by 1980. This trend towards collective and group schemes included such schemes as profit sharing; share and share option schemes; Scanlon-type schemes (based on sharing the benefits of reducing labour costs); and Rucker-type schemes (based on sharing benefits of improvement in added value). The 'added value' type of scheme became particularly popular during this period.

Profit and productivity sharing schemes currently in existence pay employees a cash sum periodically (annually, six-monthly, monthly, or even weekly or fortnightly). With profit sharing schemes a formula is used for converting net profit or net capital growth into the proportion to be given out as bonus, and this is allocated to employees either all

TABLE 2.2 *Types of incentive bonus schemes in the UK, 1968–77 (all employees receiving incentives)*

	Individual incentives	Group schemes	Company or plant performance schemes
1968	39	45	11
1977	48	41	7

SOURCE New Earnings Surveys, 1968 and 1977.

equally or with differential shares based on differential salary and wage levels.

Rucker schemes, Bentley schemes and added value schemes all base the bonus payment on a ratio relating added value to employment costs in some way. Table 2.3 shows a fairly standard way of calculating added value.

Whilst this is a reasonably standard way of calculating 'added value', there is considerable variation in the methods of calculation used by different companies. Some deduct depreciation from the sales value figure, and not from added value; some treat rent, rates and insurances in the same way; some regard advertising and professional services as part of the costs of earning the sales value, and so deduct them from sales value first.

Although some writers have implied that there is a logical or

TABLE 2.3 *Calculating added value*

ADDED VALUE = SALES VALUE LESS:

    raw materials   used in
    bought out components   goods sold
    sub-contracted processing   or scpapped
    consumable stores purchases
    loose tools purchases
    repairs and maintenance
    light, heat, power
    transport
    production services
    other purchased services
    commission, discounts and royalties

PLUS:

    any increase (or minus any decrease) in value of work-in-progress and finished stock

The following expenditure is then left to be met from the added value earned:

    profit before taxation
    wages and salaries
    depreciation
    rent, rates, insurance
    advertising
    professional services
    interest charges
    other administrative and overhead expenses

Payment Systems and Performance Improvement 27

financial/economic distinction between the items which are deducted in order to arrive at the added value figure and those which are paid out of it, the wide range of current practices belie the claim. This wide range of options has the advantage of allowing companies to make the calculations in a way which is most appropriate for their particular industry. For example, some factor which was subject to wide variation due to matters outside the control of the employees and their managers could be included in such a way as to not affect the bonus payments based on the added value figure.

Another major source of variation between companies lies in the way in which the added value figure is converted into a financial reward for employees:

1. ICI designed a new share incentive scheme where the shares earned were related to the ratio between the ICI added value performance and the added value achieved by other major international chemical companies.
2. One large public sector corporation paid a productivity bonus based on the added value performance but subject to compliance with an agreement relating to restrictive practices. Since added value was not expected to fall below the bonus-earning level, variation in this case arose only if productivity payments were withdrawn from a particular group because of non-cooperation.
3. A Scottish engineering company paid a bonus to all its employees based on the percentage improvement in added value over the base period (just prior to the introduction of the scheme). This bonus was paid on top of existing payment by results and measured daywork schemes operating in various parts of the company.
4. A North Western vehicle company paid a fixed bonus to its manual employees giving them a high wage provided the company's added value figure did not fall below an agreed level.
5. A Midlands engineering company paid a monthly bonus to all employees and staff based on the ratio of payroll to added value.

Table 2.4 shows a simple calculation of an added value bonus, in which the sales value per month in the reference period was on average £1000; costs of 'bought in' items per month were £500, and so added value was £500. The payroll bill in this reference period was £200 per month, which represented 40% of added value. This was then taken as the norm for comparing with performance in subsequent months. Suppose that in the first month of operation of the added value scheme, sales value has increased to £1100, with no change in the value of

TABLE 2.4 *Simple example of an added value bonus scheme calculation*

Improvements in the value added to 'bought in' materials and services are distributed between employees and company.

Reference Period
Suppose normal sales value per month = £1000

Normal cost of bought-in materials, services and supplies outside the company's control	= £500
Then normal added value	= £500
Normal wage bill	= £200
	= 40% of A.V.
Subsequent month sales value	= £1100
Cost of bought-in materials etc.	= £510
Added value	= £590
Payroll share of added value	= £236 (40% of added value)
Actual payroll	= £206
Saving, to go into bonus fund	= £30

stocks; but it has cost £510 for materials, services, and other 'bought in' items. Added value is then £590. If the 40% ratio is applied to this (from the reference period), the 'payroll share' of added value is £236. Comparing this to the actual payroll in this month, £206, we find a saving of £30, which is then made available for the bonus fund.

Table 2.5 shows another method of calculating an added value bonus. The difference comes in the way the calculation is related to bonus. The payroll cost of £206 is 35% of the £590 added value, an improvement over the 40% norm which is converted to a bonus by reference to a graph relating these percentages to bonus payments.

There are in fact a wide variety of ways in which one added value bonus scheme may differ from another. The following list indicates the most common variations to be found in Britain in recent years:

1 The amount of the saving which goes into the bonus fund can differ (a BIM survey found the percentage of the payroll proportion of improvement in added value which was distributed varied from 17% to 85%).
2 The method of converting payroll/added value improvements into bonus may vary, as illustrated in Tables 2.4 and 2.5.

Payment Systems and Performance Improvement

TABLE 2.5 *Added value bonus scheme calculation*

The productivity bonus is based on improvements in the value added to 'bought in' materials and services

Reference period

Sales value	= £1000
Costs of 'bought in' items	= £500 (materials, services)
Added value	= £500 (for payroll, interest expenses, profit, investment etc.)
Payroll cost	= £200
Payroll as % of added value	= 40%

Subsequent month

Sales value	= £1100 (including stock changes)
'Bought in' costs	= £510
Added value	= £590
Payroll	= 206
Payroll as % of added value	= 35%

In this example, the bonus payments were read from the following graph:

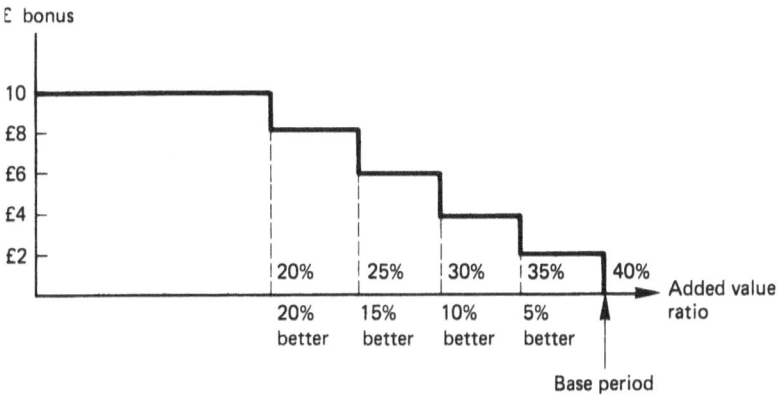

3   The method of calculating added value can differ according to the items deducted from sales value to get added value.
4   The method of relating added value to employment costs may be
    a: Added value per £ employment cost.
    b: Employment cost as a percentage of added value.
    c: Added value per employee.
5   The bonus may be paid monthly (common recently); bi-monthly; quarterly; half-yearly; or annually.
6   The bonuses may be paid in cash or shares.
7   The bonus may be paid as a flat sum to all employees or as a percentage of wage/salary.
8   The bonus may be conditional, i.e. withheld under certain circumstances such as lateness; absence; industrial action; non-cooperation.

Many advantages are claimed for added value schemes, most especially that the added value figure does not go up when prices go up if costs have also increased, whereas other systems, such as the Scanlon plan, would not be insulated in this way.

Table 2.6 shows a simple example of a Scanlon Plan calculation which can usefully be compared with the added value calculation shown in Table 2.4. In this example, the average sales value per month in the reference period was £1000 and labour costs £200, i.e. 20% of sales value. In the first month of operation of the scheme, sales value had increased to £1200 and labour costs to £210. Standard labour costs at 20% of sales value would have been £240; so there has been an improvement of £30 to be put into the bonus fund.

Viewed as incentive schemes, all of these company-wide systems have major shortcomings. The final bonus payment is too far removed from the employee's effort for him to perceive them as causally related. The final bonus is very likely to be affected by changes in prices, changes in currency, changes in the market, and the effectiveness of management's performance. Discontent and blaming other groups' efforts are likely to

TABLE 2.6   *A simple example of a Scanlon plan*

Suppose normal sales value per month	= £1000
Normal labour costs per month	= £200
	= 20% of sales value
Subsequent month's sales value	= £1200
Labour costs	= £210
Standard labour costs (20% of £1200)	= £240
Improvement	= £30 to be shared

result if a poor bonus is declared when employees have been working hard.

But as a means of rewarding improvements brought about by initiatives in other areas and informing employees of the contributions others make to the enterprise they have merit; particularly if the company or organisation can ensure that there will be fairly stable bonus payments. Figure 2.6 shows the numerous links to performance improvement which can be demonstrated.

Participation by employees in the organisation and monitoring of the entire scheme, whether it be profit sharing, Scanlon type or added value type considerably improves the chances of success, as indicated by the experience of Marchington (1977) and our own study (Chapter 5).

THE IMPORTANCE OF PAY IN MANAGEMENT

It is important to consider the role played by pay within management, not just during an incomes policy which encourages the use of incentive schemes, but more broadly as one means by which employers seek to influence the way their employees work.

Managers sometimes rely on pay for the achievement of all kinds of aims within organisations. It is a key area of managerial concern because of its potential for controlling or influencing the workforce. It is a major component of the employment contract, both formal and informal. Employees work for money and also for other rewards, but on the whole they will not work without money.

Employers have tended to see money as a component of numerous strategies for carrying out their managerial responsibilities in a wide range of areas. These include:

- recognising what jobs deserve (status, skill, responsibility, etc.)
- retaining good employees
- responding to demands for more pay
- motivating high performance
- encouraging interest in promotion
- encouraging loyalty to the company
- rewarding merit generally
- compensating for adverse conditions

and at the same time pay is a key component in
- controlling costs
- complying with government policy aims
- maintaining a company image.

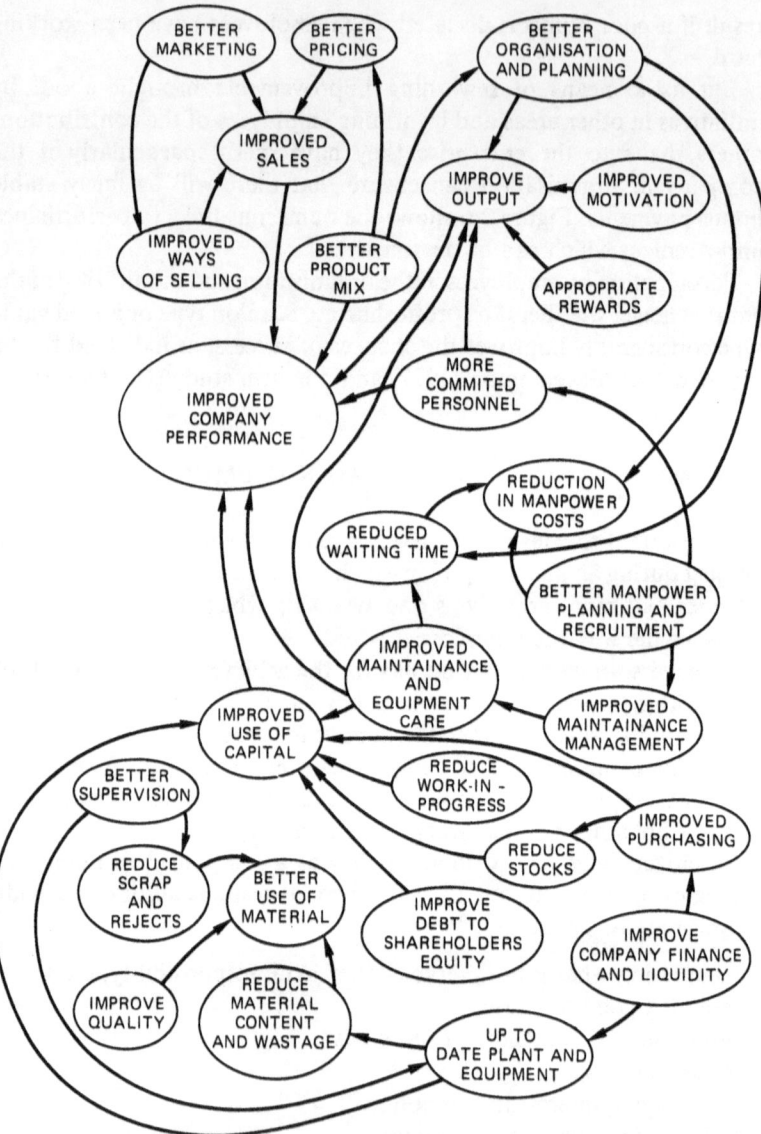

FIGURE 2.6 *Areas of activity which could contribute to improved performance*

In our view using money in all these different ways defeats its own purpose because the aim for achieving any one of the above objectives is to pay those employees to whom that particular objective applies more money relative to other employees. But by paying more money to groups of employees to whom each of the above objectives apply, the employer ends up cancelling out the impact of one differential by superimposing on it another which may go in a different direction. Nevertheless, vast sums of money are spent by British managers on designing payment systems and implementing and modifying them.

The attraction of focusing on payment system design may be that it places a large share of the responsibility for organisational success or failure on the workforce, in the belief that the organisation will succeed if only the employees can be motivated to perform their jobs better. Sometimes the payment system has very little bearing on the real problems in an organisation. Consequently payment systems are sometimes being changed in an attempt to solve problems which have very little association with the payment system, or in situations where the problems the payment system could solve would contribute very little to the organisation's real difficulties.

On the other hand, the major organisational effort required to change a payment system creates a suitable situation in which other changes can be brought about. The inter-relationship between changed payment systems and changes to other systems and procedures within the organisations, together produce benefits in those organisations which 'succeed' with a new payment system.

The underlying reason for this association between integrated packages of change incorporating a payment system with greater success, is that a payment system designed to motivate employee performance can only form part of the effort-reward bargain. Reward is much broader than pay; and effort involves far more than measured results. Table 2.7 shows, on the left hand side, some of the rewards which employees may seek or may receive from their work experience; and on the right hand side, the various dimensions of effort which the organisation may need.

One of the problems with much payment systems work in the past, is that by focusing narrowly on pay the opportunity to contribute to employee motivation through some of the other rewards may be missed, and frustration may even be caused by lack of those rewards. And by focusing narrowly on those aspects of effort which can be measured, it sometimes happens that employees turn all their attention to those efforts and neglect or refuse to give other possibly more important forms of effort.

TABLE 2.7 *Aspects of the effort–reward bargain*

Rewards	Efforts
Basic pay	Physical effort
Extra pay (bonus, overtime, etc.)	Mental effort
Fringe benefits	Willingness to work extra hours
Time off	Good attendance
Autonomy	Cooperation with change
Interesting or satisfying work	Commitment
Power or influence	Initiative
Relationships with colleagues	Cooperation with others
Sense of achievement	Enthusiasm
Self-evaluation	

In this context it is important to note that the particular characteristics of the employees concerned, the work that they are doing, and the context in which they work, will affect both the extent to which they would respond to and expect different kinds of rewards from work and the extent to which different dimensions of effort are important to their job performance.

These views about payment system design are not the dominant ones to be found in British management today. Theories about pay and motivation have been through many phases in the past half century, and there is a wide spread of points of view amongst managers concerning the role which payment systems can play in relation to employee job performance and concerning the design of payment systems.

Managers who have, at some stage in their careers, operated with a particular type of payment system which was successful at the time, sometimes believe that this particular payment system design is unquestionably the best. And managers who have been convinced by the exposition of a particular system either in texts or at seminars may also hold tenaciously to that point of view. But other managers have recognised that the best design for a payment system will greatly depend on the circumstances in which it is to be applied, and do not try to impose their 'favourite' system whatever the circumstances.

CONCLUSIONS

This chapter has considered different ways in which employers have sought to bring about improvements in productivity. These were

Payment Systems and Performance Improvement 35

individual payment-by-results incentives, improvements to human relationships at work, job enrichment, participation, and collective bonus schemes. The currently popular contingency approach says there can be no one answer to the question 'How do I motivate my employees to work well?' The manager who wishes to bring about such improvements should take a careful look at his employees, his organisation, and the environment in which he is operating. The results of recent research suggest that even this is not enough. A key factor in the successful design, implementation and operation of a new procedure for motivating employees lies in the procedures adopted by management. These must involve wide discussion of the proposed changes with all levels and functions of the organisation, and an integrated programme of complementary changes designed to ensure effective operation of the new schemes.

3 Productivity Measurement

Productivity has become an everyday word for a concept which everyone is supposed to approve but which is rarely defined satisfactorily. For the last 20 years and more, politicians, industrialists, economists and management specialists have stressed the importance of productivity improvement for the general economic state of a nation. Company executives are concerned with productivity both for making comparisons between enterprises in home and world markets and as a shorthand term for factors which need to be improved to make their own enterprise more competitive and successful. Governments stress the relationship between productivity, the standard of living, inflation and economic growth.

Over this period, whole careers have been spent addressing the problem of productivity and how it can be measured, without coming to useful conclusions. Faraday (1971) comments 'The calculation of productivity has long been a field of controversy. When attempts are made, little value is placed on the results because they seem to contain so many imperfections.' Zammuto summarised the conclusions of several authors on organisational performance and wrote: 'The search for a universal criterion or set of criteria is fruitless and ill-advised.' (1982). And yet the search continues: many people feel they need to measure productivity.

This chapter aims to provide a framework for productivity issues and bring together some of the often complex and diverse approaches to measuring productivity at the organisational level.

Productivity has generally been defined as the ratio between output(s) and input(s) of a system. It differs from production in that increasing production means increasing the output, whilst increased productivity means obtaining a greater amount of output from the same amount of input, or the same output from less input. Total Productivity Measure is the name for an index based on all inputs and

Productivity Measurement

all outputs of a system. The inputs can be man-hours of labour, units of capital, areas of land or buildings, numbers of machines, quantities of raw materials, the financial value of such inputs or some combination of inputs. And the output can be tonnes, numbers of products, clients served, sales value, profit, standard minutes of work produced, value of production, or a combination of such items.

It is sometimes helpful to visualise productivity as a tree, such that the roots denote the inputs to the system, the trunk the conversion process and the branches and leaves the system's outputs. This underlines two fundamental problems to be discussed later in this chapter:

1. Different measures of productivity can be derived by selecting different inputs and outputs.
2. The diversity of inputs and outputs make combination and analysis very difficult.

Teague and Eilon (1973) outlined four main reasons why measurement of productivity is important:

1. for strategic purposes, to enable management to assess the performance of an enterprise with competitors or similar organisations elsewhere;
2. for tactical purposes, to enable management to assess the performance of the various divisions within the organisation;
3. for planning purposes, to compare the relative benefits accruing from the use of differing inputs or varying proportions of the same inputs; and,
4. for internal management purposes, such as collective bargaining with trade unions.

Thorpe (1983) identified the following purposes for which companies commonly made attempts to measure productivity:

for rewarding labour based on measurement of work content;
for determining manning levels;
for appraisal of managerial performance;
for investment decisions;
for measuring organisational effectiveness.

These lists can be further elaborated as shown in Table 3.1.

The many problems that relate to productivity measurement and the choice of a measure will in this chapter be examined under the following headings:

conceptual problems of defining what is meant by productivity, how it may be measured, and how it can be improved;
perspectives of how different people view productivity;
operational problems relating to the uses of productivity measures in an organisation;
data problems in terms of lack of data and the synthesis of different types of data.

TABLE 3.1 *Uses of productivity measurement at the level of the firm*

Strategic
    Measuring return on capital or plant efficiency to assist decisions about investment and expansion (or closure) at different locations.
    Measuring contribution to the national economy to justify claims for government support.
    Measuring profitability and trends in financial ratios to attract investment funds.
    Measuring labour performance factors (strikes, absenteeism, labour turnover) to assist decisions about expansion or closure at different locations.

Tactical
    Measuring departmental/divisional target attainment to assess management performance.
    Measuring plant/equipment utilisation to identify areas requiring improvement.
    Assessing work content in order to judge required manning levels in various parts of the organisation.

Planning
    Comparing the contribution to productivity of alternative levels and types of automation.
    Comparing the contribution to profits or added value of alternative production programmes or projects.
    Comparing the relative benefits of using different inputs or varying proportions of inputs.

Direct Management
    Measuring work performance for purposes of incentive payment to employees.
    Measuring work content to decide allocation of employees to teams or sections of work.
    Assessing productivity for collective bargaining purposes.

CONCEPTUAL PROBLEMS OF PRODUCTIVITY

Simple Productivity Ratios

There are two types of simple productivity ratio: those which relate to organisational performance and those which relate to employee performence.

Both are simple in the sense that they take only one kind of input and relate it to only one kind of output.

The simplest organisational performance ratios assume a fixed scale of operation and no change nor independency between factors in production, and as such are unrealistic. Nevertheless ratios such as tonnes of output per tonne of raw material, volume of output per head, number of managers per manual worker, volume of output per machine or per plant, are used frequently for some of the strategic and tactical decisions shown in Table 3.1. The aim of using such a ratio is then to seek the most favourable productivity, or in the economists' terms to maximise the output from a given amount of input or to minimise the input needed to achieve a required level of output.

Simple productivity ratios can also be expressed in value terms, for example value of sales to cost of raw materials, value of production per £ labour cost, value of sales increase per £ invested in new machinery, etc. Alternatively only one part of the ratio may be expressed in value terms. For example, volume of output per £ labour cost; or cost of raw materials per unit produced.

Simple productivity ratios for measuring employee performance are usually used for the types of decisions listed under 'Direct Management' in Table 2.1. These ratios include such things as standard minutes of work produced per hour (by an individual) or per man-hour (by a group), where a standard minute of work is the amount of work which an employee is expected to complete in a minute at a specified standard of quality if he works in a brisk and businesslike fashion for the whole day. The number of standard minutes of work in any particular task would be determined by some form of work measurement either by timing the task and adjusting the observed time (rating) to take account of factors such as the speed, effort and efficiency of the employee, or by using pre-determined times from a manual of such times for each motion making up the task, or from sampling, or comparisons with previous similar jobs. The standard minutes allowed for all the tasks completed by an employee in a week would then be totalled and divided by the number of minutes he had spent on that work, to give his personal performance in terms of a percentage over the duration of the work. The standard minutes calculated for each task would include a percentage allowance for unavoidable interruptions in the work (contingencies) such as talking to the supervisor or collecting tools, as well as for breaks, which employees need to take (relaxation allowances dependent on the physical and mental demands of the task).

The British Standard Scale for measuring employee performance is based on this kind of calculation. It measures 'effort' in terms of the minutes saved from the standard minutes allowed for completing all the tasks in a given period. Thus if an employee works for 40 hours and completes 50 hours worth of work he has saved 10 hours and his performance rating would be:

50 × (the work completed) ÷ 40 (the time taken) × 100 = 125 performance
(i.e. 25% above standard)

In this context it should be noted that time taken to complete a piece of work contains many elements as shown in Figure 3.1, and many of these are outside the control of the man doing the task.

Complex Productivity Ratios

Complex productivity ratios combine the effects of several inputs in producing a given level and type of output (or combination of outputs). They are sometimes called 'production functions' and can be represented symbolically as:

x(output) = f(a function of) [(factor A) + f(factor B) + f(factor C) etc.

The coefficients are worked out by statistical analysis of the relationships in the past.

Such a formula can be used to illustrate the 'Law of Variable Proportions'. Any given ratio between output and a combination of all inputs includes those inputs which are fixed (such as the plant), i.e. do not vary with the level of output, at least in the short term. The optimum level of producing output is thus the level which produces the maximum output per unit of variable inputs, such that an additional unit of these variable inputs will not produce as much as previous units.

Productivity Measurement

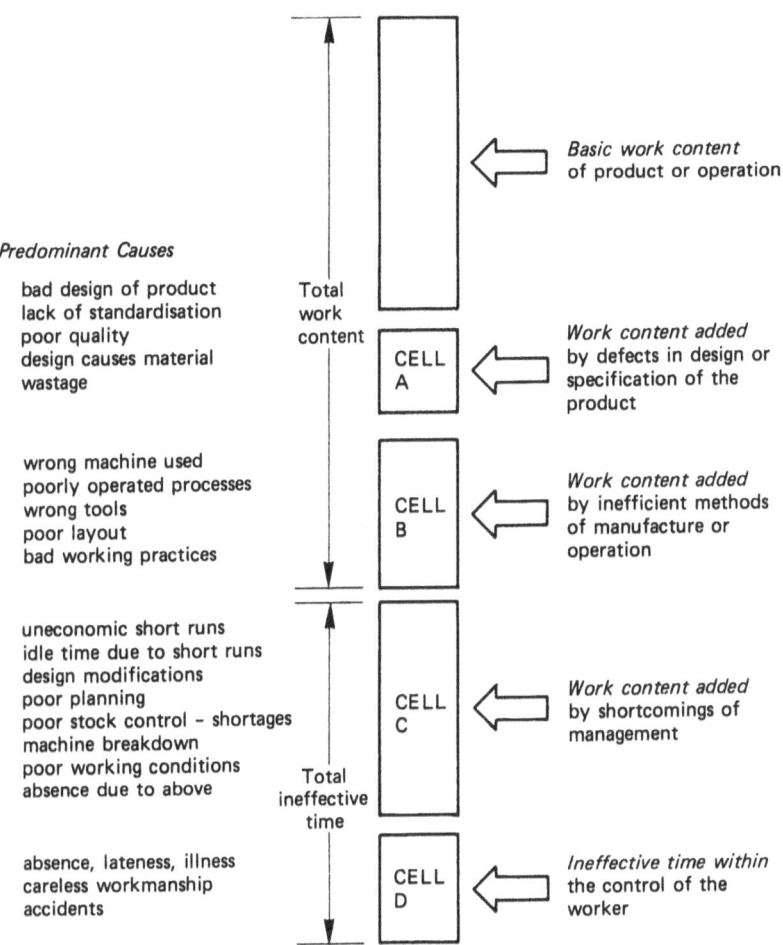

SOURCE: *ILO Handbook (1982)*

FIGURE 3.1 *How manufacturing time is made up*

This is not necessarily the same as maximum capacity, since output per additional unit of variable input may begin to fall away before the maximum plant utilisation is achieved. The purpose of this kind of analysis of productivity is to identify optimum operating levels and then to seek improvements in factor performance in order to close the gap between maximum capacity and maximum productivity.

This, crudely stated, is a theoretical economic approach to productivity measurement. It bears little relationship to the uses of productivity measures as we have observed them in employing organisations; and it has not greatly aided our understanding of the issues and problems associated with productivity measurement. However, it could be relevant if it were used for the kinds of decisions listed under 'Planning' in Table 3.1.

One final point about simple and complex productivity ratios is that their use for predicting future relations between factor inputs to achieve expected levels of output has been shown to be very questionable. Wabe *et al.* (1974) have compared the predictive power of several different productivity ratios, and found that better predictions of levels of factor inputs (specifically labour) over a ten year period were obtained by assuming that there had been no change in manning levels than by trying to calculate manning levels from productivity ratios or production functions based on levels of output.

System Productivity Measures

The measures of productivity considered above are all 'goal-based' in the sense that they assess the extent to which a particular objective has been achieved. There are other measures or sets of measures which attempt to assess the performance of an organisation as a whole, which can be termed 'system' measures. The distinction between goal-based and system measures of performance will be considered further in Chapter 4. For the purposes of considering productivity measurement it is appropriate to consider here those measures of productivity which try to assess the 'system as a whole' rather than some particular aspect(s) of it.

There are system approaches to financial performance which measure a set of financial ratios for the purposes of judging the viability of an enterprise and identifying its weaknesses. Financial analysts have achieved fame by using such systems to predict correctly company collapse before others even suspected the company was in difficulties (for example Clarkson and Elliot of Manchester Business School predicted the collapse of Rolls Royce in the early 1970s, several months before it happened).

Ingham and Harrington (1980) use such a system (or pyramid) of financial ratios to compare performance of companies in the same industry so that relative productivity can be assessed. Firms taking part in their comparative study received a confidential report explaining the reasons for differences in ratios for different firms and drawing management's attention to the possibilities for improvement.

Some of the financial ratios used in such an exercise do not assess productivity so much as risk. These include financial risk which may be measured by liquid assets/current liabilities, asset risk which may be measured by debt/shareholders' equity, operating risk which may be measured by plant and equipment value/sales or by inventory/sales. Accountants' use of such ratios is well established, but they need to be interpreted with care, paying attention to the accounting conventions they may be based on (cf. Norman and Bahiri, 1972).

More complex than the financial ratio models are the economists' models such as that of Gold (1971) shown in Figure 3.2, which combine managerial control ratios with financial control ratios in order to judge the performance of a system as a whole. These systems of productivity measures do not attempt to combine all the ratios into one formula. They apply criteria of how each ratio should be in a 'healthy' organisation, and what the relationships between some of the ratios should be, and from this identify the weak areas of an organisation and predict its potential for future performance.

Other complex system approaches developed by economists have reduced the inputs and outputs of several ratios to comparable units (usually money) and then combined them to produce one overall measure.

Smith & Beeching (1968) advocated a measure using 'corrected' monetary value of output, where the purpose was to study change and rates of change in performance of organisations or industries with complex and varying forms of output or to assess the relative importance of products. The effects of price changes had to be eliminated prior to the calculation. The method reduced the total financial value of output over a period to a base year value (by reference to a cost of living index) and related this to the value of materials used (similarly corrected to base year prices). This index was then related to the manpower employed to give a measure of productivity.

The same authors also suggest a method of synthesising an overall productivity measure from measurements for each department of a large organisation, combining these unit indices to give an index for the whole organisation. In this case the unit for comparison was man-hours, and work completed was converted into man-hours by using its standard man-hours of work content (i.e. by reference to work study). Input factors were converted into man-hours by dividing their cost by

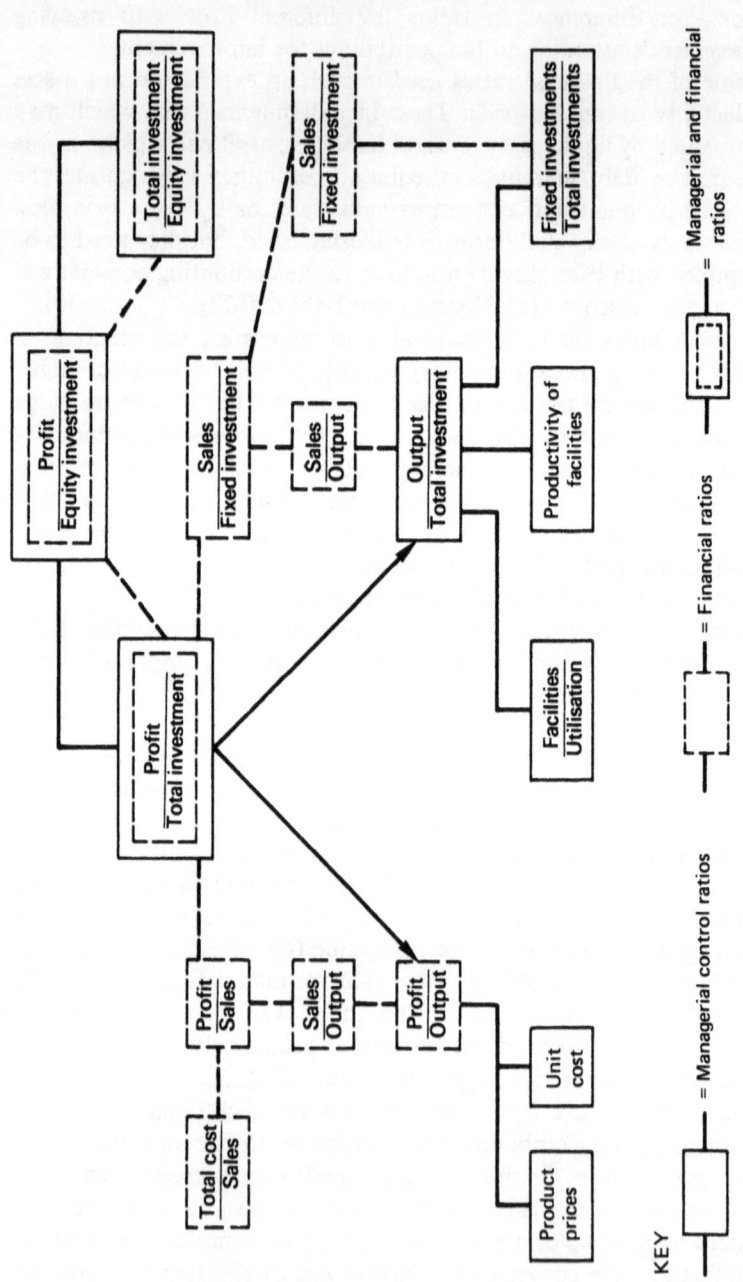

FIGURE 3.2 *Gold's hierarchy of performance ratios*

the average hourly pay for manual workers. Thus total company productivity (TP) for an organisation would be the sum of each department's productivity divided by the number of departments (n).

$$TP = \frac{\sum_{1}^{n} \frac{\text{man-hours worth of work completed}}{\text{manpower equivalent of total departmental costs}}}{n}$$

To enable annual comparisons to be made the annual index was then discounted back to a base year value of the £. The method is very ingenious, but the value of such an aggregated measure based on so many layers of estimation is questionable.

A still more innovative approach was suggested by Norman and Bahiri (1972) and termed the Integrated Systems Productivity Model. This model integrated the accountant's financial model of factor productivity with the engineers' measures of conversion efficiency and the economists' model based on added value and the concept of labour productivity. In each step the measure was the rate of generation of output for that conceptual model per related unit of input.

Teague and Eilon (1973) recorded a contingency type of approach which defined productivity per product as the efficiency of that product at making a profit. For example, Bahiri and Martin (1970) advocate measuring only that work which truly contributes to the objectives of the organisation. It is claimed that this method is of greater use for tactical, planning or management purposes and less useful than productivity ratios for strategic decision making. It does throw light on costing of industrial goods and the utilisation of plant, equipment, and manpower.

Another approach to a total system measure of productivity is to use added value, as advocated in recent years for managers by many writers including Smith (1978) and Wilson (1979) as well as for accountants by Cox (1980), Ferris (1980) and others. Its use was enhanced by support for a time from the Department of Trade and Industry and the Department of Employment in the late 1970s. Added value is the sum of money added to the value of raw materials (plus goods or services provided by suppliers) by the processes carried out by the organisation and received through the sale of its output.

There is no single accounting standard for calculating added value, but it is usually defined as the difference between sales income and the cost of goods and services, adjusted for changes in level of stocks and work in progress. An example of an added value calculation was given in Chapter 2, Table 2.3. Added value represents that amount available to cover wages and salaries, interest charges, rent and rates, company tax and depreciation, etc. Any remaining net income is profit from which dividends may be paid and retention made for further investment.

What should not be included in the calculation can be argued at length.

For example some people would say that rent and rates should be included under bought-in goods and services and not appear in the added value. However, since there is no universal accounting standard, the decision about what to include where depends very much on how the measure is to be used and the preferences of the user.

The concept has the advantage that it is reasonably easy to understand and emphasises the contribution of all those concerned in the wealth creation process (management, white collar staff and direct workers). It also uses information which is fairly readily available in many organisations (as compared, for example, to work study data which often requires a great deal of skilled manpower to collect and maintain).

However, it has a number of disadvantages as an index of performance for such purposes as motivating improved effort, linking to a bonus system, or assessing relative performance of individuals or groups. These disadvantages include the fact that any improvement in added value will be very far removed from the point of contribution of any one individual or group, such that they will see movements in added value which do not reflect their own performance (or indeed may not even move in the same direction). Also, it is a measure which is greatly affected by price changes (including those brought about by a change in currency valuation) and whilst this is a strength when viewed as an overall productivity/performance measure, it is a decided weakness when used as a measure of the contribution to productivitiy made by direct production staff.

Its other disadvantage is the lack of a universal accounting standard, a consequence of which is that organisations can choose where to put particular items in the calculation, and in doing so can virtually produce the answer they want. For example, if some specific item of cost is difficult to control and a source of poor organisational performance (e.g. current value of stocks), it is possible to devise a method of calculating added value which neutralises the effect of this item on the added value calculation. This makes it a difficult measure to use for comparisons between organisations which use different principles of calculation.

The criticism that added value is remote from the performance of individuals and groups can be applied to a great many system productivity measures, and emphasises the importance of choosing a measure which is appropriate for the purpose for which it is to be used.

Efficiency

The concept of efficiency differs from productivity in the sense that it incorporates the idea of making the best use of resources and combining them in the best way, rather than simply the relationship between input of resources and output. It implies an objective scale against which the productivity is judged. One needs a standard according to which some performance level can be judged as more or less efficient. In one sense the British Standards Scale for measuring effort provides a measure of labour efficiency, because it relates the productivity to a standard which can be widely applied. Machine efficiency is often judged in terms of the ratio of power input to power output, where a perfect machine (which is never achieved) would convert 100% of the power it used (e.g. electricity) into the power it generated (e.g. driving an engine). Machines are often given output capacity ratings, and efficiency in this sense would be the percentage of that capacity which was achieved with the recommended input of resources.

There is often terminological confusion between productivity and efficiency, and part of the reason for continued futile searching for a single index of productivity may be because of this confusion of terms. There can be a single index of efficiency for any particular productivity ratio. All that is needed is a standard against which the performance of several organisations or individuals can be compared on the output achieved from the particular kinds of inputs in the ratio. But there can be no single index of productivity because there are legitimate reasons for including different inputs and different outputs in productivity indices used for specific different purposes, as this chapter will show.

Effectiveness

Effectiveness is another concept which is often confused with productivity. There is nothing in a productivity ratio or an efficiency measure which takes account of the usefulness of the output produced, or its relevance. Yet the highly efficient production of a mountain of unsaleable products is of little use to an organisation. Or the rapid completion of specified work targets, whilst turning a blind eye to opportunities which would benefit the organisation more, is not the kind of contribution most organisations need from their employees. Effectiveness implies the combination of high productivity with relevance of that productivity; and it requires not just the optimum combination of inputs and efficient use of those inputs, but additional factors such as judgement, initiative, adaptation, flexibility, cooperation. Indeed, relevance is often more important than efficiency or productivity. And the danger with much of the work on measuring productivity is that it focuses too much attention on those factors which can be measured and too little on the qualitative components or determinants of relevance. As Minzberg claimed 'the maximisation of efficiency in practice does not mean the greatest benefit for the cost, but instead the greatest measurable benefit for the measurable cost' (Minzberg, 1982). The development of a measurement cult precludes many of the less quantifiable yet essential ingredients of effective productivity.

Another danger of over-emphasising the easily measured dimensions of productivity is that it encourages individuals to pursue measurable targets and they may refuse to co-operate with colleagues who are falling behind or refuse to assist with contingencies which arise and affect the working of others, or give less attention to maintenance of their equipment or quality of the work completed.

We would therefore like to suggest that any attempts to measure productivity which do not take account of effectiveness will produce a false assessment of the performance of the organisation and of its employees and have a misleading impact on decision-making at all four of the levels shown in Table 3.1.

Having argued the case for incorporating effectiveness into productivity measurement, let us examine what this implies. It implies that the factors incorporated into the measure are appropriate to the priorities for success of the enterprise. So an organisation which has, for example, a very poor record on meeting its deadlines for delivering orders and is losing orders because of this poor reputation, should measure productivity in terms of the key inputs which affect delivery performance and outputs which are components or dimensions of it. In another organisation where the key priority areas are reducing manufacturing costs and prices in order to maintain its share of the product market there would be a need for measures of productivity which measure the components of costs and relate them to reducing the price of the finished products. Other priority areas which organisations might need to improve include increasing plant utilisation, improving financial performance (return on capital invested or profit or added value), introducing new technology, controlling new technology, obtaining an increased market share, diversifying into a new market, etc., or some combination of these. In each case an overall productivity measure – or perhaps more accurately, a performance measure – can be devised for the whole organisation; and any measures of departmental or individual productivity/performance which are used in the organisation should flow from this and measure factors which contribute to it.

Although this approach emphasises the fact that there can be no single measure of productivity appropriate to all circumstances, it does at the same time provide an answer to the requirement for a universal standard – the standard of relevance. There is always an appropriate measure or set of measures for productivity/performance which is preferable to any other for a particular organisation at a particular time, depending upon its current priorities for improvement.

Dynamism

It follows from incorporating the concept of relevance into productivity measurement that since relevance changes with time, a dynamic element is needed in productivity/performance measurement.

Dynamism is important at two levels. In the first place it is important to review fairly frequently the measures used in order to ensure that priorities have not changed, and if they have, to change the measures to something more appropriate. One perennial danger of performance measurement is that it can rigidify patterns of behaviour which have no bearing on currently important issues.

And in the second place, dynamism is important at the level of individual performance. Criteria of performance should never be so rigid as to discourage flexibility, co-operation and initiative. On-the-spot decision-making may often be required from an individual to change activities to help someone else, or to take an opportunity to act in the best interests of the overall organisation. Narrowly defined terms of reference (such as maximising the number of standard minutes of work produced) can produce unwillingness to be diverted from one's current set of tasks. When selecting a performance/productivity measure, therefore, we would recommend that a sufficiently broad choice be made as to avoid such limitations wherever possible – team performance or departmental performance measures may achieve this.

Flexibility and the ability to take advantage of changing circumstances may mean operating with considerable levels of inefficiency on some factors, such that the costs of these inputs are not minimised. Work methods and plant should not be geared solely to maximising productivity ratios for the present state of the market, the technology and the human resources, if an alternative set of actions resulting in less efficient use of some particular factor can secure more effective achievement of current priority objectives. For example, suppose a priority objective was completing a large engineering project on time, and the most efficient schedule of work had been planned but one team could not get on with their work because an external contractor had failed to deliver vital components on time. It might be that another team could divert from their own work schedule for a time to complete another section of the project out of sequence in such a way as to allow the delayed team to work on another part of their work schedule until the components arrived. This hypothetical example illustrates the kind of practical problems which have to be resolved all the time in industry, and underlines the need for a dynamic approach to performance/productivity measurement. A good system of measurement would rank the flexible team as performing better than one which refused to co-operate. It is very easy to fall into the trap of devising a measurement system which discourages such flexibility.

Strategic Dimensions

The discussion so far has been concerned with measuring productivity in terms of current or recent work. The dynamic element incorporated in the last section needed to be stressed so that any measures used in practice would not restrict effort solely to those actions recognised as valuable when the measure was devised, and which might since have become less important. But there is another dimension of organisational performance not usually taken into account in attempts to measure productivity, and that is the extent to which the organisation has been equipped to deal with future requirements. Strategic objectives related to the long term stability, cash flow position, investment pattern, rate of growth, market share, product development, technological change, industrial relations etc., are at least as important as high productivity in the use of current resources. Although productivity factors and strategic objectives are usually interdependent, this is not necessarily so. It is possible to sacrifice long term viability in the interests of achieving short term success. For example, a departmental manager seeking rapid promotion may show a very high rate of output relative to the resources his department has used over a two-year period; but in pursuing this single-minded objective he may have allocated very little money to maintenance and renewal of machinery or tools, cooperated only minimally with R & D staff wanting to introduce new products onto the production line, and resisted disruption to his efficient production schedules when the marketing or sales division changed their forecasts of market demand. The end result could well be that he has been promoted and has left the scene before the adverse consequences of neglecting strategic considerations is recognised.

Many similar examples of the consequences of focusing on productivity targets at the expense of strategy could be cited for varying levels of executive responsibility. We would recommend that strategic considerations should be given specific consideration when productivity or performance measurements are reviewed. We discussed above the fact that productivity measurement is most useful when the factors in the productivity calculation are related to the organisation's priority areas for improvement. We would now like to add that these priorities should contain not only current performance dimensions but also factors related to future strategy. And that this can only be ensured by allocating discussion time specifically to the issue of strategy before being satisfied that a suitable measure for performance/productivity has been devised. The nature of the strategic factors which are relevant to productivity/performance measurement will depend on the stage of the growth cycle an organisation has reached.

Figure 3.3 shows one cycle of growth of an organisation or division, where the first period is marked by growth because of the advantage of offering a new product or service; the priorities are thus concerned with expanding operations fast enough to meet the market demand. Productivity measures should here assess the rate of growth and recognise the importance of initiative and responding to opportunities and problems. In the next stage more competitors have come on the scene and the priority issues relate to aggressive marketing and selling tactics and better methods of operating in order to continue growing. Productivity measures should then focus on market share and growth together with measures designed to recognise and encourage good organisational systems. The third stage is characterised by many competitors where

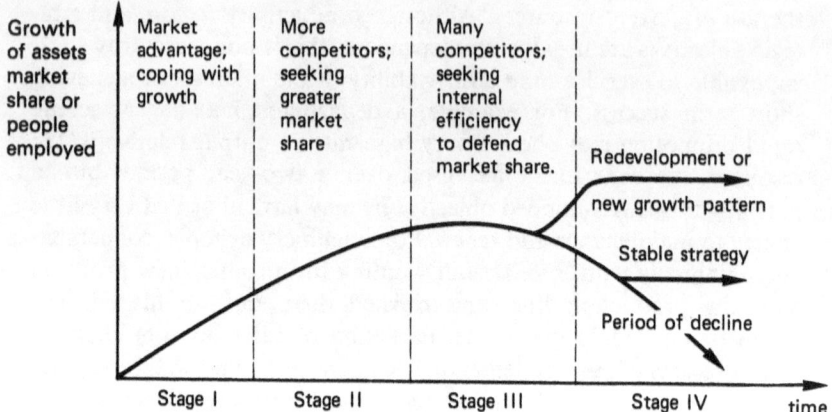

FIGURE 3.3 *Stages of organisational development*

the advantages of being first in the field have eroded and there is price competiton between organisations, making cost efficiency a major objective. It is at this stage that traditional productivity ratios and efficiency measurement are most closely related to strategic considerations. Whatever productivity measures are used here they should emphasise the importance of cost reduction and keeping prices low. In the fourth stage so many competitors have come on the scene or some product or service substitution is taking place, so the organisation must either develop in new directions or exploit some advantage it still has, to retain a stable position in a very difficult market, or it must face decline. Even if it can identify new activities to replace those in decline the organisation should be concerned with re-allocating its resources, restructuring its management and manpower, and introducing productivity measures focusing on tight control of costs in the declining areas with encouraging initiative and development in new areas.

There have been many models of organisational growth and development put forward in the literature, and we would not like to claim that the synthesis shown in Figure 3.3 is either original or better than others; only that it illustrates our points about relevance, dynamism, and strategy in relation to productivity and performance measurement. Haire (1959) compared organisational development to biological growth Greiner (1972) identified four stages of organisational development each characterised by a different philosophy of management. Hofer (1975) focused his model of organisational development on changes in the product life-cycle. And both Greiner (1972) and Webster

(1976) pointed out that there are significant differences in the kinds of management problems which arise at various stages of growth.

Cradall and Wooton (1978) made the very important point that the choice of factors which an organisation values as part of productivity will affect the future direction of the company and represent or shape its orientation towards policy issues. An organisation which focuses too much on internal efficiency measures at the expense of more important strategic factors for its current stage of development may well have a short life-expectancy or at least a poor potential for future performance.

Performance and Productivity

This chapter began by considering what is meant by productivity and its measurement through simple and complex ratios or functions. We then introduced the concepts of efficiency, effectiveness, dynamism and strategy because productivity measurement which does not take these into account is misleading and unhelpful to those who wish to base decisions on these measurements. But in doing so we have moved away from the technical definitions of productivity, and what we are really discussing is performance measurement. For the rest of the chapter we will use the term performance measurement except where productivity is the technically correct term. We hope the reader will recognise that in our view performance measurement is not something essentially different from or of limited relevance to productivity measurement. It is a fundamentally more valid concept applicable in all practical situations where productivity measurement is required.

PERSPECTIVES OF DIFFERENT PEOPLE ON PRODUCTIVITY

One of the important points about productivity measurement which is clear from the discussion above is that people with differing responsibilities in relation to an organisation have different views of what productivity means, different reasons for wanting to measure it, different requirements from such a measure, and different ideas on what it should take into account. There is no good reason for suggesting that any one of these alternative perspectives is superior to all others, or that the people who use them would be better served by one single measure of productivity. Table 3.2 identifies some of the

TABLE 3.2 *Alternative perspectives and appropriate measures for productivity/performance*

Person or group	Aim in measuring productivity	Appropriate measure
Government	Control of inflation Better international competitiveness	Unit cost (sales value of output divided by total cost of inputs)
Investors	Wise investment Protect capital	Financial measures, e.g. Return on capital (value of dividends or profits divided by shareholders equity or total assets; £ dividend per £ invested; etc.)
Top management	Attract investment Strategic decisions on location, expansion, etc.	Overall system measures, e.g. Return on capital Added value Sales value per £ labour cost Sales value per £ total cost Rate of change in market share
Middle management	Efficient use of resources Coordination of resources	Measures of performance of parts of the system, e.g. Machine running time Output per hour Output per unit of materials used, etc.
R&D management	Product and system development	Speed of acceptance of new technology Changes in hours for development time Reliability and flexibility of new technology
Work study or productivity services	Labour productivity Calculating incentive pay	Standard minutes of work produced per man hour
Supervision	Coordination of resources Achieving targets Control of workforce	Willingness of employees to comply with instructions Material utilisation Machine downtime
Employees	Extent to which they can get on with their own jobs unhindered	Provision of adequate materials and tools on time Subjective assessment of facilities and resources
Customers/clients	Good service	Prompt delivery Good quality Competitive price Quick response Adequate stocks

people who may need or wish to measure productivity, shows the purposes for which they typically wish to use it, and indicates the type of measure which is suitable for such purposes.

It is often the case that in pursuit of these different kinds of performance they pull in different directions, each detracting from the potential success of some other. This is not a necessary outcome of all these different aims and measures, since in theory it would be possible for them all to be complementary. But in practice they are very rarely all complementary.

For example, the manager from productivity services whose aim is to ensure that times are provided for all tasks and used to calculate incentive payments for employees may be creating the situation in which cooperation with the R & D manager's aims of introducing new technology rapidly with full employee cooperation is thwarted (and vice versa). If the order book is low and employees are short of work, the same productivity-related incentive payment system may be resulting in high payments (due to waiting time compensation) and high labour costs which could affect adversely the performance improvement aims of top management, the government, investors, and so on.

In their efforts to secure employee compliance and cooperation, supervisors very often agree to work schedules which suit the employees but which waste materials or machine-running time. Top management in pursuing their aim of expanding to secure a greater market share could well invest in technology which, perhaps temporarily, increased costs and made the investors' return on capital less attractive, at the same time as increasing unit costs and adversely affecting inflation, albeit in a small way. And past Government's aims of reducing inflation via incomes policy has at times in some places caused problems of recruitment and retention of key staff, so creating less efficient use of other resources. Policies designed to improve international competitiveness through reducing the value of the currency may cause worsening of productivity, measured in financial terms, for organisations importing raw materials or parts from overseas.

It would be possible to quote many more examples of the conflicting effects of different groups pursuing productivity improvement as they understand it. Whenever such conflicts occur the parties concerned would almost always feel justified that their own aims were of greater importance than those they thwarted. To some extent this is an inevitable consequence of their different perspectives on the issues. To some extent it is a consequence of failure to understand the complexity of productivity and the interconnections between its forms.

We would like to recommend that those concerned with improving the productivity or performance of an organisation should bring together a wide range of people within the organisation to discuss the organisation's priorities and to derive from those priorities a set of consistent productivity–improvement aims for each separate level and section of the organisation.

OPERATIONAL PROBLEMS OF USING PRODUCTIVITY MEASURES

Certain kinds of problems arise when productivity or performance measures are put into practice in an organisation. They are intended to affect the way people perform their jobs in ways which benefit the organisation, but they can have a detrimental effect on that performance or the performance of others in the organisation. And they can also have other unintended consequences. A number of these problems have been mentioned elsewhere in this chapter, but are drawn together in this section. The problems may be avoided by careful selection of appropriate productivity measures.

Changes in the System

Organisations experience change from numerous sources, for example from the introduction of new technology or changes in the skill levels of employees. Changes are occurring all the time, and therefore there is no constant relationship between the structure of input factors used and the package of outputs produced. In other words the constituents of productivity are constantly changing, in some cases at a much more rapid rate than others.

It is therefore very difficult to make comparisons over a period of time, as the base from which one seeks improvement is constantly shifting. And there is a great danger that any measurement system set up at one point in time will, after a period, be measuring inappropriate matters for the decisions which are based thereon; or worse still, will be diverting effort towards those inappropriate matters and away from more important current priorities.

Focus on Manual Workers

Those productivity measures which place heavy emphasis on the amount of 'work' completed by the workforce relative to labour costs are often taken to imply that improving productivity is mainly a matter of reducing what the workforce costs the organisation. This can provoke shopfloor resentment. It can also lead to a complacent management attitude which places responsibility for poor performance on the workforce and gives scant attention to management's own responsibility for improving productivity through better organisation.

Error of Aggregation

Many measures of individual productivity, particularly those based on work study, incorporate compensation for periods when the employees cannot get on with their job because some other person has failed to carry out their responsibilities adequately. For example, employees may receive compensation if they do not have an adequate supply of materials for their work, if their machine breaks down, or if there is a hold-up in the supply of work. Time is allowed for these delays in calculating his productivity, and consequently the individual productivity figure is a fair reflection of the extent to which the individual has been ready and willing to expend effort in performing his job. But by aggregating such figures to give overall performance or productivity for a number of people one is subsuming, within a so-called productivity figure, allowances for all the inefficiencies resulting from poor organisation or administration. This is a false figure for overall productivity.

Detraction of Effort from Some Aspects of Performance

By emphasising those aspects of work which are readily measured – and rewarding improvement in these aspects – productivity measurement can reduce the attention given to other aspects of the work, such as discretion, initiative, flexibility, and may make their exercise more difficult. This is sometimes seen as impoverishing the jobs of employees and/or their managers, and resented. It can also have a seriously adverse effect on commercial performance of the organisation, where such things as discretion and initiative are needed for success.

Discretionary Adjustments

When compensation is made in calculating performance level for disruption beyond the control of the individual or group, there is usually a large area of discretion in the allowances which enable the supervisor, the work-measurement staff, and sometimes the individual worker, to adjust the figures in such a way as to produce an answer they think is correct. This is usually done because the person making the adjustment believes the unadjusted productivity measure does not adequately reflect the effort expended by the worker. Adjustments are made in the interest of what is regarded as fair or acceptable, and in order to make the system operate more smoothly. However, it may lead individuals into making adjustments which amount to falsifying records about the work done, which does not contribute to a healthy climate of relationships at work. It also produces inaccurate information for planning and pricing purposes.

Individual Focus

By focusing on individual performance, productivity measurement can detract attention away from much needed group cooperation.

Shortage of Work

The measuring of productivity when there is not sufficient work to keep the workforce occupied throughout the day can have a very peculiar effect on patterns of work and of pay. Unless the organisation can produce more work in the time saved by employees who increase their productivity, there is little value in a productivity measurement scheme tied to a system of rewards, other than to provide information for potential changes to manning levels. The adverse effects can be quite serious. For example in one organisation which we studied where there was a shortage of work for one particular department. The employees in that department worked very hard for the first two hours, not taking any breaks or slackening their pace, and in those two hours completed all the work that was available for that day. They recorded waiting time for the rest of the day, which was paid at the same bonus rate as had been earned for the first two hours. Consequently the employees were recording very high productivity levels and receiving very high bonus during a period when the organisation was experiencing great difficulties and was certainly not benefiting from this pattern of work. Managers facing this situation sometimes also resort to creating work for their employees which is not actually necessary. This in turn consumes other resources, and may result in stocks of output which subsequently cannot be sold or used.

Discretionary Factors

Some productivity measures, particularly company-wide performance measures, incorporate many discretionary decisions about such matters as the valuation of stocks, how to handle depreciation, the valuation of work in progress, etc. There are so many choices to be made before a figure is finally reached, that it is easy for management to produce the answer they require and difficult to know how to make a wholly objective assessment. Such a figure is no more than a management control mechanism; and it should not be taken as an objective measure for comparison purposes.

Proxy Measures

Because some aspects of productivity and performance may be difficult to measure, organisations may resort to proxy measures, for example using absenteeism is a proxy for commitment. This can lead to problems where employees are not convinced of the reasoning for the proxy measure, or where they respond to the heavy emphasis placed on the proxy measure of their work performance by improving it independently of the matter it is intended to reflect. In the example quoted, absenteeism may be reduced, but commitment remain unchanged.

Link Between Measurement and Pay

By associating work measurement with bonus payments managements produce intense interest from the workforce and their representatives in the efforts of the work study and O & M department staff. It has been well documented elsewhere (Lupton, 1963; Roy, 1952) that employees go out of their way to ensure that 'rate fixers' make a generous measurement of the time it takes to complete a job. This is largely because such activity then results in loose times being given for the jobs, which subsequently enables the employee to earn high bonus payments. This distorting effect is often exacerbated by inaccurate recording of actual performance, which is presented in such a way as to disguise the loose rates. Consequently the productivity measurement figure obtained by management may be quite incorrect, and can be very misleading when they are used either for price calculations (to calculate the labour force input), for manning level calculations or for productivity comparisons. Since reasonably accurate performance figures based on measured productivity can be of great value to management, it is questionable whether the distortion in these figures which results from tying them to an incentive payment scheme is beneficial to the organisation overall.

Mickey Mouse Jobs

One effect of productivity measurement, especially where it is tied to bonus payment, is to produce an increase in the amount of activity, but not necessarily an increase in the amount of useful work. For example one sewage works which we studied showed a substantial increase in productivity, but this was obtained from a growth in relatively useless work, for example cutting the grass three times a week rather than only once. There is no financial benefit to the organisation from such productivity improvement. Another organisation which we studied showed a large cost saving resulting from a reduction in manning. However, the manning reduction was achieved by transferring the employees to another department not included in the productivity calculations, and there was little, if any, net benefit to the organisation.

Transfer Pricing

Some measures of performance are based on the sales value of work completed, e.g. added value ratios, sales/costs ratios; but organisations which are part of a larger group are frequently in the situation of selling their products as inputs to another part of the group, and therefore not receiving a market price for their output. Determining an equitable transfer price for the value of output from subsystems of an organisation is fraught with difficulty, especially where the output which is being priced could not readily be provided from the outside market. The problem is confounded when international currencies complicate it as products or services are passed between different parts of an international group. In such situations the managers and employees of subsidiary may feel aggrieved by the manner in which the transfer price of their output is calculated and then used to measure the performance of their organisation. They may feel that indices based on these transfer prices are not a fair assessment of their performance.

DATA PROBLEMS

Another kind of problem in relation to productivity measurement concerns the kind of data needed for the measurements and both the availability and compatibility of that data. The main problems concerning data are discussed below.

Diversity of Outputs

There is considerable variation between organisations in the extent to which their output can be treated as homogenous. At one extreme are organisations which span several industries and produce a wide range of completely different products and services; and at the other extreme are organisations producing only a small number of different lines, all of which are similar and may differ only in quality or grade from one another. Where there are several diverse outputs it becomes difficult to total them in order to produce an index of output, and even where the several products or services produced are reduced to their value in monetary terms in order to total them, there is still the complication that their production will have required differing amounts and combinations of inputs. The structure of the package of outputs may be as important therefore, as its total value when assessing the 'productivity' of the inputs used to produce it. In such cases the problem may be overcome by aggregating separate contributions to added value for each type of product in a given period. Alternately the work content, in man-hours, of each product can be used to convert total sales in a period into a labour productivity measure, but this is an approach which has limitations. Or progress can be judged by comparison to a set of production targets.

Diversity of Inputs

A similar kind of problem arises from the diverse nature of the several inputs which an organisation uses to produce any given level of output. It is very often possible to substitute more of one input factor for less of another, and whilst one package of inputs may be more expensive to produce a given level of output than another, it may have long term benefits such as enabling other work, with a value of output which will not come into the productivity equation until a much later stage, to progress more efficiently. It is therefore difficult to achieve a single measure for the value of inputs which is satisfactory, and strategic considerations should be borne in mind whenever assessments are made of the use made of resources.

Quantifying some of the Factors

Some of the factors which are important to the productivity or performance of an organisation, as was discussed above, are essentially qualitative and very difficult to quantify. Factors such as flexibility, cooperation, initiative or adaptability are fairly easily measured by the subjective judgement of participants of the organisation or of observers, but such qualitative measures are of very limited value for comparisons. Finding proxy measures which will quantitatively assess these factors is very difficult, but where they are important dimensions of productivity it is necessary to make the attempt if it is thought necessary to measure productivity/performance.

Diachronic and Static Characteristics of Productivity/Measurement

Productivity measurements attempt to relate inputs to outputs at a specific point in time. This diachronic approach does not enable one to take any account of the dynamic nature of the processes which are being evaluated by the measurement. Such a cross-sectional view is an unrealistic way of considering a dynamic process, and for organisations experiencing a period of change diachronic measures may be of limited immediate value and potentially harmful to successful change.

Ordinal, Cardinal and Ratio Types of Measurement

There are problems involved in trying to add together factors which have been measured according to different types of scale (ordinal measures, cardinal measures, and ratios). However, it may not be necessary to aggregate different kinds of measures if the information they contain can be interpreted and used adequately by comparing like with like for different time periods or different organisations.

Lack of Data

Many organisations simply do not collect certain types of data which would be needed for adequate productivity measurement. Other organisations collect the data in an aggregated form, so that looking at the productivity of a division or department is extremely difficult. Another problem about the availability of data is the adequacy of the data collected. Organisations which do keep records of productivity may nevertheless not record a sufficient range of factors for the information to be of value. And in addition, in some organisations the reliability of the data is questionable. It may be collected without sufficient attention to accuracy or without adequate checks to ensure it is up-to-date or accurate or that it reflects what it purports to reflect. Or it may be distorted in the process of being used for another purpose – such as bonus calculation.

Comparability of Data

Data may be collected in different formats in different parts of an organisation, making it impossible to produce indices, ratios or scores which could be compared between different parts of the organisation. Data may sometimes be collected and analysed so long after the time to which it relates that it is of little value. And even the various constituents of a productivity index may be recorded for different time periods and with different time lags, so that incorporating them all into one index becomes fairly meaningless.

Comparisons between organisations are even more difficult. Data may not be available at a sufficiently disaggregated level for comparisons to be feasible. Data is often presented in relation to a base period, and different base periods are often used. And it is very rare to find two organisations collecting exactly the same performance data and analysing it in exactly the same way, even supposing that it was appropriate for them to do so bearing in mind their current performance priorities.

CONCLUSIONS

There can never be a simple answer to the question 'How should we measure productivity?' The type of measure which is appropriate will depend greatly on the purposes for which it is to be used. The following recommendations may serve as guidelines:

1 Because of the problems discussed above, the simplest possible measure which will adequately serve the purpose should always be used.
2 Because of the problems created by distorted data and the tendency for some kinds of incentive schemes to encourage such distortion, information collected primarily for calculating bonus or incentive payment should be avoided in deriving a productivity measure for other purposes.
3 Figures which have incorporated into them allowances for inefficiency (waiting time, unmeasured work, etc.) when deriving a productivity measure for strategic, tactical planning or management purposes other than assessing individual effort, should be avoided.
4 Measures used should take account of qualitative and strategic factors where these are relevant to the purposes of the measurement (e.g. where it would be undesirable to encourage employees to neglect them, and where the measures used are likely to influence job performance.)
5 There is often no need to collapse all the important inputs and outputs into one single index or formula. A set of measures covering a range of types of productivity components may be quite adequate for comparison purposes. In the study of productivity improvement described in Chapter 4 we chose this alternative, and measured productivity improvement according to the degree of improvement in twelve different indices, namely:
   Manning reductions; increased output; financial improvements; improvements in quality; other general quantifiable improvements; industrial relations improvements; improved attitudes to work; generally better standards; improved pay situation (terms of differentials and relativities); improved customer service; improved internal relations; improved general state of the company.

It would have been impossible to produce an index or formula which incorporated all of these factors in any adequate way. Equally, it would have been unjustifiable to leave any of them out, since they were all based on statements made by managers we interviewed about the ways in which their scheme had improved productivity.

Some of them could have been incorporated into an index – for example manning reductions and increased output – but it would have lost some important information in the aggregation process, namely the ability to differentiate between those companies whose productivity improvement had come about because of reducing their labour force and those where the level of activity had, on the contrary, increased. In addition, incorporating the data into a combined index would have required a standard format; and the 63 companies in the study did not collect their data according to a standard format.

As will be shown in later chapters, this method of assessing productivity improvement proved quite adequate for our purposes. We did not find ourselves trying to explain fine differences in the degree of improvement between firms, because the differences were substantial, with some firms not obtaining any improvement at all on many of the factors. However, this is not to suggest that the method used in our study is suitable for other circumstances or other purposes. It would only be suitable for a similar study of relative improvements in productivity in a large number of dissimilar organisations.

Measuring productivity and performance can be vitally important to a wide range of purposes as was shown in Table 3.1. It is viewed in a different way by many different people, as indicated in Table 3.2. And there has been considerable confusion created by the many problems of trying to measure productivity referred to in this chapter. We hope that the points we have highlighted have demonstrated the need to develop appropriate productivity measures for the specific purpose to which they will be applied, bearing in mind the current priorities for performance improvement and availability of adequate information.

4 Payment Scheme Decision Choices

This chapter compares the decision choices in 63 organisations which introduced new payment schemes between 1977 and 1980 with the decision processes implied by a normative approach to contingency theory and a relativistic multiple constituencies model for the evaluation of organisational performance. The relatively poor impact of these payment scheme changes on organisational performance (judged from three major perspectives) derives at least in part from the discrepancies between the decision choices actually made and the normative theoretical model proposed. There are certain key strategic choices made by organisational decision-makers (whether deliberately or by default) when a change is made in a payment system, and these are discussed and analysed from the empirical evidence of the longitudinal study discussed in more detail in the next chapter.

Those organisations which fitted the model of positive descriptive or structural contingency theory (termed deterministic or positivist in this chapter) designed their payment schemes primarily in response to external contingent factors, and had the worst results, so casting further doubt on the validity of such a model.

ALTERNATIVE CONTINGENCY THEORIES

Contingency theory is now a well-established approach to management decision making. Two conceptually very different theoretical approaches have been given the label 'contingency theory'. The first, termed Structure-Contingency Models (Pennings, 1975) or Positive Descriptive Contingency Theory (Legge, 1978) assumes that the structural characteristics of an organisation (such as its management style, spans of control, degree of centralisation, type of payment system, etc.) are *determined* by the state of various contingent factors in its environment, such as its technology, its market, its economic environment, etc. This theory postulates that the survival of the organisation is dependent on the 'right' structural and procedural arrangements being set up, and therefore a statistical association is expected between contingent factors and organisational characteristics. This view has been strongly criticised (for example by Shreyögg, 1980; Bobbitt and Ford, 1980; Wood, 1979; Child, 1972) on the grounds that there is often no such relationship, because several factors may intervene, most particularly the strategic choices about structure and procedures made by managers in the organisation; and also because organisations do exist and survive within a similar set of contingent constraints with a wide variety of characteristics (Child, 1972; Galbraith, 1977), so proving that these structural characteristics are not *determined* by the contingent constraints.

Contingency theory was based on the empirical findings of such people as Woodward (1959; 1965) and Burns and Stalker (1961), and was consistent with prevailing developments in sociology (structural functionalism and its emphasis on inter-dependence of organisations with their environment, cf. Gluckman, 1964). With this background it was welcomed as a great improvement on previous theories of organisational effectiveness (which primarily assumed one best way of organising, structuring, managing, etc. cf. Urwick, 1943; Fayol, 1949). Nevertheless, it has received a prodigious amount of criticism in recent years. So much so, that some have been moved to question whence the environment – structure model derives its tenacity for survival (Sherif, 1982 for example).

Part of the reason for its survival is that the crude deterministic model of environmental-structure interdependence described above, and illustrated in Figure 4.1, is quite different from the version of contingency theory which underlies much of the work which relates contingency theory to management practice (Feidler, 1967; Vroom and Yetton, 1973; Lupton and Gowler, 1969).

This latter work is consistent with the model of motivated action

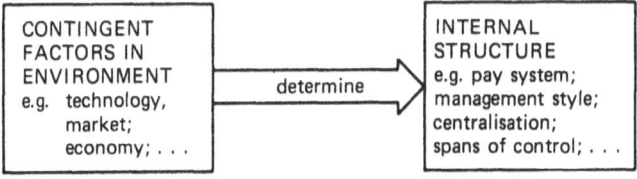

FIGURE 4.1 *Determinist or positivist contingency theory*

shown in Figure 4.2 where the action of organisation members influences and in turn is influenced by the context of economic, political, and social structure within which it takes place; and where such action and these contextual factors combine to produce the results of the action.

This 'action theory' approach (cf. Silverman, 1970) translates into a version of contingency theory as shown in Figure 4.3. Here the contingent factors (which may be external or internal to the organisation, so obviating any need to define environment or organisational boundaries) influence and are influenced by the strategic choices made by managers which in turn combine with the contingent

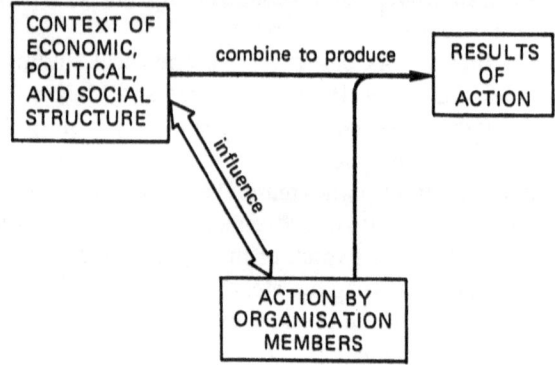

FIGURE 4.2 *Simple model of motivated action by organisation members*

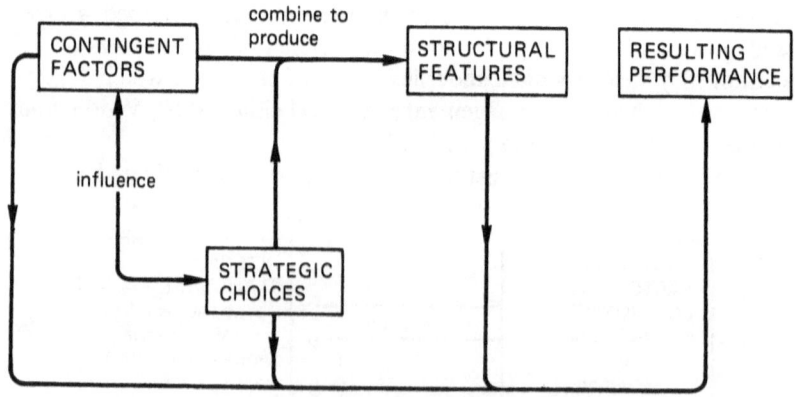

FIGURE 4.3 *Contingency model based on action theory*

contextual factors to shape structural features of the organisation about which strategic choices are being made, and to determine the resulting organisational performance.

This second contingency theory approach has been termed normative contingency theory (Legge, 1978) or the 'best fit' approach (Lupton and Gowler, 1969). Here the dependent variable is seen as the effects or outcome of the structural and procedural arrangements, which in turn are dependent on strategic choices. Management decisions about structure and procedures are viewed as intervening variables between the contingent constraints within which the organisation operates and the effects on organisational performance. Contingent factors over which managers have little or no control may influence their strategic choices to varying extents, but do not *determine* them. For example in the study of payment systems reported in Chapter 5 the choice of objectives for their payment systems (and consequently some characteristics of those payment systems) was greatly influenced in many organisations by the constraints and exhortations of the prevailing national incomes policy. But these did not *determine* the objectives nor the type of payment systems selected. They only affected the strategic choices made by management and this indirectly affected the eventual outcome in performance terms. Other contingent factors, such as technology and type of market had a less marked effect on these choices.

The difference between the two approaches to contingency theory can be illustrated diagramatically as shown in Figures 4.4 and 4.5. In these figures the type of payment system is the aspect of structure which, in the positivist or determinist model of contingency theory (Figure 4.4) is seen as determined by internal and external factors, and in the normative model of contingency theory (Figure 4.5) is seen as the resultant of management decisions.

One of the key differences between the two models is the recognition in the second that there can be all kinds of different dimensions of performance influenced by a payment system choice and that organisations survive with a wide range of performance levels on each of these. It is therefore not the payment system that is contingent on the constraints, it is the eventual performance of the organisation. The reason this model is termed the normative model of contingency theory is that it implies managers *should* make decisions about, say, their payment systems in such a way as to achieve the impact on organisational performance they are aiming towards, i.e. by taking account of the various contingencies in deciding what the objectives of

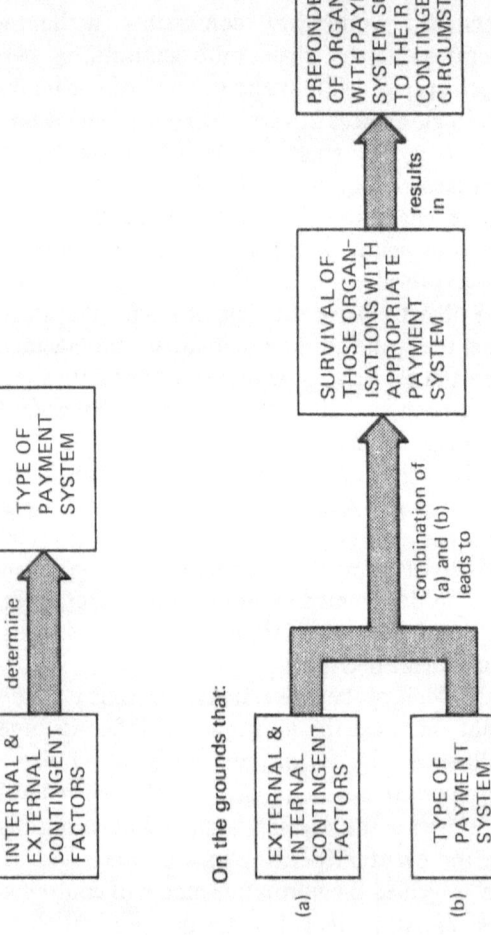

FIGURE 4.4 *Positivist or deterministic model of contingency theory applied to payment systems*

Payment Scheme Decision Choices

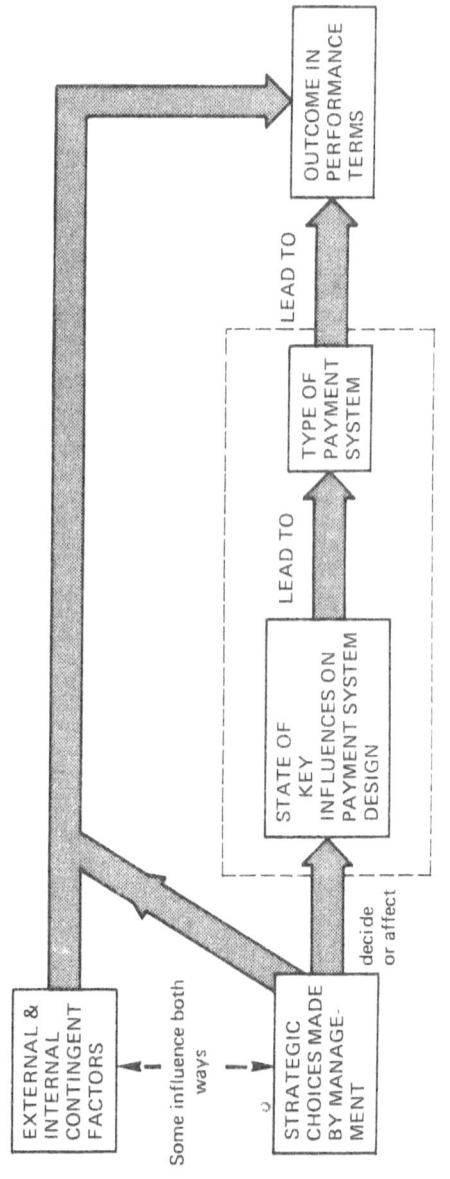

FIGURE 4.5 *Normative model of contingency theory applied to payment systems*

the scheme should be and what kind of scheme should be introduced.

The data for the study used in this chapter and the next were collected using fixed choice questionnaires (1040) and open-ended interviews (438) of selected personnel from 63 UK organisations which had introduced incentive payment schemes between 1977 and 1980. The research began in 1978 and this phase of the data collection stopped in 1981.

The underlying assumption in this chapter about the role of payment systems within organisations is that they form part of the control procedures introduced by management with the aim of influencing the way employees perform their jobs and thereby influencing organisational effectiveness. The following analysis is based on the proposition that characteristics of the relationships linking priorities for organisation success, payment scheme objectives, and payment scheme design principles, greatly influence the effects of a payment scheme on organisation performance. The relationships are influenced by external and internal contextual factors and by the different goals being pursued by different people within the organisation (see Figure 4.6).

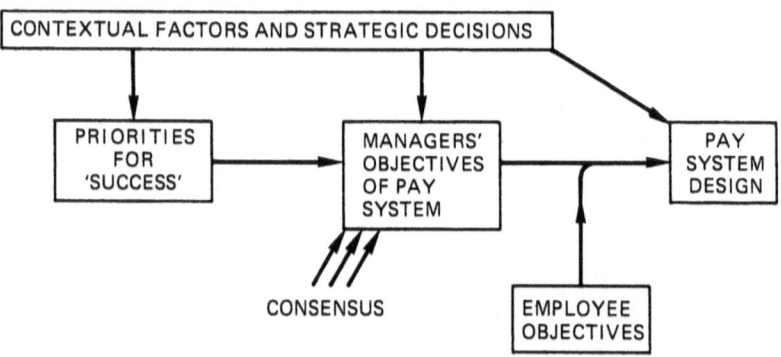

FIGURE 4.6 *Key influences on pay system design*

This kind of approach to studying organisational behaviour still leaves difficult questions to be answered. But they are not the same questions as the critics of deterministic contingency theory pose as stumbling blocks (such as how one defines the boundary between organisation and environment). The most important question this approach poses is how one evaluates organisational performance.

Evaluating Organisational Performance

Previous studies of effectiveness have identified three alternative approaches to defining and evaluating organisational performance – goal-based models; system models; and multiple constituency models (Zammuto, 1982). Goal-based models may focus on any of four views of the appropriate goals for assessing effectiveness – operational goals for the organisation; manager's goals; a contingent choice of goals; or the social scientists' view of what the goals should be. The latter often take the form of concepts associated with the viability of the organisation and form the basis of the systems approach to assessing organisational effectiveness. A multiple constituencies approach is one which recognises that there are several alternative perspectives as to what an organisation should be achieving, depending upon the point of view of, say, an employee, a manager, a shareholder, a member of the wider society, the government, or an observing social scientist. The manner of reconciling these alternatives may either be to leave such evaluations for others to make (relativistic multiple constituencies); to place emphasis on the goals of powerful groups; or to place more emphasis on the goals of weak or deprived groups (social justice approach). Figure 4.7 shows a summary of these alternative approaches.

The goal-based model which accepts that there are 'goals of the organisation' and judges organisational performance by how well these goals are achieved is probably the oldest and most common evaluation mode (Strasser *et al.*, 1981). But there are problems in trying to distinguish between individual goals and organisational goals (Katz and Khan, 1966; Perrow, 1961); and in identifying these organisational goals, since it has been found that organisation members are often unwilling or unable to clarify them unambiguously (Katz and Kahn,

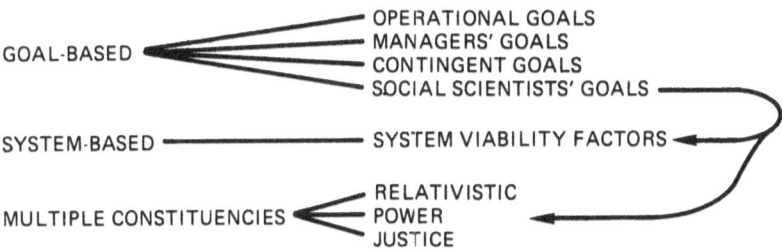

FIGURE 4.7 *Alternative methods of assessing organisational performance*

1966, page 15, quoted in Strasser *et al.*, 1981). Indeed Weiss (1970) has argued that researchers should not attempt to evaluate organisational performance unless there is a clearly specified set of operational goals for that organisation. However, such a limitation to research is not helpful. The key question about identifying 'organisational goals' is whether and in what form they do exist. The evidence seems to indicate that they are no more than constructs used by organisation theorists and to a limited extent by some organisation members. As such they do not provide a valid basis for assessing organisational performance.

An alternative goal-based approach is to ignore the problem of distinguishing between operating organisational goals and individual goals and to accept the goals set by managers as those against which organisational performance is to be evaluated (as advocated, for example, by Etzioni, 1960, and by Price, 1968). However, the value judgement that the objectives of the wider society (or the employees or shareholders) are of no importance in evaluating organisational performance is definitely questionable.

Dubin (1976) tried to resolve the problem by proposing a contingency approach to determining the appropriate goals for evaluative purposes according to the actions being evaluated and the intended aims of those actions. But actions have implications for goals they were not aiming towards, and there seems to be little justification for excluding from an analysis of organisational performance the effects on goals of groups within or affected by the organisation other than those initiating the selected goal-oriented actions.

An alternative contingency approach is to select the goals appropriate to the purposes of the evaluation. That is, if the evaluation is being performed in order to guide managers in their decisions, then managerial goals are appropriate. If the purpose of the evaluation is to inform or assist outside agencies in their decisions, then the goals of the relevant outside agency are the appropriate ones. If the purpose of the evaluation is for a research team to make an objective evaluation of organisational performance, then either some concepts relating to system viability will be postulated, or one is led to a 'multiple constituencies' model which takes account of the variation in goals-for-the-organisation as envisioned by different groups.

The dominant alternative to the goal-based approach is the systems approach, which evaluates organisational performance from the overall strength or viability of the organisation, as indicated by its behavioural dynamics. It focuses on the processes occurring within the organisation in order to evaluate organisational effectiveness in terms

Payment Scheme Decision Choices

of the capacity for successful resolution of internal problems and for adaptation to the external environment, using such factors as flexibility, adaptability, conflict-handling capacity, etc. (see for example Katz and Kahn 1966; Yuchtman and Seashore 1976; Georgopolous and Matejko 1976). The approach is consistent with the recommendations of Thompson and McEwan (1958) and Parsons (1956) amongst others, who argued that the appropriate goals for evaluating organisational performance should be derived from the wider society.

The drawbacks of a systems approach have been referred to many times and in many different contexts (e.g. Silverman 1970; Weiss 1972; Bowey 1974; Strasser et al., 1981). Some of these drawbacks can be summarised as follows:

- the approach is difficult to operationalise and no consistency has developed in the concepts applied (Weiss, 1972; Strasser et al., 1981);
- by emphasising the functions served by various processes for the maintenance and survival of the organisation the model suffers from the same conservative bias often laid at the door of structural functionalist developments (Silverman, 1970; Bowey, 1974);
- the assumption that system models are value free (made, for example, by Evan 1976; Mahoney and Frost, 1974; Duncan 1973) is in error since the social scientist is merely substituting his own values for those of others (Zammuto, 1982; Spray 1976), in deciding that the viability of the system is the goal which should be aimed for.

More recently, dissatisfaction with the models discussed above has led to the development of multiple constituency models of effectiveness (for example Connolly et al., 1980). Early work had pointed out the significance of alternative criteria for success applied by different groups (Bass, 1952); and the lack of close correlation between scores for these different criteria (Freidlander and Pickle, 1967). Multiple constituency models can either make no attempt to evaluate the relative importance of the criteria used by each constituent group, and present the data for others to assess (termed relativistic multiple constituency models, for example Connolly et al., 1980); or they may define effective organisations as those which satisfy the demands or preferences of some particular group, such as the organisation's most powerful constitutency (power-oriented multiple constituency models, for example Pfeffer and Salancik, 1978; Hrebiniak, 1978; or the organisation's least advantaged constituency (termed the social justice criteria as propounded by Keeley, 1978; or Rawls, 1971).

There is no requirement for a researcher to confine his approach to assessing organisational performance to only one of the pure types described above. Strasser *et al.* suggested that goal-based and system models could usefully be conceptualised as two ends of a continuum (1981). Zammuto pointed out that each approach can be developed so as to incorporate elements from the others (1982). There have been several comprehensive and useful reviews of the alternative models for evaluating organisational effectiveness (for example, Campbell *et al.*, 1974; Steers, 1975; Dubin, 1976; Weiss, 1972; Zammuto, 1982; Barton Cunningham, 1977).

This present study started out with multiple constituencies each with a legitimate interest in the results of its evaluations. These were the Social Science Research Council and the Department of Employment who funded the work; a team comprising ex-managers and social scientists who carried out the work; and many managers and trade unionists within organisations whose cooperation was required for its successful completion. The Department of Employment were particularly keen to use our research results to evaluate the government policy of encouraging companies to introduce self-financing productivity schemes as a means of reducing unit costs and thereby helping to bring down inflation. The managers who cooperated with us wanted feedback to help them assess the effects on their own goals of the changes in payment systems they had introduced. The trade unionists were interested in the effects of these schemes on their members. And our research team were interested in assessing the effectiveness of the changes introduced in order to compare the different strategies adopted by different organisations, and apply a normative contingency theory analysis to these.

We therefore made separate assessments of organisational performance from each of these perspectives. This involved us in a form of contingency-based composite goal and systems model, taking into account the goals of all the groups relevant to the purposes of the study, plus a range of 'system health' measures.

The measures of performance used were constructed from answers to our questionnaires given by up to six different managers in each organisation (differentiated by function and including a supervisor), a shopsteward and a group of up to 20 shopfloor employees. Approximately half of these people were subsequently interviewed (open-ended) and the interview summaries coded and scored to give a quantitative analysis. From this data two methods of performance measure were derived. The first consisted of variables selected as typical of the range of objectives, at least one of which any organisation is usually pursuing when introducing an incentive scheme. Scores were judged from answers to a question asked of the person in the organisation most likely to have accurate information on this point.

The ten performance variables measured were:

1 Unit cost reduction;
2 Increased volume of production;
3 Number of blue collar employees reduced;
4 Reduced prices to customers;
5 Decreased lead time on deliveries;
6 Reduced reject rate;
7 Product quality improved;
8 Output increased;
9 Morale improved;
10 Cooperation with management improved.

The second measurement method was to construct composite indices, each one cumulatively taking account of answers from each respondent to several questions and their interview comments on the same topic. The twelve performance indices so constructed were:

1 Manpower reductions;
2 Increases in output;
3 Financial improvements;
4 Quality improvements;
5 Other specific improvements (e.g. reduction to wastage; stockholding reduced; material costs reduced);
6 Improvement in industrial relations;
7 Improved work attitudes;
8 Better standards of work;
9 Pay relativities or differentials improved;
10 Better customer service;
11 Better inter-personal relations;
12 Generally improved state of the company, e.g. future prospects of the company, or economic condition of the company.

It can be seen that some of these indices are direct managerial criteria of performance; some are criteria shareholders or investors would use; some relate to the Government's objective of bringing down inflation; some relate to criteria the employees applied to evaluating organisational performance as it affected them; and some were essentially system criteria of performance. Our research took account of the extent to which each type of criteria had been improved as a result of the introduction of the new payment system. We accepted the view of the participants in the system as evidence of such causal improvements, with two safeguards. Firstly, by asking several respondents for their views and aggregating them; the strength of consensus (and thereby the likelihood of a genuine improvement) was reflected in the index scores. And secondly, we made considerable efforts to follow up the assertions of our respondents by collecting quantitative information about performance from company records and by examining company reports and other sources.

Empirical Application

An important factor which correlated significantly with good results on most of our criteria was the decision process on which the new payment system had been designed and implemented. Figure 4.8 shows the model of this decision process as we postulated it would be operated by 'good management'. We identified four factors as being of significance: 1: the link between the management priorities for organisation success and management's payment scheme objectives; 2: the link between these payment scheme objectives and the principles incorporated in the payment scheme design; 3: the degree of internal consensus about payment scheme objectives; and 4: the link between labour force motivational requirements and payment scheme design. The impact of internal and external contingent factors upon each component of the model was also taken into account.

Evaluation of the impact of these schemes on organisational performance was undertaken from five perspectives: 1. achievement of organisation priorities for success; 2. achievement of managerial objectives; 3. achievement of national incomes policy objectives; and 4. achievement of criteria considered important by other organisation members; 5. achievement of improved organisational performance judged from an external managerial perspective.

PRIORITIES AND OBJECTIVES

Managers' opinions as to the variables considered most necessary for

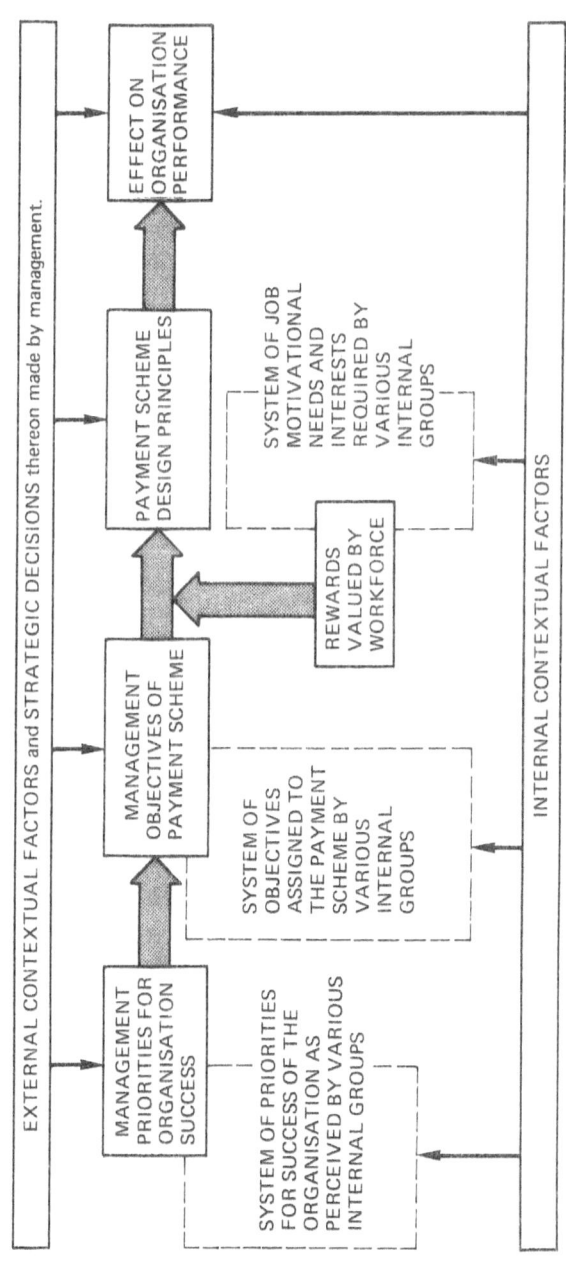

FIGURE 4.8 A normative contingency model of payment scheme design and implementation

organisation success (Table 4.1 first column) indicated strong preference for 'maintenance of quality' and 'meeting delivery dates'. We were interested in asking about the objectives for organisational success so that we could assess the extent to which the new payment schemes had been designed with these objectives in mind. The normative contingency approach to studying payment systems would lead one to conclude that an effective payment system ought to be designed with the priorities for organisational success in mind. By examining the extent to which this occurred, we could make an

TABLE 4.1 *Senior managers' priorities for organisation success and payment scheme objectives**

*Priorities for organisation** success*

*Incentive payment scheme*** objectives*

	frequency (N = 57) %		frequency (N = 57) %
Maintenance of quality	67	Increased employee earnings	74
Meet delivery dates	40	Increased output	70
Retention of labour	22	Increased motivation & employee commitment	58
Keep prices low	21	Increased profits	39
Production throughput	21	Increased labour mobility and flexibility	35
Continuous running of plant	14	Improved product/service quality	32
Customer or client relations	7	Reduced manpower	32
		Reduced labour turnover	32
		Improved delivery performance	16

*The analysis for this table was completed by Lawson Savery
**Priorities were measured by asking managers judged likely to know what was important for the success of their organisation to choose a maximum of 2 factors (from a list of 14) which they thought were the most important.
***Objectives for the payment system were judged (in this instance) by asking senior managers most closely involved with designing and implementing the scheme to choose a maximum of 5 factors from a list of 15.

assessment of the extent to which this aspect of a contingency approach had been adopted.

In spite of the finding that quality of output and meeting delivery dates were the two most commonly occurring priorities for success, these factors were not given high priority as objectives for the incentive payment schemes introduced (see Table 4.1 second column). The majority of senior managers reported that they had introduced their incentive scheme in order to offer increased earnings to employees in the belief that this extra money would motivate them to produce more.

Our questionnaire survey was followed by open-ended interviews with the same respondents in which they were encouraged to discuss the new payment system freely. Just less than half our total sample of managers and employees were interviewed and Table 4.2 provides a

TABLE 4.2 *Most common interviewee perceptions of payment scheme objectives*

Objectives most frequently mentioned by interviewees	Proportion of total mentioning this objective (N = 449) %
Increase employee earnings	55
Increase productivity	26
Increase production	21
Circumvent Incomes Policy	19
Increase efficiency	17

summary of the five objectives most frequently mentioned by organisation members in their interviews. No other objective was mentioned by more than 8% of the sample. Note that the objective 'to circumvent incomes policy' had not been offered for selection in the questionnaire. Our respondents volunteered it in their interviews.

In approximately two-thirds of the organisations studied there was substantial interview evidence indicating that increasing employee earnings was a major objective of introducing the incentive scheme.

There were three broad groups among those senior managers who introduced an incentive scheme with a primary objective of increasing earnings for employees. Each group differed in its secondary objective, and these were:

a. To improve productivity by completing more work;
b. To circumvent the incomes policy;
c. To facilitate a reduction in manning levels.

Approximately one third of the surveyed organisations fell into the second category and were pursuing the objective of increasing employee earnings.

OBJECTIVES AND DESIGN

Features about which decision-makers need to make choices in the process of designing a payment scheme include:

1 the number of people (or size of groups) whose work is to be used as a basis for incentive payment;
2 the aspects of work performance to which incentive payments are to be linked;
3 the period of work time on which the payment is to be based;
4 the length of time after the work period that the payment is made;
5 whether the bonus payments are to be equal for all members of a group (in group based schemes), or to be higher for those on higher basic pay;
6 the proportion of total pay to be constituted by bonus payments;
7 the method by which improved performance is to be measured and related to pay;
8 the arrangements for feedback to employees about their performance and its consequences for pay;
9 which employees are to be included in the scheme, and which excluded.

Unless the design of a payment scheme is based explicitly on the objectives it is intended to achieve (and those objectives in turn give due regard to contextual factors), then it will be sheer luck if it achieves them. For example: a 'group' incentive payment scheme suits the objective of encouraging closer employee co-operation and increasing flexibility; a 'machine running time' scheme suits the objective of increasing production throughput or the amount of work completed with existing machinery; a 'quality improvement' scheme suits the objective of reducing customer complaints.

In many of the organisations in our study a blanket supposition had been made that incentives would motivate employees to contribute to company priorities, even though there had been no close examination and identification of what those priorities were, or of how they could be translated into objectives for a payment system. This made it unlikely that these schemes were designed so as to contribute to organisational priorities. There was, indeed, little evidence in many of our cases that the schemes had been through a process one could label 'design' with the aim of achieving specific objectives. To do this would have required detailed discussions and consultation with a wide range of people within the organisation, a lengthy planning period and considerable preparatory work. Only a small proportion of our schemes had these characteristics.

CONSENSUS ABOUT OBJECTIVES

Payment schemes and organisations do not in themselves have objectives, they can only be assigned objectives by people. The extent to which different members of an organisation assign closely similar objectives to a new payment scheme will depend upon the amount of time which has been spent discussing those objectives and the range of people who have been involved in such discussion. Lack of consensus about a scheme's objectives can contribute to the failure of a scheme (Thorpe, 1980). This arises when organisation members perceive the payment scheme as intended to achieve different aims from those intended by the decision-makers who introduced it. Their efforts may in consequence be directed towards goals which are inconsistent with those of line management, or are of no value to the organisation.

Table 4.3 shows the frequencies with which different groups ranked each factor from a choice of 15 as one of the 5 (or fewer) main objectives of their new payment scheme. The factors on which management, particularly senior management, focused attention to a greater extent than shopfloor workers and their supervisors were 'increasing employee earnings', 'increasing motivation/commitment', and 'reducing labour turnover'. The factors which shopfloor workers and, to a lesser extent, their supervisors, emphasised more than the managers were 'to reduce wastage', 'to increase company profits', and 'to reduce/avoid industrial action'. The sales and marketing managers were one group with a view distinctly different from other managers, and they placed more emphasis on the importance of 'increasing profit', 'reducing industrial conflict', and 'improving delivery times'. It can be seen that these perspectives on the payment schemes reflect the particular interests and position in the organisation of the respondents.

A comparison was made between the perspectives of male and female and between blue and white collar employees and there was a

TABLE 4.3 *Questionnaire responses indicating each payment scheme objective*

Payment scheme objectives (From fixed choice questionnaires)	Senior management (N=57) %	Personnel (N=53) %	Sales marketing (N=36) %	Supervisors (N=53) %	Employees (N=640) %
Increase employee earnings	74	62	53	64	51
Increase output	70	64	75	79	77
Increase motivation & employee commitment	58	53	59	38	21
Increase company profits	39	–	66	47	57
Improve labour mobility & flexibility	35	34	34	26	35
Improve product-service quality	32	34	38	25	27
Reduce manpower	32	26	13	17	26
Reduce labour turnover	32	17	9	17	14
Reduce overtime working	28	26	13	25	29
Reduce lead time on order deliveries	16	17	41	23	16
Reduce stoppages or industrial action	14	–	34	15	25
Reduce wastage	7	22	41	25	31

N.B. Percentages represent % of category selecting this objective as a main objective of the scheme; each respondent was asked to choose up to 5 from a list of 15.

similar pattern of seeing the payment scheme differently and focusing on objectives in which they had a special interest (Table 4.4). White collar women attached more importance than their male counterparts to the 'adjustment of pay differentials between groups in the plant' and to 'reduce absenteeism'. Blue collar women placed more emphasis than blue collar men on 'improved labour flexibility', 'mobility', and 'manpower reductions' as objectives for the incentive schemes.

The observed lack of consensus in many of the organisations about the objectives of their new payment systems led us to expect that many schemes would not be effective in achieving these objectives.

MOTIVATIONAL NEEDS AND PAYMENT SYSTEM DESIGN

The fourth link in the normative model underlying this work concerns the extent to which payment scheme design had taken account of the motivational needs and interests of people to whom it was to be applied and integrated these requirements with the objectives the scheme was intended to achieve.

If it is intended that a payment scheme should achieve a particular objective by changing the way a certain group of people do their work, then it should be designed so as to offer rewards to those employees that they would value, and not detract from other rewards they think are important. This requirement is fundamental, for example, to the expectancy theory of payment systems (Lawler 1971) which states that an effective incentive payment scheme must meet the following requirements:

a. the employees must value and seek the reward being offered;
b. they must believe that the reward will follow if they improve their performance;
c. they must believe that they are capable of improving their performance to the extent required to earn the reward.

For the analysis that follows, information on job satisfaction was obtained from questionnaire answers which required the respondent to indicate which three factors from a list of nineteen were the most important to their job satisfaction. The results are summarised in Table 4.5. The factors which these employees and supervisors indicated as being of great importance were job security and regular increases in pay.

Blue collar workers tended to place greater value on those facets of

TABLE 4.4 Payment scheme objectives as indicated by men and women in joint white collar or blue collar payment schemes*

Payment scheme objectives
(from fixed choice questionnaires)

	White collar		Blue collar	
	Men (N=37) %	Women (N=25) %	Men (N=66) %	Women (N=87) %
Increase employee earnings	62	64	56	55
Increase output	73	80	76	80
Increase motivation & employee commitment	49	24	29	20
Increase company profit	54	68	73	45
Improve labour mobility and flexibility	41	32	17	48
Improve product-service quality	32	20	24	28
Reduce manpower	27	16	6	22
Reduce overtime work	27	24	27	28
Reduce lead time or order deliveries	22	36	24	9
Reduce wastage	24	32	35	38
Reduce absenteeism	11	32	41	39
Change earnings differentials	5	24	18	21

N.B. Scored from same question responses as table 3.2.
*The data for this table was analysed by Lawson Savery.

TABLE 4.5 *Blue and white collar employees' and supervisors' job satisfaction requirements*

Job satisfaction requirements (from fixed choice questionnaires)	Blue collar (N = 420) %	White collar (N = 82) %	Supervisor (N = 45) %
Regular increase in wages	55	32	40
Guaranteed job security	48	43	44
Opportunity for promotion	9	22	13
Fringe benefits, eg. subsidised meals, discount buying, social facilities	4	1	–
Generous holiday/sick pay allowances	27	7	16
Shorter hours of work	15	1	13
Opportunities for overtime	10	1	–
Good union representation	10	5	2
Healthy and safe working environment	22	16	20
Extra payment for effort	24	20	20
Job status/prestige	2	4	7
Opportunity for leadership or responsibility	4	22	18
Opportunity to learn and develop skills	8	20	11
Participation in decision-making	6	18	22
Recognition and praise for job well done	10	15	18
Good working relationships	21	33	22
Reputation of the organisation	2	10	11
Fair allocation of work load	12	4	–
Management attitudes	4	10	16

job satisfaction which measured extrinsic rewards of the job (such as pay and job security) than did white collar workers. And for the majority of factors which measured psycho-sociological aspects of job satisfaction (such as opportunities for leadership, learning new skills, and good working relationships) the white collar group indicated significantly greater preference than the blue collar operatives.

The supervisors' responses fell between the blue and white collar groups, indicating preferences for shorter working hours, generous holiday and sick pay allowances (in common with the blue collar group) and opportunities for leadership, for responsibility and for participation in decision making (in common with the white collar group). Many of these first line supervisors had been promoted from the ranks of the shopfloor workers, and the majority (93%) were in charge of blue collar workers, had to work the same hours and usually worked in the same conditions as their subordinates. Supervisors ranked the highest of the three groups on factors that suggest that they wished to be recognised and given status by their superiors, and they indicated a stronger orientation to the management of the company than the other two groups.

An examination of male and female job satisfaction requirements was also carried out, but this yielded only three factors on which there was a statistically significant difference between male and female preferences (at the 5% level or better). Both white and blue collar women saw good working relationships as more important than did men. White collar women did not seek opportunities for leadership and promotion, which was not the case for male white collar employees, although this could have arisen because the women were in lower graded white collar work than the men. The other major difference was that white collar women saw good union representation as more important than did men. This concern is reflected in the evidence from other studies that women form a major new growth area for unions (Department of Employment, 1981, page 23; Bain and Price, 1980, tables 2.1 and 2.2).

The above analysis suggests that some employees will respond better to certain kinds of reward systems than others. The study casts considerable doubt on any proposals for a blanket approach to employee motivation based on universalistic assumptions about the satisfactions they seek from their work. There are major differences in the extent to which the three groups (blue collar, white collar, and supervisors) valued the range of possible rewards from work, and little evidence of any desire amongst blue collar employees for those facets of job satisfaction normally associated with job enrichment programmes.

Many of the incentive payment schemes introduced by the organisations in our study were, in broad terms, likely to be appropriate for blue collar employees. There is, however, some room for doubt about their appeal to the white collar and supervisory groups. Those schemes which were intended to facilitate reduction in manning ran counter to the second most important priority of the blue collar groups and the top priority of white collar and supervisory employees, namely guaranteed job security. It is therefore unlikely that these employees gave their wholehearted support to this kind of scheme.

EXTERNAL CONTINGENCIES AND OBJECTIVES

This chapter has argued that if any of the four key aspects of the normative model so far referred to are not adequately managed, then it is highly unlikely that a payment scheme will succeed in improving organisational performance. And the poor results from many schemes can be traced back to these kinds of failures.

Every payment scheme operates in an organisational context of structure, technology, human relationships, control procedures, etc. And the organisation in turn operates within an external context of markets, technological developments, government policies and controls, legislation, social structure, training systems, other organisations, etc. These factors, internal and external to the organisation, can also influence the corporate performance achieved by the introduction of an incentive payment scheme, and have been the focus of previous contingency studies (Lupton and Gowler, 1969: Lupton and Bowey, 1974).

This chapter adds to the contingency approach the recognition of four key aspects of the design and implementation process (Figure 4.8) which require 'strategic decisions' to be made by management (Child, 1972; Bobbitt and Ford, 1980), and which are major influences in the effects of the payment system on organisational performance.

It is the decisions which are made about payment scheme objectives in relation to organisational priority, the degree of consensus about payment scheme objectives which is generated, the links between these objectives and the links between scheme design and rewards sought by employees, and payment scheme design, which form the key influences on eventual results. They mediate between contextual contingent factors, which cannot in themselves affect the payment scheme design.

The results of our study show a considerable effect from external economic conditions and government policy upon the four key strategic decisions discussed above. However, it is certainly questionable that these influences shaped the decisions in such a way as to enhance organisational success. In other words the influence of certain contextual factors (such as the prevailing incomes policy) on managers' strategic decisions caused, in many cases in our study, decisions to be made which had an adverse effect on organisational performance. The predominant external factors influenced the key strategic decisions made by managers in the following ways:

a. they encouraged management to set objectives for payment schemes which did not adequately match the operating priorities for organisation success or improved performance,
b. they generated a short-term consensus that payment scheme objectives were to increase earnings above incomes policy guidelines, which effectively hindered the development of consensus about organisation performance objectives,
c. they encouraged the design of bonus schemes which were easy and fast to introduce and which took little account of organisation success requirements or of factors important to the motivation and job satisfaction of a large part of the staff to whom they were applied.

The managers in our sample demonstrated a range of responses to the external influences on their decision making. And the best results were not obtained by those whose main objective had been to respond to the external pressures. This provides yet further empirical evidence that the determinist or positivist mode of contingency theory, discussed at the beginning of this chapter is inadequate.

Chapter 5 considers the results achieved by these payment schemes.

5 Payment Scheme Performance

Previous chapters have considered management approaches to the design of payment systems and some of the shortcomings of these approaches. This chapter looks at the results of a substantial research study of newly introduced incentive payment systems in Britain. The project which began in 1978 and was completed in 1981, was carried out by a team of six researchers at the Pay and Reward Research Centre (Strathclyde University)* and examined the effects which these systems produced. The results identify certain pre-requisites of successful new payment systems.

At the time the study began in August 1978 many organisations in Britain were considering introducing self-financing productivity schemes which involved changes to their wage payment systems. This provided the project team with a unique opportunity for a large-scale comparative study supplemented by in-depth studies of a smaller number of organisations. In the process of our study 1040 questionnaires were completed by 320 managers, 58 shop stewards and 662 employees in 63 organisations; 438 semi-structured interviews were held, and further data was gathered from company reports and follow-up questionnaires completed 12 months later by 29 of the companies. This data was supplemented by three in-depth case studies, one of a large engineering company, one of a large public sector enterprise, both in England; and a third covering two different branches of a large insurance company, one in Scotland and one in England.

The main thrust of the study was to answer the following questions:

1 had the new payment systems achieved improvements in factors which had previously been indicated to be the objectives of the scheme, i.e. had they achieved what they set out to achieve?

---

* The project was funded by the Department of Employment and the Social Science Research Council. The report of the study was published in 1982 (Bowey *et al.*, 1982). The research was carried out by a team consisting of Angela Bowey, Richard Thorpe, Fanny Mitchell, David Gosnold and Geoffrey Nichols, who were joined for part of the time by Bob Ferris, Lawson Savery and Phil Hellier.

2 had they achieved improvements in factors important to the national government's aim in imposing this kind of incomes policy on the companies, i.e. had they contributed to national priorities?
3 had they achieved improvements in factors previously indicated as being important to the success of the organisation, i.e. had they achieved anything of commercial value to the organisation?
4 what were the distinguishing characteristics of the more successful schemes?

The short answer to the first three questions is: yes, they largely achieved what they set out to do, namely to increase pay in an acceptable way; no, they did not contribute to national priorities which had been to reduce inflation by controlling unit costs; and no, on the whole they made little contribution to the priorities for success of the organisations, although some were better than others.

The study then went on to examine the differences between these new schemes and between the companies to find out why some had done better than others.

CHARACTERISTICS OF THE STUDY

Before examining the analysis of the data it is useful to have an understanding of the types of firms included in the study, and the nature of the incentive schemes examined.

The 63 organisations for study came from a wide spread of industries within the manufacturing and service sectors (see Appendix, Tables A.1 and A.2). These organisations were located throughout Britain with the majority centred in the industrial areas of Scotland, London, the North-West and the Midlands (see Appendix, Table A.3).

The sample covered a spread of sizes from very small companies with fewer than 35 blue collar employees, to very large ones with more than 3000 workers. The age distribution and union membership of employees is provided in the Appendix, Tables A.5 and A.6. Three quarters of the employees surveyed held union membership whereas less than one-quarter of their supervisors belonged to a union. There was a reasonably even distribution of skill levels among the organisations studied; 12 companies had highly skilled workers, 24 had moderately skilled employees and 14 had semi-skilled and unskilled workers, while 4 companies recorded a complete range. (Nine companies did not answer this question.)

Almost all the incentive systems in the study were introduced during the operation of the government's 'Phase III' incomes policy. Table 5.

TABLE 5.1 *Summary of dates of negotiation and implementation of the schemes in the survey*

Policy	Negotiations started	Negotiations finished	Scheme introduced
August 1975–July 1976	5	1	1
August 1976–July 1977	3	4	1
August 1977–July 1978	27	17	24
August 1978–April 1979	14	23	27
May 1979 onwards (No policy)	1	3	8

shows the dates of negotiation and implementation of schemes in this survey.

As was expected, the 63 organisations surveyed were instituting a wide variety of incentive schemes. In fact, the number of dimensions on which payment systems varied were so numerous and had so many varied forms that trying to categorise payment systems became a futile exercise, as mentioned in earlier chapters.

The majority of the schemes paid a basic rate plus a variable bonus of some kind. Of the 63 companies, 38 were using work study techniques, and 32 based the incentive pay on work-measured performance figures. Some of these were directly work-measured payments by results, whilst others had devised output targets or machine operating speeds based on work measurement data. Sixteen of the schemes were versions of added value or profit sharing or sales value related schemes, which were popular at the time. Seven had introduced fixed sum bonuses of one kind or another (the categories are not mutually exclusive). Fifteen paid bonus linked to individual performance; twentyseven linked it to group performance; and thirteen schemes were based on plant-wide performance figures. There was a much higher proportion (63%) of group and company-wide schemes than was to be found at the time in existing schemes in Britain as a whole, indicating a move towards this kind of scheme at the time (discussed in Chapter 2). Of the 33 companies that gave figures for their bonus as a percentage of total pay, three-quarters paid a smaller bonus than the United Kingdom average of about 33% (New Earnings Survey). This may have reflected a trend towards smaller bonus payments as a form of pay increase rather than as an attempt to motivate employees.

RESEARCH DESIGN AND METHODOLOGY

Research design is illustrated by the model shown in Figure 5.1. The

94 Payment Systems and Productivity

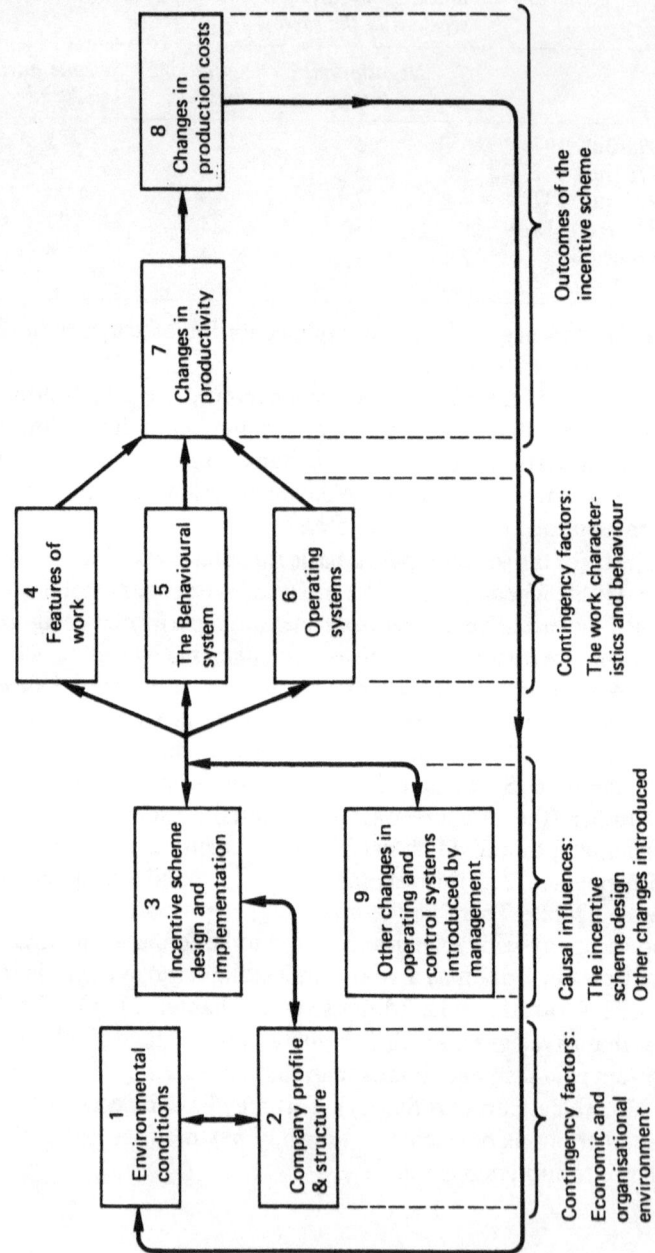

FIGURE 5.1 Model of processes and factors influencing the outcome of a new incentive scheme

study involved an examination of the strength of relationships and the causal influences between the variables in the cells of this model. Data was collected on each of the 9 component cells.

1. Cells 1 and 2 represent external contingency factors impinging on the success of any new incentive scheme. Cell 1 examined hypothesised contingent factors at a macro level, while cell 2 examined hypothesised contingent factors at the company or micro level.
2. Cell 3 explored the incentive scheme, its implementation and its design.
3. Cells 4, 5 and 6 represent hypothesised contingent factors internal to the activities of the organisation which related to incentive scheme success; cell 4 exploring features of the work, cell 5 exploring the behavioural system and cell 6 examining the operating systems of the company.
4. Cell 7 provided information on changes in performance and productivity.
5. Cell 8 examined changes in production costs.
6. Cell 9 related to any other changes in the operating and control systems of the organisation (other than the payment system) which may have been causal influences on changes in cells 4, 5 and 6.

Multiple methods of data collection, sometimes termed 'triangulation', were used with the aim of improving the analysis by collecting different kinds of information on the same phenomenon. The term triangulation is taken from the navigation and military strategy that uses multiple reference points to locate an object's exact position (Smith 1975, p. 273). The use of this technique in social science research is based on the premise that the weakness in a single data generation method will be offset by the counter-balancing strength of another. The assumption is that the multiple and independent measures do not share the same weakness or potential for bias (Rohner 1977, p. 34).

With the overall objective of maximising the amount of data we were to collect we adopted several research techniques to complement each other. First, we distributed fixed-choice questionnaires to a number of individuals in each of our sample of companies; second, we carried out semi-structured interviews with a high proportion of questionnaire respondents; third, we sent out a questionnaire to each company approximately 12 months after our interviews to monitor changes resulting from the incentive scheme; and finally we carried out in-depth studies in several companies which entailed either a researcher working as a participant observer or members of the work-force writing diaries over several months. Wherever possible we also acquired data from other company sources, such as company reports. Our analysis took into account all these sources of information, and consequently it was both complex and extensive.

Our research team normally consisted of five or six members with complementary experience. As will be imagined with an interdisciplinary research team, different views were often held. For instance some saw an inherent conflict between the objectives of management and employees, whilst others took a more unitary approach and believed it possible to devise payment systems which would benefit both parties involved.

Whilst a common perspective shared by all members of a research team might avoid some of the variability in approach, it would also reduce interpretations of the data. In all, and with one short-term exception, our research team was mutually supportive and worked well as a team.

Table A.7 (Appendix) shows the calendar of main stages in the work carried out. Apart from conducting a literature search and establishing a system of reference articles, most of the first few months were spent identifying a suitable sample of companies and persuading them to participate. We tried to achieve a representative sample in terms of types of payment system, industry, geographical location, size and type of ownership.

The next stage of the research was the questionnaire survey which was aimed at obtaining as broad a range of information as possible. For example, information about the kinds of incentive schemes introduced and how they were introduced, the objectives they were designed to meet, the initial results following their introduction and the expectations of the managers and employers involved in the schemes, together with data on the motivations of the employees and management. Most of the questions were of the 'forced choice' type.

In all, eight different self-completion questionnaires were designed to cover eight distinct organisational functions, namely:

senior management
personnel manager
finance manager
sales or marketing
   manager

management services manager
supervisor
shop steward
employees (usually 10–20
   working as a group)

A total of 167 questions were designed. Each individual or group was asked only those questions that were relevant to their function within the organisation. In many cases the same question was asked of more than one group. This enabled checks to be made for data accuracy and conflicting individual or group perceptions.

Several versions of the questionnaire were drafted and piloted in two different companies. The longest of the eight questionnaires took nearly 30 minutes to complete, and the shortest just over ten minutes. These were distributed in April and October 1979. Examples of the questionnaires are included in Appendix II.

The distribution of questionnaires was sub-contracted to a commercial survey organisation, but their interviewers were all carefully briefed by our research team, who also provided a list of named individuals to whom the questionnaires were to be delivered personally. The interviewer was left to pick at random some 10 to 20 shopfloor workers in the area or department chosen for study (selecting a whole team or section wherever possible). As a result of their persuasive efforts the response rate was quite good. From the named individuals there was a response rate of 90% and including the shop floor workers it was 79%.

Data obtained from questionnaires is more or less limited to factors and hypotheses which have been specified precisely beforehand. One aim of our research was that it should be exploratory as well as testing known theories. There could be many factors which might affect the operation of incentive schemes in ways hitherto not predicted, and one way to obtain this information was by the use of open-ended interviews.

Our initial intention had been to carry out interviews in half of the proposed sample of organisations, but due to the fact that our sample of organisations was smaller than we had hoped, it was decided to carry out interviews in all the companies that would co-operate. Very few refused, so at that point (October 1979) almost our entire sample was covered, (52 companies). Companies which joined the study later were not given interviews. In each organisation we aimed to interview all the managers who had completed a questionnaire (including the supervisor), plus the shop steward, about 4 shopfloor workers and a maintenance worker related to them. The execution of the interviews went very smoothly; in very few organisations was there a refusal to participate, and in most cases the respondents were extremely helpful to the interviewers.

In order to obtain an objective and quantitative summary of each interview, to which computer analysis could be applied, a coding framework was devised by the research team and all the interviews scored on this in a systematic way. The technique developed for this was based on methods used on content analysis. Three coders were employed on the task of using this framework on all 437 interviews, and care was taken to ensure consistency between the three.

Data from the interviews was then computerised and combined with data from questionnaires to permit cross-referencing between the different sets.

In order to gather longitudinal data about the effects of these incentive schemes over time, we sent out a 'monitoring' questionnaire to each company some twelve months after our interviews. The monitoring questionnaire was long and detailed, and was sent out through the post in April 1980. Frankly, the response was not as good as we had hoped, and the completed questionnaires were returned by 19 companies. However, most of the monitoring questionnaires we did receive had been completed with great care and attention.

The data which was received from these questionnaires was duly processed and coded in a form to make it compatible with our other data sets.

Further to our aim of obtaining in-depth information, during the Autumn of 1979 and the Spring of 1980 we carried out four in-depth case studies, using two different research methods, the first, participant observation, and the second, a novel use of work diaries. These detailed studies provided considerable insight into the operation of payment systems. They helped us to generate propositions which could then be tested more formally from our other data sources. And they helped us to understand the dynamic operation of payment systems, the causal relationships and behavioural responses which underlay the statistical data subsequently generated.

The three months long participant observation study involved one of our research team going to work on the shop floor in the summer of 1979 in a high technology light engineering company. In addition to participant observation, data was gathered by a questionnaire from management and a cross-section of the workforce. The researcher worked as a company employee under the same conditions and tried to act in the same way as other workers, so that he could experience their situation at first hand and observe behaviour in detail. Thus he was able to understand their attitudes, feelings and reactions to the incentive scheme and the reasons for their behaviour.

In the other three case studies we used work diaries; groups of employees and their immediate managers and supervisors from two different companies were asked to write a daily account of their work experiences, the events occurring at work, how they reacted to and interpreted these events, and in particular anything that related to the incentive scheme.

The first organisation in which we conducted a diary study was one which we were particularly anxious to include and our original intention was to send one of the research team to work as an observer. However, safety regulations would have required several months training before this would have been allowed, and it was not feasible. The alternative of getting the employees to write their own accounts was adopted. In the second organisation in which we used diaries, the work required a level of skill which would have taken months to acquire, so again participant observation was not feasible.

All those selected in consultation with management and the union to participate in writing a diary agreed to do so, and in one case we organised a training weekend to involve them more closely in our study and to help them to write the kind of accounts we were looking for in the diaries.

Following this introduction, a member of the research team was put in charge of each study, with responsibilities for maintaining continued contact and encouragement to the diarists, and for analysing the diaries as they came in. The diaries were to be returned direct to us each week. The researcher then read them and wrote back asking for clarification of specific points to aid our analysis and to encourage the writers further. This maintained a good relationship between the research team and the diarists, and showed that we were reacting to, and taking an interest in what they were writing. Members of the team visited the work sites on a number of occasions during the study and talked to as many of those involved in the study as possible.

The diaries were supplemented by systematic interviews of several members of management and union officials, and by statistics collected from Head Office and Regional Offices, so that a balanced report of the schemes could be written.

RESULTS OF THE STUDY

An effective incentive payment system should improve the work performance of employees and increase the productivity of the organisation. In the rest of this chapter the effects of the incentive payment schemes in the Strathclyde study are examined in a two stage analysis. First, the overall success of the schemes is considered – were their objectives achieved? Second, an attempt is made to determine the characteristics of successful schemes.

How Successful Were the Incentive Payment Schemes?

It has already been demonstrated that the performance of an incentive scheme can be evaluated from several viewpoints. The approach taken here is to consider the success or failure of incentives schemes by:

a. determining whether the objectives of the managers who introduced the schemes were met;
b. determining whether the goals of the national incomes policy were achieved;
c. examining the judgement of organisation members as to each scheme's effects.

The Achievement of Managerial Objectives

To determine whether managerial objectives had been achieved, a set of fourteen performance factors were developed from managers' questionnaire and interview responses. Table 5.2 summarises these results by indicating for each of the evaluation factors (objectives) the percentage of organisations which definitely aimed for that objective and the percentage of those who were aiming for it who definitely achieved it.

From the point of view of the objectives as understood by the managers who introduced and operated the payment schemes, and provided it is accepted that increased employee earnings was a legitimate objective, then most of the surveyed organisations succeeded in their primary objective. The proportion who achieved their secondary objectives varied considerably depending on what that objective was; the success in reducing manning (for example) was much higher than the success in achieving an increase in the amount of work done (78% compared to 42%). On the whole, the achievement of quantifiable performance improvement objectives was poor.

TABLE 5.2 *Comparison of objectives and achievements: a management evaluation*

Performance criteria (management questionnaire and interview responses)	No. of firms with this objective. (total 52)	% of those firms with this objective who definitely achieved it
To increase earnings	40	85
To reduce manning	9	78
To motivate employees, increase effort; provide an incentive etc	24	71
To improve efficiency or productivity	22	68
To improve quality	11	55
To improve absenteeism or timekeeping	5	50
To increase output	33	42
To reduce labour turnover	7	29
To increase profits	16	25
To increase flexibility	15	20
To improve differentials or relativities	5	15
To reduce overtime	9	11
To reduce costs	1	100 (1 firm)
To change organisation	3	0

NOTES
1. Most organisations reported more than one objective, and some reported several.
2. Several objectives which organisations reported they were trying to achieve did not occur amongst the items mentioned as having been achieved, and were therefore not included in this table (for example: to circumvent incomes policy).
3. An objective was recorded as definite when two different managers in the same organisation reported it either in their interviews or in their questionnaires, or where the one and only manager questioned so reported. Only the 52 companies where interviews were carried out were included in this part of the analysis.
4. *The percentage who achieved their objective* is calculated on a firm by firm basis and is the percentage of those firms who definitely had an objective who also definitely achieved it. (Some firms who indicated they had achieved certain objectives had not originally been aiming for them. This most often occurred when they had *not* achieved the objectives they had reported they were aiming for.)

Achievement of Incomes Policy Objectives

Under the prevailing government incomes policy guidelines, the general level of pay increases were to be kept below 10% per annum, unless any additional increase was justified by a self-financing productivity scheme which could be introduced after 31 July 1977 (Government papers Cmnd. 6882; 6151; 6507 and 7293). According to the Department of Employment a self-financing productivity scheme was one:

...whereby the savings achieved in unit costs outweigh the costs of the scheme such as the extra payments to those directly or indirectly involved, and any extra capital or running costs. Such schemes do not raise prices. The scheme must be demonstrated to be self-financing and be subject to regular checking that it remains so. (Department of Employment, June–July, 1977)

Essentially, the basic aim of the government policy of encouraging self-financing productivity schemes was that these should reduce an organisation's operating costs. From this point of view it is disappointing that only one surveyed organisation convinced us that this had been its definite objective and in only six others was it mentioned at all by management as an objective. Six of the fifty-two firms reported consistently that costs had been reduced: and a further five gave some indications which suggest that they probably achieved a reduction in costs. Taken together these represent only a fifth of the total sample. It is possible that some organisations were able to hold their product costs constant, while increasing employee earnings, by reducing overall manning levels. However, very few senior managers or sales managers saw the schemes as actually bringing about a decrease in price to the consumer.

From the point of view of the national economic policy directed towards reducing production costs and the rate of inflation, it must be concluded that the majority of these incentive payment schemes, as evaluated by management, were a failure.

Achievement of Organisation Priorities

There was little evidence of close links between the factors which managers thought were important for the future success of their organisations, and the objectives being sought via their payment systems. It is not surprising therefore to find that there was little evidence of these incentive schemes making a positive contribution to improved organisational performance. Table 5.3 compares the relative ranking, by management, of priorities for organisation success and of factors improved by the payment system. Only two of the priorities even appear in the list of factors improved, and their importance as priorities is not by any means reflected in the figures for achievement. Two-thirds of our sample of organisations needed to improve quality, but only a quarter reported that quality had definitely improved as a

TABLE 5.3 *Priorities for organisation success compared with the improvements achieved by payment schemes (from management questionnaire responses)*

Priorities for organisation success	Organisation frequency (N=57) %	Improvements achieved by payment schemes	Organisational frequency (N=57) %
Maintenance of quality	67	Increased take home pay	84
Meet delivery dates	40	Increased output	73
Retention of labour	22	Improved morale	67
Keep prices low	21	Improved co-operation between employees	49
Production throughput	21		
Continuous running of plant	14	Improved co-operation with management	49
Customer or client relations	7		
Flexibility to respond to customer specifications	5	Increased differentials	25
		Improved quality	19
Development of new products/services	3	Increased skill	18
Balance of work or operation between sections	2	Improved safety	8
		Reduced prices to the customer	6
Elimination of waste	2		
Keeping up to date with technology	2		

NOTES
1. Priorities for organisation success were measured by asking managers to choose two from a list of 14.
2. Improvements achieved were measured by asking managers to indicate whether each of these factors had increased/improved, stayed the same, or worsened.

result of introducing the incentive scheme. The reason for this poor link is undoubtedly the intervention of other influences on management objectives, primarily the national incomes policy. Managers were aiming for objectives not linked to the commercial success of their organisations, and consequently the payment schemes made relatively little contribution to the commercial success of most of our sample.

Achievement of Other Members' Priorities

Earlier it was established that one of the major factors for employee work satisfaction was job security. The questionnaire responses indicate that different groups within an organisation had different expectations about the effects their payment scheme would have on manning levels (Table 5.4). Shop Stewards were the most optimistic about schemes not resulting in manning reductions. But taking the senior managers' views as likely to be the most accurate, almost two-thirds of the organisations expected the incentive scheme to lead to fewer jobs.

TABLE 5.4 *Anticipated reductions in manpower: questionnaire responses (Bowey, 1980)*

	Senior managers N=55 %	Supervisors N=50 %	Shop stewards N=47 %	Employees N=633 %
NO	38	44	55	50
YES	62	56	45	50

Six to twelve months after the pay schemes had been introduced, the labour force had declined in about one-third of the organisations as a result of the Scheme (Table 5.5). Given the relatively short time period between the introduction and evaluation of the schemes there was still the possibility that further reductions could follow.

The increases in pay (which were achieved in all except one of our organisations) were, of course, welcomed by the employees who received them. But from the perspective of the large number of employees who placed job security at the top of their priorities, and the even larger number who ranked it second (after regular pay increases), many of these incentive payment systems conflicted with their interests.

TABLE 5.5 *Organisations that experienced labour force changes as a result of the payment scheme (Bowey, 1980)*

	% Increased	% Same	% Decreased
Blue collar	8	30	35
White collar	8	51	6

In addition, many of the white collar and supervisory groups had priorities associated with leadership, responsibility, opportunities for participation, etc. There were very few cases where there was evidence that the new payment system had brought about any positive changes in these areas, and some where these aspects of the jobs had been limited by the new systems.

We therefore concluded that the new payment systems had a mixed effect on employee interests; but their negative effects were particularly undesirable if it was hoped that the schemes would positively motivate improved performance.

Summary of Incentive Scheme Achievements

In summary, it can be said that generally the payment systems were successful in increasing employee earnings. For some organisations this had in part been financed in one or more of the following ways: reduced manning levels; greater employee effort; increased output volumes; improved efficiency and productivity.

Very few organisations had actually reduced unit costs of production, reduced consumer prices or reported an increase in profits as a result of the schemes. Less than one quarter of the 55 organisations for whom a financial benefits index (reduced costs, improved profits, etc.) could be reliably constructed, had scores indicating an improvement (Bowey et al., 1982). We therefore concluded that the majority of these payment schemes enabled organisations to increase employees' pay and in some cases to improve efficiency and reduce manning levels, but rarely were production costs per unit actually reduced.

The decisions made in our sample of organisations were compared in the last chapter to the decisions which would have been made had they been pursuing a normative contingency theory approach. This showed that only a minority of organisations made decisions consistent with this model. Since the resulting impact on organisational performance was poor it is in our view likely that a normative contigency approach would have been better.

On the other hand, approximately a third of our sample of organisations made decisions which were consistent with a positivist or determinist contingency model – they merely responded to the strongest contextual influence on them. According to this contingency model, these organisations should have consequently performed better than others. However, viewed from a multiple constituencies perspective of organisational performance, the net conclusion is that this was not the case. The organisations whose decision-making processes fitted this model performed particularly badly from the perspective of national priorities, commercial results and employees' interests. We conclude therefore that there is no empirical support in our study for the positivist or deterministic model of contingency theory.

Which Incentive Schemes Were Successful?

The above summary of overall results does not focus specifically on the differences between the relatively more successful schemes and the others. In this section an attempt is made to determine the characteristics which were common to successful schemes. The isolation of the characteristics of incentive schemes that explain performance variations may enable the identification of those features which should be designed into a payment scheme to achieve a particular set of objectives.

In terms of our analytical model, this section involves an examination of the relationship between incentive scheme design and implementation (Cell 3) with changes in productivity (Cell 7) and changes in production costs (Cell 8).

As Opsahl and Dunnette (1966), Grinyer and Kessler (1977) and Yetton (1979) have pointed out, there has been little empirical research undertaken on the impact of different types of incentive payment schemes upon an organisation's *economic* (output, cost, productivity, profit) performance. This stands in marked contrast to the research undertaken on the relationship between worker satisfaction and productivity (Brayfield and Crockett, 1955) and the work group's *social* responses to different payment systems (Roethlisberger and Dickson, 1939; Dalton, Collins and Roy, 1946; Roy 1952, 1954; Marriott, 1957; Brown, 1962; Lupton, 1963; and Millward, 1968).

Payment Scheme Performance

Even if the exogenous variables affecting payment scheme economic performance were isolated, the many internal characteristics by which payment schemes may vary, make a comparative economic evaluation of different schemes quite difficult. (cf. White, 1981, pp. 123–6). For example, payment schemes may be classified according to any one or a combination of the following factors:

the basis for reward calculations, e.g., output, cost reduction, reduced wastage;

the procedure for calculating rewards, e.g., set formula, supervisor assessment;

the process of establishing the norms entering such calculations, e.g., management initiative, time study, joint determination;

the frequency of incentive payments, e.g., weekly, monthly, annually;

the size of the group to which the payment is made, e.g., individual, group, plant;

the stability of the incentive payments, e.g., fixed, variable, partially guaranteed;

the staff included in the scheme, e.g., process workers, maintenance workers, white collar workers;

the size of the bonus as a percentage of total pay;

the period of time over which the bonus calculation is based;

the conditions attached to the payment, e.g. can it be withheld in certain circumstances such as absence or industrial action?;

the way the bonus is shared out, e.g. as a flat sum or to all as a percentage of basic pay.

As a result there is no adequate typology suitable for economic evaluation of payment schemes, although there have been attempts to produce one (e.g. ILO, 1951; Lupton and Gowler, 1969).

Given this dearth of incentive payment scheme performance information, managers have often responded by either:

following the latest fashion in payment systems as sold to them by consultants;

or adhering to their own particular preferred payment system as a panacea for all situations;

or superimposing more than one type of payment system (sometimes overlaying one on another) in an endeavour to cope with the complexities of worker motivation and changing work environments. White (1981) reported that 130 (32.4%) of the 401 British manufacturing plants he surveyed in 1979–80 were applying more than one type of payment system simultaneously to process or maintenance workers.

One advantage of the contingency approach which was discussed in earlier chapters is that it forces managers to consider the objectives of their payment systems along with the characteristics of their organisation in an analytical manner. It assists them to make those decisions on payment systems that are more likely to bring positive economic benefit to their organisations. In the past the contingency approach has been largely concerned with selecting the payment scheme design that will 'best fit' the environmental and job profiles of the organisation. In terms of our analytical model (Figure 5.2), this implies the effects of environmental conditions (cell 1), company structure and profile (cell 2), features of work (cell 4), the behavioural system (cell 5), and operating systems (cell 6), upon incentive scheme design and implementation (cell 3).

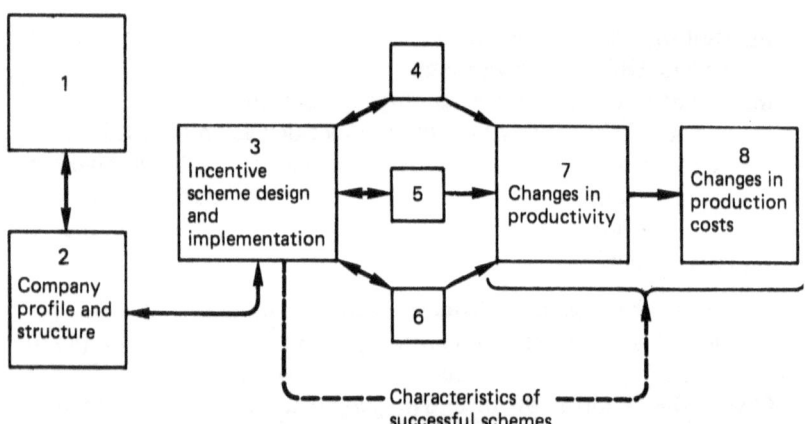

FIGURE 5.2 *The analysis of payment scheme design as it affects performance*

The assumption is that schemes so selected will perform better than schemes where these contingent factors have not been taken into account in the design of the payment scheme. To design a scheme in this way requires an understanding of the factors affecting payment scheme performance. Previous texts on this subject have based their advice on case study evidence and expert knowledge of the way particular kinds of payment systems operated under certain circumstances (Lupton and Gowler 1969; Lupton and Bowey 1974, 1983).

The study reported in this chapter was the first large scale intensive study of the operation of payment systems from which we can draw conclusions about the factors which influence payment system results.

Independent responses about features of the payment system, the organisation, its context, the relevant action taken by managers, attitudes of managers, unions, workers, and the resulting organisational performance were tested for inter-relationship. The findings in this section therefore do not say anything about management's reasons for selecting particular schemes, but only that certain factors show a significant level of association with good or bad results. Our perspective on 'good performance' was that of an objective outsider, as opposed to the perspectives of company management, the government and the employees. Here we were looking for the kind of improvements one might reasonably expect to result from the introduction of a performance-related incentive scheme.

There can be no single measure of success which applies to all organisations because of the wide variations in aims and points of view. We therefore drew up a list of ten items covering the various types of performance – improvements that companies might seek if their scheme were a straightforward attempt to improve performance. This list included some very specific items such as 'reduced prices to the customer' and some very general ones, such as 'morale improved'. Table 5.6 shows the full list. We are confident that any genuine scheme to improve productivity should be aiming to improve at least one of these.

Each of our companies was given a score (yes = 1; no = 0) for whether or not they had achieved each item. The scores were derived

TABLE 5.6 *Selected performance variables*

1 Unit cost reduction
2 Increased volume of production
3 Number of blue collar employees reduced
4 Reduced prices to customers
5 Decreased lead time on deliveries
6 Reduced reject rate
7 Product quality improved
8 Output increased
9 Morale improved
10 Cooperation with management improved

from answers to the questionnaires or from comments made on the topic in interviews. But in each case, only one score was allowed, based usually on one question, asked only of the person most likely to have the information. This did not take into account the views of other respondents within an organisation in relation to that aspect of performance – for example, from the evidence of related questions or substantiating comments from interviews. A second method of measuring performance was constructed to overcome this problem. Composite variables combining relevant responses from different people and substantiating evidence from different questions and from the interviews on the same topic, were used to produce this further set of performance indicators. The variables used in the construction of these indices are outlined in Appendix II. Five indices were developed to measure direct economic improvements and seven to measure indirect benefits, which organisations could have experienced as a result of their introduction of a payment scheme. These are listed in Table 5.7. The advantage of these indices was that each company could be given a score on a range for each index, based on the amount of evidence supporting the view that this aspect of performance had improved. The higher the scores, the more certainly it had improved, and the greater the likelihood of major improvement (i.e. because there was consensus).

These scores on performance improvement were then used to identify possible causes of the differences between the organisations.

TABLE 5.7 *Composite performance indices (questionnaire and interview responses)*

Direct Improvements	*Indirect Improvements*
1 Manpower reductions	6 Improvement in industrial relations
2 Increases in output	
3 Financial improvements	7 Improved work attitudes
4 Quality improvements	8 Better standards
5 Other specific improvements, e.g.,	9 Pay relativities or differentials improved
reduction in wastage	10 Better customer service
stock holdings reduced	11 Better internal relations
material costs reduced	12 Generally improved state of the company, e.g.,
	future prospects of company
	economic condition of company.

Payment Scheme Performance

We were interested in finding out:
a. whether certain kinds of payment systems were more successful than others;
b. whether certain payment systems worked better in some situations than in others, and what the characteristics of these situations were;
c. whether any other explanations could be found of the differing results obtained by different organisations.

Comparison of Types of Scheme

In order to make comparisons of the results obtained with different payment systems we first needed to classify the 63 different schemes in some way. This proved to be an extremely difficult task because of the numerous important ways in which these systems varied. Four different approaches to the task were considered, namely:

a. taking one feature of the payment systems at a time (such as how soon the payment was received after it was earned or whether the system was based on work study or not);
b. classifying schemes according to the motivational theory underlying their design;
c. classifying schemes according to the mechanics of their operation and the ways in which they impacted on employees;
d. classifying schemes according to the clustering of their scores on a wide range of characteristics.

Taking each of these in turn, the analysis of questionnaire data discovered few statistically significant relationships between aspects of the incentive scheme and specific performance variables. That is, it showed that very little of the variation in results achieved by the 63 firms could be explained by features of the payment system they had introduced.

A substantial number of 'payment system characteristics' and 'performance' factors were examined from answers in our questionnaires and tested for correlation. Only those with a significant correlation (above 0.25) are shown in Table 5.8. This table must be read with caution because in some cases small numbers were involved. Analysis of the cross-tabulations which showed how many cases fell into each category indicated that:

1 Schemes based on time standards were more easily manipulated than other kinds of schemes. This may have been because other

TABLE 5.8 Correlation coefficients between selected scheme effects and selected features of the schemes

Performance: Characteristics	Carry over of work to next day	Reduced no. of blue collar employees	Reduced reject rate	Increased volume of production	Output increase	Co-operation with management improved
Immediacy of bonus payment		−0.27				
Staff included in scheme			−0.26			+0.29
Work study required					+0.3	
Based on time standards	+0.28		+0.37			−0.26
Tightness of specified work practices				+0.77	+0.27	

types of scheme were not so tightly controlled on a day-to-day basis, and such manipulation would therefore be irrelevant.
2 Schemes based on time standards had a much greater likelihood of having an adverse affect on cooperation with management except for those schemes which incorporated bonus payments to managers. Again this is something we would expect, since time standards involve close managerial control rather than cooperation, and are sometimes resented by employees. There was also a tendency for the reject rate to have fallen where the scheme was based on time standards, although the statistical relationship was not highly significant.
3 A possible causal relationship, indicated by the correlation coefficient (0.3), between the use of work study and an increase in output was not adequately substantiated at either the firm or employee level, due to the small numbers in some cells of the cross-tabulation matrices.
4 A close link was found between tightly specified work practices (as opposed to understood or ad hoc work practices) and increases in production volume and output increases. The organisation numbers in this cross-tabulation were small, however, making the conclusion somewhat tentative. It appeared that firms with tightly specified work practices more easily achieved production volume increases.
5 Schemes where the labour force size had been increased as a result of the incentive scheme tended to be those where the bonus was paid fairly soon after it was earned.

When considering these findings it should be kept in mind that:

a. the analysis does not take into account the impact of contextual variables, emphasised as important by contingency theorists;
b. payment scheme characteristics and effects were defined in a simple manner from questionnaire data;
c. it may be that certain characteristics of payment schemes only have an influence when in combination with other characteristics.

Further analysis was carried out to overcome these restrictions.

The second approach to studying the types of schemes and their effects was to draw up a typology based on the underlying motivation theory about the type of effort required as a result of the scheme. This approach is firmly rooted in much of the literature on payment systems (e.g. Lupton and Gowler 1969) and ties in with the design principles evident in past and present managerial fashions about payment systems (namely, day rates; payment by results; measured daywork; added value systems; and merit-based incremental scales all fit neatly into this classification). It produced the four categories shown in Table 5.9.

This typology might be very useful for some kinds of comparisons; but it was of little use for our purposes because almost all of our schemes fell in the second category. The results would therefore not have been sufficiently differentiated for any lessons to be drawn about the effects of the different types of scheme.

TABLE 5.9 *Payment scheme classification based on inherent motivational assumptions*

Scheme classification examples:	Inherent motivational assumptions
1 Flat weekly wage	Payment for being present
2 Payment by results	Payment for producing results
3 Merit rating	Payment for appropriate attitude or commitment
4 Profit sharing	Payment for being employed by a successful organisation.

The third approach to devising a payment scheme typology was based on the mechanics of operation of the scheme, on the assumption that the time spent in deliberating about these mechanics by management indicated that they were important to the eventual results. The following characteristics were used:

a. the length of time after performance that the bonus was paid (short term/long term, where long term meant one month or longer);
b. whether or not the bonus varied with performance (fixed/variable);
c. whether the bonus was paid on individual or collective performance.

These three characteristics were chosen because they differentiated between our schemes better than other characteristics and because they were particularly relevant to current views about good and bad features of incentive schemes. Combining the two alternative scores on each of the characteristics produced eight possible classes into which the payment schemes in our survey could be classified. Three of these classes contained no cases and the 63 incentive schemes in our survey fell into the remaining five classes, as shown in Table 5.10.

Because there was only one case in the second category, the first two categories were combined into one and labelled Variable Individual Bonus, which gave a total of four payment system groups for analysis from this method of classification. Since there were major differences which managers had designed into their schemes, we expected to find interesting variations in their effects.

TABLE 5.10 *Payment scheme classification based on mechanics of operation*

Scheme classification		Number of schemes in this class
1 (a)	Short term, variable, individual bonus	16
1 (b)	Long term, variable, individual bonus	1
2	Short term, variable, collective bonus	31
3	Long term, variable, collective bonus	10
4	Short term, fixed, collective bonus	5

The results of this analysis are shown in Table 5.11. These results were, on the whole, disappointing. The four types of scheme had lower correlations with the variables measuring effects than the single features of payment schemes examined earlier (Table 5.8). Although most of the correlations were of only moderate statistical significance, the following tentative conclusions can be reached:

1 variable individual bonus schemes had, on the whole, favourable effects, whilst long term variable collective bonuses had unfavourable results;
2 short term variable collective bonuses had more negative results than positive ones; and
3 short term fixed collective bonuses had mixed but mainly negative effects.

Examination of the cross-tabulations for the more significant of these relationships removed the spurious ones which had arisen from small numbers and left only the following results:

1 Short term variable collective bonuses were more likely to be associated with reductions in manning than other schemes. When combined with variable individual bonuses they accounted for 80% of schemes where blue collar manning was decreased. This

TABLE 5.11 *Correlation coefficients* between four types of schemes and selected independent performance variables*

Scheme type: Performance variable	Variable individual bonus	Short term variable collective bonus	Long term variable collective bonus	Short term fixed collective bonus
Increased volume of production				
Reduced no. of blue collar employees		+.2	−.25	
Reduced prices to customers	+.2			−.22
Reduced reject rate			−.21	
Improved product quality	+.23			
Output increase		−.23		
Morale improved				
Cooperation with management improved				

NOTE Correlation coefficients less than 0.2 have been omitted.

association between manning reductions and short-term variable bonuses may have been spurious in the sense that both these kinds of schemes and manning reductions were commonly applied at this time to the same employees, namely unskilled and semi-skilled manual workers in declining manufacturing industries.

2 Allowing for ambiguity due to small numbers in some cells, there did seem to be a tendency for short term fixed collective bonuses to have an adverse effect on prices, more so than the other types of scheme. This result is not surprising since fixed bonuses were more often the choice of organisations whose primary aims were to raise employees' earnings, and this would almost certainly feed through to increased prices in many cases.

3 Variable individual bonuses were more likely than other schemes to be associated with reduced prices to the customer (although this related to a very small number of cases) and to improved quality of the product. It had been anticipated that good results might not be generated from examining correlations with each performance

variable separately, and for this reason composite performance indices had been developed as discussed earlier. The effects of the four types of schemes on the five indices of direct improvements and seven indices of indirect improvements from Table 5.7 are shown in Table 5.12. Only the correlation coefficients which were significant at the 5% level ($p \leq 0.05$) will be considered.

The results showed that variable individual bonuses tended to have poor results and in particular an adverse effect on employee attitudes at work but a beneficial effect on resolving problems associated with differentials and relativities. The payment systems in this category would include all those schemes where pay was linked to individual performance, including all those which used work measurement or time standards to assess that performance. This kind of close control and monitoring of work is often resented by employees, and indeed there are a number of trade unions in Britain whose members refuse to allow their work to be measured using work study techniques. It is not surprising, therefore, to find that those incentive schemes which related pay closely to individual performance had on the whole this adverse effect on work attitudes. The index of work attitudes was compiled from statements relating to cooperation, morale, industrial relations, employee loyalty, employee identification with the company, effort and safety.

The second category of payments systems, short-term fixed collective bonuses, were associated with the improvement index which related to better standards of work. This index was compiled from statements relating to increased flexibility, increased work capacity, better communications, better management standards, and increased skill application in the work. In other words, by paying a fixed weekly or fortnightly bonus for improved collective performance these organisations indicated that they had improved dimensions of job performance which would enhance the standard of work of the management and the workforce.

The next category was that of short-term variable collective bonuses. These schemes provided for a bonus which varied with the job performance of a group of employees (which could be any size from a small team to the plant as a whole) and was payable shortly after it was earned, so maintaining a reasonable relationship between effort and reward. There were a number of significant relationships between this category of scheme and the various dimensions of results. They had been more successful in reducing manning, improving output, and

TABLE 5.12 Correlation coefficients between four types of scheme and composite performance indices

Performance indices: Scheme type	Manpower reductions	Output improved	Better attitudes at work	Better work standards	Pay issues resolved	Better internal relations
Variable individual bonus	(−0.03)	(−0.14)	−0.25 P=0.03	(−0.12)	+0.21 P=0.05	
Short term fixed collective bonus	(+0.16)			+0.22 P=0.04	(+0.18)	
Short term variable collective bonus	+0.22 P=0.04	+0.24 P=0.03	+0.24 P=0.03	−0.21 (Q) P=0.05	−0.27 (Q) P=0.02	−0.26 P=0.02
Long term variable collective bonus				(+0.14) (I)	−0.23 (I) P=0.04	

NOTES
(i) There were *no* statistically significant relationships at the 5% level with any of the six performance indices excluded from this table.
(ii) (I) = Interview responses only
(iii) (Q) = Questionnaire responses only
(iv) P = probability of results occurring due to chance with repeated samples of the same size.

improving employee attitudes at work than the other three types of scheme, but they had had an adverse effect on working standards, differentials and relativities problems, and internal relations within the organisation. Of the four categories of payment scheme, this was the only one which had significant relationships with the indices of *direct* improvements. Their adverse effect on some of the indirect indices of success probably arose because paying variable collective bonuses can indeed produce problems relating to differentials between different groups of workers. Whilst the intention of group schemes is normally to improve cooperation and internal relations, these could deteriorate as a result of jealousies over differential earnings, discontent with the contribution to collective bonus from other groups and other similar problems. These results are generally supported by the study by White (1981).

This association of short term variable collective bonus schemes with direct benefits, and their success at reducing manning, suggests they should be the preferred scheme type. However, the following considerations need to be borne in mind. First, about half of the total sample fell into this category, which casts a little doubt on the validity of the findings; and second, the correlation coefficients between this type of scheme and the direct performance indices were less than comparable coefficients for some individual payment scheme characteristics, such as tightness of work specification (Table 5.8).

It had been our expectation that the fourth method of classifying payment schemes, using a wide range of variables, and applying a form of factor analysis to create clusters of schemes with similar profiles on several dimensions, would produce the best results from the point of view of testing relationships between the types of scheme and their effects. Thirty-eight characteristics of payment systems were used and the schemes clustered according to their scores for these variables using a statistical computer package, Clustan (available on SPSS). The clustering process grouped the 63 schemes in the study in such a way that those within each group had relatively similar scores to one another and less similar scores to those in other groups, so producing a typical profile of scores on the 38 variables for each category. It was not easy to apply comprehensive and meaningful labels to the six categories which were generated from this method of classification as they did not match any familiar types of system and key factors were common between some groups. Table 5.13 attempts to put a name to each payment scheme group and also indicates the distribution of the 63 schemes.

TABLE 5.13 *Payment scheme classification based on cluster analysis*

Scheme classification			Number of schemes studied
1	Type 1:	Plant wide, fixed bonuses	11
2	Type 2:	Variable, work measured bonuses, mostly individual	22
3	Type 3:	Group schemes where bonus based on basic pay levels; some work measured	13
4	Type 4:	Mostly plant wide bonuses	7
5	Type 5:	Group, variable, work measured, schemes	6
6	Type 6:	Mostly waste reduction bonuses	4

Table 5.14 shows the correlation coefficients between the six types of schemes derived from cluster analysis and the composite performance indices.

The results for each type of scheme were as follows:

Type 1 schemes, mostly plant-wide fixed bonuses, were not associated with any of the improvement indices, suggesting that on the whole they achieved little for the organisations which introduced them except, of course, to raise employee earnings.

Type 2 schemes, mostly variable work measured bonuses based on individual performance, were not associated with any of the improvements, but correlated negatively with work attitudes, internal relations, and the general state of the firm. This would indicate that this kind of scheme was also one to avoid, particularly since its effects were all detrimental to the organisation.

Type 3 schemes, which were mostly group schemes where the bonus was shared out as a proportion of basic pay, some of them work measured, and type 5 schemes, which were mostly group work measured variable bonus schemes, both had positive correlations with the output improvement index. This fits also with some of the data discussed earlier and begins to build up a consistent pattern of output improvements being associated with group work measurement and with group incentives. Type 3 payment schemes were also associated with financial improvements, but since so few organisations in our sample had achieved financial improvements this relationship must be treated with caution.

Type 4 schemes, the plant wide variable bonuses, had produced improved quality and indirect benefits such as better work attitudes, pay issues resolution and a general improvement in the state of the organisation. These schemes were the only ones that

TABLE 5.14 Correlation coefficients between six cluster scheme types and composite performance indices

Cluster scheme types	Manpower reductions	Output increases	Financial benefits	Better quality	Improved industrial relations	Better work attitudes	Better work standards	Pay issues resolved	Internal relations better	General state of firm better
Type 1 Plant wide fixed bonuses										
Type 2 Variable work measured bonuses, mostly individual		+0.33 N=52 P=0.01	+0.23 N=52 P=0.05			−0.43 N=52 P=0.00			−0.23 N=52 P=0.05	−0.36 N=52 P=0.00
Type 3 Group schemes where bonus based on basic pay levels, some work measured							+0.25 N=52 P=0.04			
Type 4 Mostly plant wide variable bonus	−0.23 N=52 P=0.05			+0.24 N=61 P=0.03	−0.25 N=52 P=0.04	+0.33 N=52 P=0.01		+0.22 N=61 P=0.05		+0.23 N=52 P=0.05
Type 5 Group variable work measured schemes		+0.26 N=52 P=0.03								
Type 6 Monthly waste reduction bonuses				−0.27 N=52 P=0.03				−0.28 N=61 P=0.01		

NOTES
(i) N = number of cell cases.
(ii) P = probability of result occurring due to chance with repeated samples of the same size.

correlated with manning reductions. The negative coefficient indicated that type 4 schemes were less likely than other schemes to lead to manning reductions. This is consistent with the finding discussed above that variable bonuses based on individual effort and paid soon after they were earned tended to be the ones which *had* been associated with manning reductions.

Type 5 schemes, mostly group, work-measured, variable bonus schemes, were not associated with any other improvements than increasing output.

Type 6 schemes, which were predominantly waste reduction monthly bonuses, had adverse effects on quality and on relative pay problems. Although the numbers were very small, this was another scheme type with no positive benefits.

None of the schemes produced an association with the direct performance index which measured 'other specific improvements', such as waste reduction, not even scheme type 6; nor with the indirect performance index which measured improvements in customer service.

However, two things stand out fairly clearly from these results. Firstly, the results are mixed; there is scarcely enough evidence to condemn any type of scheme as totally useless; nor to raise any type of scheme above others as the best. And secondly, better explanations of the differences between organisations were obtained from considering the separate features of their incentive schemes, one feature at a time, than by comparing the results of *types* of schemes (compare Table 5.8 with Tables 5.11 and 5.12). This suggests that when we combine the various features into a 'type' of scheme, the explanatory power is reduced. Why should this be? The most reasonable explanation is that the features were not being combined in a sensible way to produce schemes which performed well. The process of combining features to make up a scheme, whether it was done by managers or by consultants, was done without sufficient understanding of their effects, and the results were therefore poor.

THE EFFECTS OF CONTEXT ON PAYMENT SCHEME RESULTS

In order to assess the effects of the context in which a payment system is applied on the eventual results, we examined the statistical relationships between types of scheme and the results under varying conditions of context. So if there was a stronger relationship in some situations than in others indicating better results from a particular type of scheme in certain circumstances than in others, this would show up as a clear statistical relationship when the relevant dimension of the circumstances was held constant. Only a small number of the many contextual variables tested did affect the relationships to any meaningful extent. The contents of this section can be summarised in terms of our analytical model, as shown in Figure 5.3.

The relationship between 'Payment Scheme Design' (cell 3) and 'Changes in Productivity' and in 'Production Costs' (cells 7 and 8) – see Tables 5.8, 5.11, 5.12 and 5.14 – is now adjusted to take some account of the effects of 'Environmental factors' (cell 1) and 'Company Profile and Structure' (cell 2). The resultant matrix as shown in Table 5.15 was then produced.

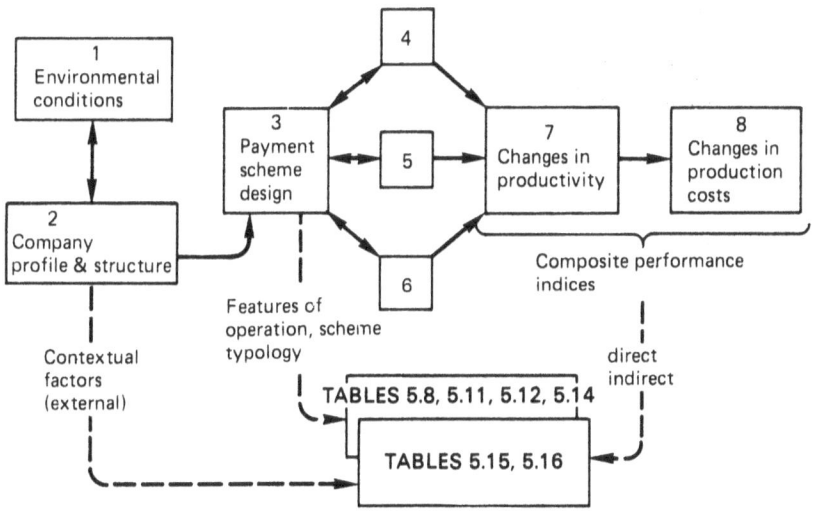

FIGURE 5.3 *The analysis of contextual effects upon specific design–performance relationships*

The two most sophisticated methods of classifying payment systems developed above were used for this analysis, beginning with the typology based on three 'mechanics of operation' variables (shown in Table 5.10) which had divided our sample into four types of scheme. Table 5.15 shows the effects of holding constant six contextual variables upon the relationship between these four types of scheme and

TABLE 5.15 *Effects of contextual variables upon scheme type performance correlation coefficients*

Scheme type	Organisation variable held constant	Composite performance indices					
		Manpower reductions	Output improvement	Better attitudes at work	Better work standards	Pay issues resolved	General state of the organisation
Variable individual bonuses	None (Table 5.12)	(−0.03)	(−0.4)	−0.25	(−0.12)	+0.21	(−0.08)
	Size of blue collar labour force		−0.28	−0.20	−0.22		
	Market competitiveness	−0.30					
	Market buoyancy			−0.31			−0.38
	Technological change			−0.16			
	Supervisory span of control		−0.23				

Payment Scheme Performance 125

Short-term fixed collective bonuses	None (Table 5.12)	(+0.16)			+0.22	(+0.18)
	Market competitiveness	+0.21				+0.23
Short-term variable collective bonuses	None (Table 5.12)	+0.22	+0.24	+0.24	(+0.14)	
	Size of white collar labour force		+0.29			
	Size of blue collar labour force		+0.41		+0.26	
	Market buoyancy		+0.30	+0.31		
	Technological change	+0.18		+0.17		
	Supervisory span of control		+0.30			

NOTES
(Table 5.12 = figures in this row obtained from Table 5.12)

the twelve composite performance indices listed in Table 5.7. The partial correlation coefficients were examined between scheme type and performance index under different conditions of each contextual variable in turn. If the partial correlation coefficient was better (i.e. a larger negative or positive number) than the original one, this indicated that the contextual variable was an intervening variable, the effect of which was to enhance the relationship. In other words this was an aspect of the context which affected the way this kind of scheme performed, producing better or worse results depending on the state of this aspect of context. If, on the other hand, the partial correlation coefficients were worse (i.e., a smaller negative or positive number) than the original one, this particular contextual factor was an intervening variable which explained some part of all of the original relationship. The relationship between scheme type and performance index in such a case would be a spurious one arising from association of both with the state of the contextual variable. Numerous situational factors were held constant and six were found to be important, namely: size of the organisation's blue collar and white collar labour forces, competitiveness of market, buoyancy of market, rate of technological change and supervisory span of control. The range of factors tested were selected because contingency theory on payment systems suggested that they would be important. These six did, in fact, have a significant effect on the way in which some schemes performed, as will now be explained (see Table 5.15).

Blue Collar Labour Force Size

The size of the blue collar labour force on site was a factor which greatly influenced the way two types of bonus schemes affected output. When the bonus was variable, based on individual performance and paid shortly after it was earned, the size of the blue collar workforce adversely affected the relationship with output. This changed from a non-significant negative relationship to a significant negative correlation of -28, indicating that variable individual bonus schemes had a worse effect on output in large organisations than in small ones (as was substantiated by examining the cross-tabulation tables for the relationship). On the other hand, the short term variable collective bonuses increased their correlation with output improvements from $+.24$ to $+.41$ when size of blue collar workforce was held constant. This indicated (after examination of the cross-tabulation) that they were more likely to improve output when applied in small organisations than in large ones.

Similar results were obtained for the impact of blue collar labour force size upon the results in terms of work standards. Short term individual bonuses were more likely to produce an adverse effect on work standards in firms with a large blue collar workforce than in smaller ones; and short term variable collective bonuses were more likely to produce an improvement in work standards in small firms than in large ones.

There is a substantial management literature on the impact of size on organisational effectiveness and on management practices appropriate to organisations of varying sizes. This literature recommends that it is well worth taking account of the size of the unit when considering the most appropriate payment system to introduce. Our study indicated that large units might do better to avoid individual incentives, and small units might expect reasonably good results from paying bonuses dependent on group performance shortly after it is earned.

Size of White Collar Labour Force

This contextual factor affected only one of the relationships between payment scheme types and performance indices. It showed that output was slightly more likely to have improved when short term variable collective bonuses were introduced in firms with a small white collar labour force than when they were introduced in firms with a large white collar labour force. This reinforces the above statements about the suitability of these kinds of schemes in small organisations.

Market Competitiveness

For those organisations operating in highly competitive markets variable bonuses based on individual effort were negatively associated with reductions in manning, a significant relationship which had been negligible until the state of competition in the market was taken into account. This type of scheme was therefore even less likely to be associated with manning reductions when the market was highly competitive. Also, when the markets were uncompetitive, this type of scheme was negatively associated with the general state of the company, something else which did not appear before the state of the market was taken into account. Highly competitive markets had, on the other hand, led to a short term fixed collective schemes being more likely to lead to manning reductions than they had been for the sample as a whole. These results suggest that competitiveness of product market may have been a key factor in whether or not an employer was seeking manning reductions and probably also influenced his payment system preferences.

Market Buoyance

When the market for the organisation's output was particularly buoyant at the time the scheme was introduced, there were closer positive correlations between better attitudes to work and short term variable collective bonus schemes indicating that buoyant market conditions made it more likely for this kind of scheme to have been associated with improved attitudes. There was also a slightly greater probability of a link with improved output. On the other hand when the market was poor there was an even greater probability of an adverse effect from short term variable individual bonuses on attitudes at work than for the sample as a whole. Achieving improvements when the market was buoyant was undoubtedly easier. These results also indicate that a buoyant market situation is well suited to the introduction of incentive systems which relate the level of bonus pay to the level of performance of groups of employees and provide for the payment of the bonus shortly after it is earned.

Technological Change

The next contextual factor with a significant effect was the rate of technological change. Since Burns and Stalker (1961) there has been considerable debate about the importance of the rate of technological change for the way in which an organisation is structured and operated. Organisations with a rapid rate of technological change have been shown to operate better with a flexible structure and fluid pattern of communication and inter-relationship, organisations with a slow rate of technological change appear to have been more successful with a more stable structure of specified regulations covering channels of communication and interaction, incorporated in an almost bureaucratic structure.

In considering the technology factor, it was expected that the more tightly structured types of incentive schemes (such as short-term variable individual bonuses) would be more suited to organisations with a slow rate of technological change than others, and would therefore produce better results in those circumstances. However, the results of holding constant the rate of technological change were that some of the previously significant relationships were largely explained away by this factor, and no relationships were strengthened when it was taken into account. These relationships were seen to have been caused largely by the common association of type of payment scheme and performance index with the rate of technological change rather than by a strong relationship directly between the two. Rate of technological change was not a factor which made any one type of payment scheme preferable to others.

Supervisory Span of Control

The supervisors' span of control was another factor examined for its effects on correlation coefficients. It was found that it increased the adverse effect on output of variable bonuses paid for individual effort and the beneficial effect on output of variable bonuses paid for collective performance in the short term. In other words, where the supervisors had a very large span of control the adverse effect of variable individual short term schemes on output was worse. As with previous results discussed, these could have been due to the interaction of particular dimensions of these types of schemes (such as tightness of work specification) with supervisors' span of control and also to the fact that such a large proportion of our sample fell into the category of variable collective short term bonuses. They do suggest, however, that organisations in which the supervisors have a large number of subordinates to supervise might be well advised to avoid variable individual bonuses, and to consider instead short term variable collective bonuses.

Results from Alternative Typology of Schemes

We also examined the effects of contextual factors on the correlation coefficients between the six types of scheme derived from cluster analysis of 38 dimensions (Table 5.13) and the composite performance indices. The results of this analysis were inconclusive. Although several of the organisational characteristics had a strengthening effect on some correlations, they did not produce such significant changes as they had in the analysis above (Table 5.15).

Multivariate Analysis

In addition, a multivariate analysis was carried out holding constant multiples of the contextual factors at the same time, to test whether it was *combinations* of situational characteristics which influenced the results obtained from different payment schemes. For some combinations of contextual factors this produced such small numbers in the cells that no valid conclusions could be drawn. In cases where the numbers were sufficiently large, considering several factors at once did not produce significantly improved correlations; that is, there was no strong evidence that combinations of different situational characteristics helped to explain the relationships between type of scheme and resulting performance.

For the relationship between type of scheme and simple variables measuring scheme performance (Table 5.6), several runs of multivariate analysis were made to find some set of relevant contextual variables which, when held constant together, produced improved correlations. Table 5.16 shows the results of holding constant one such

TABLE 5.16 5th Order partial correlation coefficients for type of payment scheme with performance variables*

Scheme type: Performance variable	Variable individual bonus	Short term variable collective bonus	Long term variable collective bonus	Short term fixed collective bonus
No. of blue collar employees reduced		+0.35	−0.27	
Reduced price to customers	+0.29			−0.26
Reject rate reduced			−0.31	
Quality improved	+0.28			
Output increased		0.25		

NOTE
*Only coefficients above .25 included.

set, namely expectation of a rise in investment over the next 5 years, the rate of introducing new machinery or technology, skill levels of labour force, extent to which effort could be measured, and whether new capital expenditure was occurring.

Although these results look particularly encouraging by comparison with Table 5.11 where no contextual factors had been held constant, it must be remembered that holding five contextual variables constant all at the same time inevitably produced small numbers in some cells. On the other hand, the indications are that the conclusions discussed in the text about links between type of scheme and effects on performance were reinforced by examination of mulitple partial correlation coefficients.

THE IMPORTANCE OF SITUATION

The above results to a limited extent substantiate the view that a combination of payment scheme type and the situation into which it was applied affected the performance achieved. Although this supports the contingency perspective on incentive scheme design, the results were nevertheless a little disappointing. The main reason for disappointment, as will be indicated below, was that the correlation coefficients between performance and situation were larger than those between performance and type of payment scheme even when the contextual factors were held constant. In terms of the analytical model, the following examination can be illustrated as shown in Figure 5.4.

There was a significant impact of the contextual factors external to the pay-work situation (cells 1 and 2) and the contextual factors internal to the pay-work situation (cells 4, 5 and 6) directly upon performance (cells 7 and 8), as summarised in the correlation coefficients of Table 5.19. In other words, characteristics of the organisation and its situation were more important determinants of the results obtained with a new payment system than the features of the payment system itself.

In this analysis of the influence of context upon performance, seventeen variables were used to measure features of the organisation or its situation. Table 5.17 provides a list of these variables.

These seventeen contextual variables were tested for association with the ten independent performance variables previously listed in Table 5.6. The correlation coefficients (those greater than 0.25) are shown in Table 5.18. Some of the larger correlation coefficients have arisen

132 *Payment Systems and Productivity*

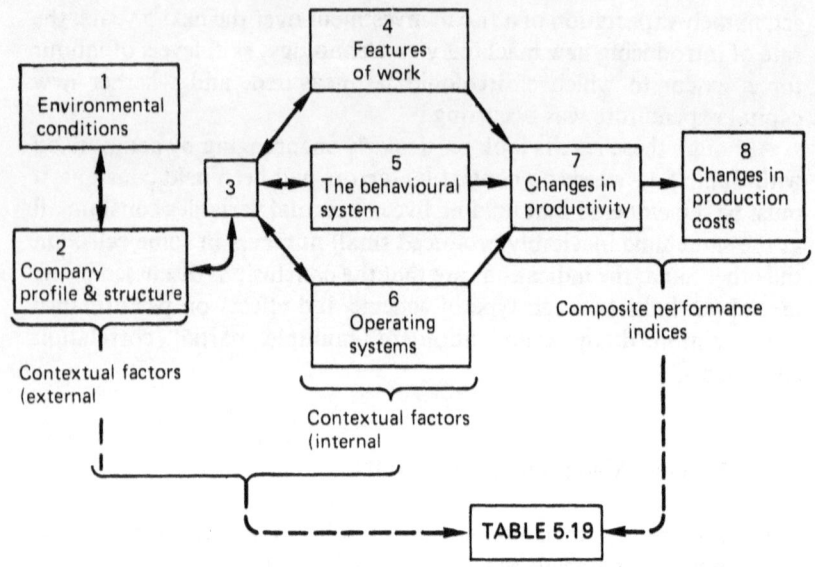

FIGURE 5.4 *The analysis of context–performance relationships*

TABLE 5.17 *Variables which measure features of the organisation and its situation*

1 Market requirement to increase production (Senior management estimate)
2 Market requirement to increase production (Marketing management estimate)
3 Investment increase over next 5 years
4 Rate of introduction of new machinery or technology
5 Time between receipt of order and delivery
6 Skill levels of labour force
7 Ability to measure work effort effectively
8 Importance of quality standards
9 Degree of employee control over output
10 Degree of repetitiveness of work
11 The adequacy of supervisors
12 The existence of previous incentive schemes
13 New capital expenditure occurring
14 Pay differentials as a source of difficulty
15 External pay relativities as a source of difficulty
16 Favourable pay comparison with other groups
17 Current application of other incentive schemes.

because of the small numbers in some categories, and some of the relations were fairly obvious. Nevertheless several of the relationships, when examined further (cross-tabulations), were of considerable interest.

A brief comparison of Table 5.18 with the correlation coefficients in Table 5.11 (where the largest was -0.25), Table 5.12 (largest -0.27), Table 5.14 (largest -0.43) and Table 5.15 (largest 0.41), shows that the correlations obtained here were substantially higher than these for the links between types of payment scheme and results.

The particularly interesting conclusions to be drawn from Table 5.18 relate to the contextual factors of market conditions, skill levels and quality standards, and the existence of multiple incentive schemes. Several of the other contextual variables also correlated closely with performance variables, but these three have been selected as of particular interest, and are the most consistent.

Management Assessment of Market Conditions

Organisations where it was thought desirable to increase productive capacity had a much greater tendency to experience an increase in volume of production than otherwise and vice versa. In other words, there were organisations in the sample for whom an increase in output would not have been desirable because their market would not buy very much more from them. They were consequently less likely to experience an increase in output after introducing their incentive scheme than other organisations without this constraint. This factor explained the variation in output increases far better than the type of payment scheme or any other characteristic of the organisation. At the very least, this suggests that organisations were not choosing a payment scheme to match one of the most important features of their situation, namely whether or not they could market more of their product or service if they managed to produce it. If contingency theory recommendations were being applied by these organisations, we would have expected this strong link between state of the market and increased output to have been reflected in a correspondingly strong link between a suitable payment system for increasing output and the resulting increase.

Another feature of situations where the market could accommodate an increase in volume, was that the price to the customer was more likely to have decreased than in situations where such an increase in

TABLE 5.18 Correlation coefficients between selected contextual features and selected independent performance variables

Performance variables: Contextual variables (See Table 5.17)	Decreased unit costs	Increased production volume	More blue collar employees	Lower customer prices	Improved delivery lead time	Reduced reject rate	Improved product quality	Increased output	Improved morale	Greater co-operation with management
1 Potential for increased sales	+0.35	+0.54		+0.36				+0.40	+0.27	+0.42
2 Potential for increased sales (2nd opinion)				+0.63				+0.36		
3 Investment increase		−0.27	+0.27			+0.52	+0.26	−0.28		
4 New machinery or technology		−0.36				+0.43				
5 Length of order delivery time	−0.50			−0.44	+0.39	+0.29		−0.54	−0.57	
6 Labour skill level		−0.28			−0.32	−0.36				
7 Importance of quality	−0.32	−0.39			−0.39 +0.27	−0.48		−0.27	−0.31	
8 Repetitive work										
9 Supervisor adequacy			+0.27			−0.27				
10 Pay differential conflict	−0.29			−0.28						
11 External relativities conflict		−0.30								
12 Favourable pay comparisons						+0.37				
13 Other incentives								−0.50		

NOTE
Correlation coefficients less than 0.25 have been omitted.

volume was unlikely to find a market. We had previously found little evidence of financial benefits (such as reductions in costs, increases in profits or price reductions) being associated with any particular features or types of payment scheme. In those organisations where a reduction in prices was reported, this was linked with the fact that the market would buy more of the products or services if they were available, so enabling increases in the scale of operations to contribute to a reduction in price. The results suggested that where price reductions were not going to lead to increased sales, there was little or no likelihood that the incentive scheme would lead to reduced costs which would be passed on to the customers in the form of lower prices.

This again raises queries about the decision-making processes which failed to link the market situation to any identifiable type of payment scheme. And more importantly, it shows that the situational characteristic (state of the market) was far more important in explaining results than the type of payment system. Indeed, we might have hoped to find the opposite kind of association between capacity of the market to absorb increased output and reductions in price, as this would have indicated that in situations where there was no scope for increasing output the incentive schemes had produced the alternative benefit of reducing costs. This was not so. Rather, the market had provided the opportunity to reduce costs in precisely those situations where output increases were also feasible.

Skill Levels and Quality Standards

In those organisations with a skilled workforce and also in those organisations where quality was important, there were high negative correlations with several of the performance variables. A firm with a highly skilled workforce was less likely than others in our sample to have increased its volume of production or to have improved its delivery times or to have reduced its rejection rates. An organisation where quality was important was less likely than others to have decreased unit costs, increased production volume, improved delivery times, reduced its rejection rate, increased output, or improved morale. These results suggest that organisations with high skill levels and quality standards may have little interest in these kinds of performance improvements. Indeed, it is possible that incentive schemes aimed at achieving these kinds of results are inappropriate to these kinds of organisations.

Multiple Incentive Payment Schemes

The existence of another incentive payment scheme seemed to be a particularly bad sign. In the small number of firms which had more than one scheme operating a very high proportion of organisations had not increased output. This contrasted with those organisations where no other scheme operated.

In most multiple scheme cases the new scheme was not the primary means by which management were hoping to motivate employees to improve their performance. It was seen as an additional bonus paid on top of the existing incentive scheme. This finding is supported in later analysis, when the degree of management effort put into introducing a new scheme is considered. It is worth noting in this context, that White (1981) found almost a third (32.4%) of the organisation in his sample (401 U.K. manufacturing units) were applying more than one payment system simultaneously to some of their employees.

MOST SIGNIFICANT SCHEME DESIGN EFFECTS: CONSULTATION

The section above considered the effects of different types of payment systems on the various dimensions of success which an organisation could have achieved with the introduction of its scheme, and also the effects that the contextual factors had on these results. One of the problems faced by the above analysis was the difficulty of classifying types of payment scheme, since they vary in so many different ways and do not fall easily into categories. Indeed, better results were obtained by considering payment system features one at a time – for example, to see whether schemes which were based on work study performed better than schemes which were not – than were obtained from looking at whole schemes. This suggests that the compilation of features to produce whole schemes had not been done very effectively by management. Nevertheless, some general results about the effects of different types of scheme did emerge and were described above.

When the effect of context were considered on the results obtained from different payment schemes it was found that some types of scheme did perform better in certain circumstances than in others. However, it was also observed that the context itself was an even better predictor of results in terms of improved performance than either features of schemes, types of schemes, or combinations of types of scheme and particular circumstances. In other words, in the right circumstances, employers had improved performance irrespective of the kind of changes to their payment system.

There was still considerable variation between organisations in the degree of success achieved with their new incentive schemes which could not be explained by reference to the features of the schemes, types of schemes, or features of the context. We therefore made an exhaustive investigation of our data to identify the variables or combinations of variables which *would* explain these results.

From this search through the 'triangulated' data (questionnaires, interviews, case diaries and participant observation reports) the significance of scheme implementation was highlighted. Preliminary examination of the interview data and case study experiences generated the proposition that an organisation's performance was significantly affected by the amount of management effort involved in establishing and implementing the payment scheme. The coding framework for our interviews therefore picked out certain aspects of the implementation process which had been frequently mentioned, and produced quantitative scores for their occurrence.

In this attempt to find variables (from amongst, literally, hundreds on which we had data) which correlated highly with results, we ran numerous tests on single variables, and one of these produced dramatically better results than any other. This approach to seeking explanations of data by examining the data in detail and from numerous angles is often referred to as 'grounded theory' – that is, where one's theory is grounded in the data to which it relates (Glaser, 1978).

The variable which produced these good results was taken from our interview data, and measured the length of time that interview respondents said had been spent on payment system consultations. It was recorded as extensive if more than three weeks had been spent on consultation; brief if less than three weeks had been spent on consultation; and non-existent if the respondent indicated there had been no consultation.

When this single variable was cross-tabulated with a wide range of performance variables, it produced some striking results. Table 5.19 lists the performance factors by their association with this measure of extent of consultation.

This identified 'extent of consultation' as a major variable for the purpose of explaining payment scheme performance. The remainder of this section explains the analysis which systematically tested the

TABLE 5.19 *Associations between consultation and performance factors*

Performance factors with a positive association with consultation	Performance factors with no association with consultation
Output increase	Increases in earnings
Favourable industrial relations	Employee identification with firm
Favourable comments and relations with:	Reduced production costs
management	Reduction in wastes or rejects
supervisors	Overtime reduced after scheme introduced
other employees	Wage differentials and relativities after scheme introduced
young workers	Number of employees
Favourable comments about:	Composition of work group
work	Process of machinery change after scheme introduced
labour flexibility	Information available after scheme introduced
work flow	Safety
the organisation and its economic state	Attitude to previous scheme
Labour force stability	Current absenteeism
Increase in profits	Current labour turnover
Increase in productivity	Time spent with colleagues
Increase in labour flexibility	Frequency of mechanical breakdowns
Reduced absenteeism after scheme introduced	Timekeeping
Quality of output	
Increased worker effort	
Decreased labour turnover after scheme introduced	
Increased supervisor control	
Satisfaction with payment scheme	
Understanding of payment scheme	
Level of productivity.	

proposition that the process of implementation has a significant influence upon payment scheme results. Figure 5.5 outlines the general approach of the analysis.

Composite indices measuring aspects of scheme implementation (cell 3) were examined for their effects on scheme performance (cells 7 and 8). The results are summarised in Table 5.20. The impact on these relationships of environmental conditions (cell 1) and organisational characteristics (cell 2) were then considered, and this analysis is summarised in Table 5.21.

The Composite Implementation Indices

Utilising questionnaire and interview data, four composite indices were

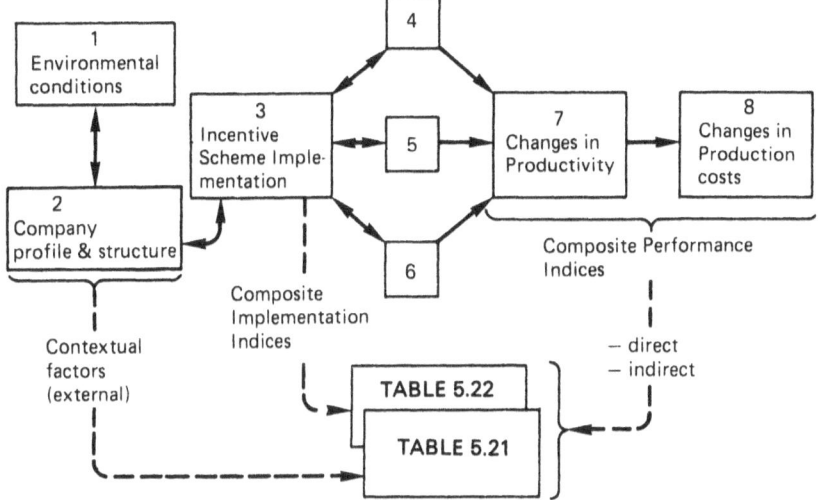

FIGURE 5.5 *The general analysis of context, implementation and performance relationships*

constructed to measure different aspects of the payment scheme implementation process. The four indices measure:

1. the extent of consultation and negotiation;
2. the information collected before the scheme was introduced;
3. staffing changes to maintain the scheme;
4. extra monitoring information (non-financial) required.

The variables that constitute each index are contained in Appendix III.

The association between these four composite indices of scheme implementation and the twelve composite indices of performance (used in earlier analysis discussed above) is indicated by the correlation coefficients in Table 5.20. The effects of each of the four aspects of the implementation process will be examined in turn.

Extent of Consultation and Negotiation

This comprehensive index included:

a. whether specific levels and types of management had been involved in the design, consultation and negotiations of the scheme;
b. whether shop stewards had been consulted;

TABLE 5.20 Correlation coefficients between composite implementation indices and composite performance indices

Implementation indices \ Performance indices	Manpower reductions	Output increase	Financial index	Better quality	Other specific benefits	Better work attitudes	Better standards	Pay issues resolved	Internal relations better	General state of the firm better
Extent of consultation and negotiation	+0.32 (Q) P=0.01 +0.28 (I) P=0.02	+0.44 P=0.00	−0.27 P=0.03	+0.41 P=0.00		+0.48 P=0.00	+0.30 (Q) P=0.02 +0.57 (I) P=0.00	−0.36 P=0.01		
Information gathering before scheme					−0.38 (Q) P=0.00 −0.46 (I) P=0.00			+0.29 P=0.02	+0.29 P=0.03	
Staff changes to maintain scheme	−0.49 (Q) P=0.00 −0.27 (I) P=0.04					+0.40 P=0.00				+0.34 P=0.01
Extra information gathered to monitor scheme		+0.24 P=0.05		+0.25 P=0.04	−0.27 P=0.03	+0.30 P=0.02			+0.31 P=0.02	

NOTES
1 (I) = interview responses only.
2 (Q) = questionnaire responses only.
3 P = probability of results occurring due to chance.

TABLE 5.21 Effects of contextual factors upon scheme implementation–performance correlation coefficients

Scheme implementation indices	Organisation variable held constant	Composite performance indices					
		Manpower reductions	Output increase	Financial benefits	Other specific benefits	Improved industrial relations	Internal relations better
Extent of consultation and negotiation	None (from Table 5.20)	+0.32 (Q) +0.28 (I)	+0.44	−0.27		(+0.18)	
	Market competitiveness	+0.36		−0.32		+0.23	
	Market buoyancy	+0.24	+0.39	−0.23			
Information gathering before scheme	None (from Table 5.20)						+0.29
	Market buoyancy						+0.22
Extra information gathered to monitor scheme	None (from Table 5.20)		+0.24		−0.27		+0.31
	Size of blue collar labour force		+0.19				
	Market buoyancy		+0.14		−0.32		+0.13

NOTES
(i) (I) = interview responses only.
(ii) (Q) = questionnaire responses only.

c. whether the marketing departments knew how the scheme worked;
d. the time spent on negotiations, consultations and explanations of the scheme;
e. the adequacy of the information provided about the negotiations, consultation and the details of the scheme.

Throughout the entire study, this index performed better than any other in explaining the results achieved by payment schemes. The extent of consultation and negotiation was strongly associated positively with manning reductions, output increase, improvements in quality, better work attitudes and better standards of work; and negatively associated with the financial index (a reduction in which implied an improvement) and the resolution of problems concerning relative pay.

The breadth and extent of consultation and negotiation in preparation for the introduction of incentive schemes was the major determinant of the degree of success eventually achieved with these schemes. It should be noted that this was not a finding that the project team deliberately set out to prove or disprove. It arose from detailed investigation of the data and the construction of indices which best explained the findings. When evaluating this result one should keep in mind the very wide range of variables which were studied through the questionnaires and the complete freedom given to interviewees when discussing their scheme's results.

Over the past ten years, and particularly due to the Bullock Report (1976), there have been a considerable number of books and articles written which advocated increased participation and involvement of employees in the decision-making processes within organisations. Participation was advocated both as a means of improving the quality of working life and improving organisational effectiveness. But when one looks for empirical evidence that organisational effectiveness has been improved by the introduction of greater participation, there is little to be found (Marchington and Loveridge, 1979; Ramsay, 1977; Loveridge, 1980).

We consider that the findings of our study make an important contribution to the debate about consultation and participation. The major difference between the results of this study and many other studies of participation and involvement is that the project examined consultation in relation to a *specific change* which was subsequently implemented. This study was not concerned with assessing the general management style or *general* procedures for decision making, such as participative committees or representation by trade unions on the board of directors. In the case of incentive payment schemes, the specific decision was something about which the employees and managers consulted had relevant knowledge and points of view to contribute. Also, their cooperation and understanding of the scheme was required for the payment scheme to achieve beneficial results for the organisation. From this study of payment schemes, it is clear that involvement in the decision-making process, at least to the extent of consultation and involvement in the design of the new scheme, had very positive effects on the results obtained from the schemes.

We then went on to consider possible explanations of our findings. The extent of consultation may, or may not, be an indicator of the degree of seriousness with which management approached the implementation of their incentive schemes. There was a large proportion of managers (and employees) who indicated that 'getting around' the constraints of the prevailing national incomes policy was a major objective when introducing their incentive payment scheme. Therefore, it was necessary to assess the extent to which 'seriousness of implementation' could also explain scheme results, and whether our findings on consultation could be explained in this way.

Three indices were designed to complement the 'extent of consultation and negotiation' index as measures of managements' seriousness when implementing the new payment schemes. The components of these three indices are also outlined in Appendix III, and their results discussed below.

Information Collected Before Scheme Introduced

This second index measured the procedures adopted for gathering information in preparation for the introduction of the incentive scheme. This was not positively associated with any of the direct benefits indices, but it did relate to improved internal relationships and the resolution of problems regarding pay relativities. It had a very high negative correlation with the index measuring 'other specific benefits' (minus 0.46).

From this it was concluded that schemes reporting benefits such as reductions in wastage or absenteeism were very unlikely to have been schemes where a great deal of information was gathered prior to the introduction of the scheme. This was interpreted as indicating that those schemes reporting such benefits had not, on the whole, been well prepared. Many of these were schemes where few other benefits were reported, and usually the benefits which the scheme had been designed to obtain had not been achieved. It should also be noted that 'other specific benefits' was the only index of direct success which did not correlate with extent of consultation.

Staffing Changes to Maintain Scheme

The third index was based on questions and statements related to increases in staff required to maintain the incentive scheme. This index had a very high negative correlation with the index for manpower reductions. This suggested, quite reasonably, that in organisations where the scheme had led to reduced manning there had been a tendency to avoid increasing the staff complement, or even that managerial manpower had also been reduced. The other indices of success with which this index was associated were better work attitudes and a generally better state of the firm. It would appear that where more staff were recruited to maintain the incentive scheme, indirect benefits were obtained rather than specific direct improvements.

Extra Monitoring Information (Non-Financial)

The final index was compiled from statements and answers relating to the information gathered by management in order to monitor the scheme after its introduction.

This index correlated positively with increased output, better quality, better work attitudes, and better internal relations; and negatively with other specific improvemens. This was a better result than obtained by the previous two indices. It was therefore concluded that the increase in management effort to control and monitor an incentive scheme after its introduction was an important factor in the performance of the scheme. However, the relationships were not so strong as those for extent of consultation.

In the summary, it can be said that the seriousness of implementation (as measured by the three latter indices) was clearly a factor affecting payment scheme performance. But it was not so important as to explain away the major impact which extent and degree of consultation had on payment scheme results. That is, the extent of consultation was a major factor in its own right.

Context and Scheme Implementation

In our earlier analysis of the effects of payment scheme design it was noted that the situation within which the scheme was operating had a significant influence on some of the results, particularly such environmental factors as degree of market buoyancy and the extent to which the market could absorb increased output.

We therefore examined the impact of situational factors upon the association between scheme implementation and results by again holding constant each of several contextual variables in turn. Table 5.21 shows the results obtained from those contextual variables which did change the relationships. Very few contextual variables had any important impact upon the relationship between scheme implementation and performance.

When the degree of market buoyancy was held constant there was a reduced association between performance and 'information gathering before the scheme' and 'extra monitoring information gathered' (implementation indices). This indicated that the good results obtained from these two indices had to some extent arisen because organisations whose markets were buoyant at the time the scheme was introduced had also been more careful than other organisations in the attention paid to gathering information.

The contextual factors had little effect on the good results obtained with extent of consultation, except that the correlation coefficients increased when degree of competition in the market was held constant. This suggests that in a highly competitive market the extent of consultation is even more significant than when the market is not so favourable. This further supports the view that it was the extent and nature of consultation, in its own right, that had the greatest impact on scheme performance of all the factors we considered.

CONCLUSION

In this large scale study of the results obtained when organisations changed their payment systems, there was considerable variation between organisations in the degree of success in improving performance.

However, when the results obtained were compared to the original objectives of those who introduced the schemes, and of the government of the day which encouraged this kind of scheme, the results were seen to be poor. If we exclude the objective 'to increase employee's pay' (an objective which most achieved fairly easily through their incentive schemes), the majority of organisations failed to achieve their stated objectives and were particularly poor at achieving quantifiable – as opposed to subjective – improvements.

The aim of the government of the day, was to decrease unit costs and thereby reduce inflation, but almost all these organisations failed to achieve this aim, and in fact, they appeared to ignore it. On the other hand, there was variation between the organisations and some performed considerably better than others. Most of this chapter has been concerned with identifying why they did.

One of the most striking findings is that managements' efforts to design incentive schemes seem to be singularly unsuccessful. They put together the separate features of incentive schemes in such a way as to worsen the end result – in other words the sum of the parts of a payment system was worse than the results from those parts separately. In particular, the extent to which the jobs of employees were rightly specified (as opposed to being unclear or worked out as the job went along) was closely associated with good results in terms of performance improvement. But when this factor was combined with other factors to produce an actual payment system, the association was less close; i.e. some of the factors it was combined with or the manner of combination had the opposite effect. The same was true of other features of payment systems.

Another indication that managers or their consultants did not perform well in designing payment systems was that there was a closer association between the organisational variables in a situation and performance improvement than there was between the organisational variables, the payment system, and performance improvement. In other words, the particular design of incentive scheme applied to an organisation did not enhance the performance improvement.

Part of the reason for this poor showing is no doubt the inadequacy of payment system literature to date. Even where the literature is helpful we found many managers sceptical of academics and more inclined to follow fashionable trends in management practice. There is a strong tendency in the literature and amongst specialists in the area to use familiar names for payment systems which grossly over-simplify the complexity of payment system design. Very often the same name is used for very different schemes. There is very little advice for managers on how to decide about the specific dimensions of their payment system (like size of the group, aspect of performance to be used as the basis, time delay before payment, time period covered, what to do about waiting time, etc). Indeed, until this present study, there was little information on which to base such advice.

The research showed that one factor had a greater impact on the eventual success of a payment system than any other. And that factor was consultation – the amount of time spent consulting with a wider range of people in the organisation in preparation for the introduction of a new incentive scheme. This extremely important result will be considered further in the next chapter. It far outweighed the significance of the type of scheme which was introduced or the suitability of the scheme to its circumstances.

However, there were some lessons to be learned about payment system design characteristics from the study. Firstly, the extent to which the jobs of employees were tightly specified was related to good results. Clearly there is a case for more effort to be put into spelling out exactly what an employee's task involves when an incentive scheme is introduced.

Secondly, incentive schemes which paid a variable sum of money related to the work performance of an individual tended to produce poor results. They had an adverse effect in particular on attitudes to work, and this effect was worse in large organisations than in small ones. It was also worse when the market for the organisation's output was buoyant. When the variable individual bonus was based on work measurement the results tended to be poor in terms of attitudes to work, internal relationships, and general perspective on the organisation.

Thirdly, when the amount of money to be earned from an incentive scheme was a fixed sum which was paid weekly or fortnightly on the basis of group performance, there was a tendency for prices to the customer to be increased. This kind of scheme was also unlikely to have been associated with manning reductions, especially if the market was buoyant.

Where the bonus payment varied with the performance of a group rather than an individual, and was paid weekly or fortnightly, the results tended to be better. This kind of scheme was associated with manning reductions in some organisations. In an organisation with a small blue collar workforce it was linked with improved output and better work standards, and where the white collar work force was small there was also a link with improved output.

Group schemes where the bonus was related to group performance based on work-measured assessment were associated with output improvements.

In general the study indicated that good practice in payment system design would involve clear specification of tasks, a variable bonus based on group performance, and extensive consultation with a wide range of people from all sections and levels of the organisation during the process of design. In our view these findings are of major importance.

Chapter 6 contains details of three case studies which show how the degree of effort put in by management to consultation, and the consequent modification of the schemes prior to introduction and during implementation, were the major factors explaining eventual performance. The chapter focuses primarily on the dynamic processes involved in managing a payment system once it has been introduced.

6 Payment Scheme Processes

The research described and analysed in Chapter 5 indicates that the success of a payment system depends not so much on the type of scheme that is adopted, or the characteristics of the organisation, but on the way in which the scheme is designed and implemented.

The most important elements in the design and implementation process were isolated and are represented in Figure 6.1.

But to tell managers and trade unionists that the answer to their problems with payment systems is simply to introduce consultation is not very helpful.

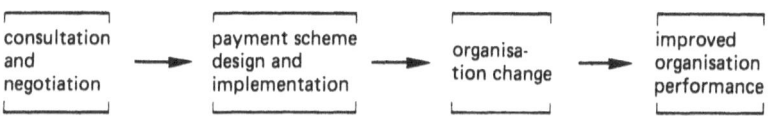

FIGURE 6.1 *Significant factors of incentive payment scheme success*

In this chapter we are concerned to identify the processes which are made possible through consultation and the reasons why consultation about the payment scheme is related to successful performance. This will give a clearer indication of what is meant by extensive consultation in payment system design and implementation and how it can be achieved.

What has been explained so far is that with careful and competent preparation in terms of consultation and discussions about the design and implementation of a new incentive scheme, a good management team can achieve good results with many different types of incentive schemes. This does not mean that the kind of incentive scheme is totally unimportant, but that the process of matching a payment system to an organisation is one which requires considerable management time and effort.

This represents a considerable step forward in management theory. Lawrence and Lorsh's work (1969) advised managers on the design of their organisation but it ignored the whole question of the motivation of the members of the organisation and the problems involved in matching individual objectives to 'organisational goals'. These problems have been recognised by others (Child, 1972) who have tried to make realistic proposals to resolve them. Our contribution is to a theory of behaviour in organisations which may form the basis for designing methods of influencing behaviour.

Matching the payment system to the social and economic system of the organisation, with its attitudes, motivations, inter-relationships, past history, expectations and interpretations, is more important than matching the type of payment system to non-social characteristics of the organisation and its environment (such as technology, market, location and size), even though some of these structural contextual factors may have a significant effect on the results of those companies examined.

The relative importance of the type of scheme adopted, the characteristics of the organisation and the way in which the scheme is implemented is shown in Figure 6.2. This general model will be referred to throughout the chapter.

This chapter is broken into two parts and shows the processes involved in payment systems that underly these findings.

PART A: Describes the characteristics of the variable 'extent of consultation' and how the process of consultation can lead to better management of:
1 organisational objectives
2 design and implementation of an incentive scheme
3 understanding contextual variables
4 understanding motivation
5 attaining commitment to scheme success
6 organisational changes which are needed to reinforce the new scheme

This section concludes with a discussion of some factors which have been found to inhibit consultation about a payment system.

PART B: Examines three detailed case studies of the introduction of new payment systems which throw light on how schemes are affected by 'extensive consultation' and serve to pinpoint the crucial factors in the process. The three examples were introduced under quite different circumstances.

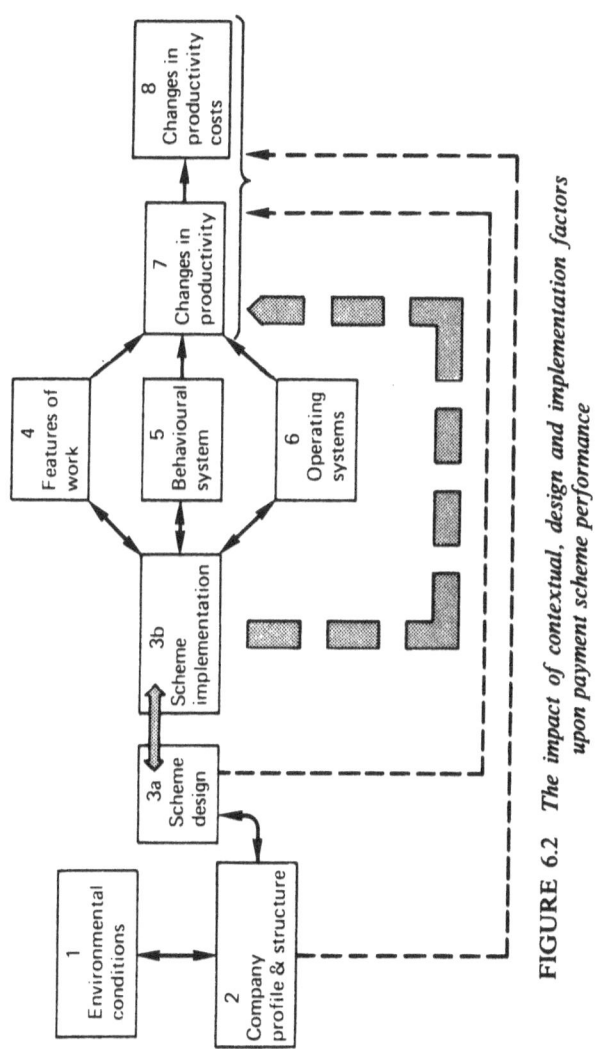

FIGURE 6.2 *The impact of contextual, design and implementation factors upon payment scheme performance*

PART A: THE PROCESS OF CONSULTATION AND NEGOTIATION

From our data, described in Chapter 5, and from empirical results published by other researchers, a more detailed explanation of the relationship outlined in Figure 6.2 can be constructed.

The component variables of the index 'extent of consultation' indicate that organisations with successful schemes actively endeavoured to increase their understanding of the contingent factors in their organisations and relate these to the strategic choices available to them, before designing and implementing incentive schemes.

Figure 6.3 shows how the contingent factors and strategic choices were found to be key influences on payment scheme design and how they affect performance.

Figure 6.4 enlarges on this model and shows how contextual factors and strategic choices pervade each stage of the pay design process from

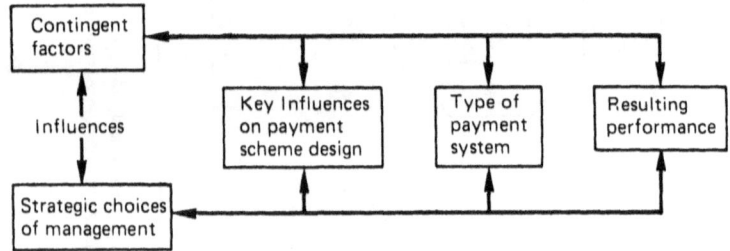

FIGURE 6.3 *Normative contingency theory related to payment systems*

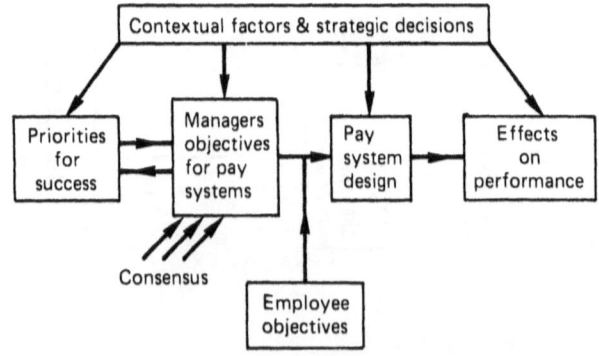

FIGURE 6.4 *The role of consultation in relation to objectives*

the establishment of priorities for success, linking these to the management's objectives in implementing a scheme, developing a consensus about what these objectives are, learning about the aims and interests of all affected employees, designing the payment system taking all of these factors into account and producing the final effect on performance.

At each stage in this process the linking mechanism was found to be consultation, communication and participation.

D'Aprix (1982) states that as well as creating trust, effective consultation will provide employers with information about objectives and motives both in relation to the roles of others in the organisation and from their personal point of view. This information is often all the more important because it is the sort of information about which management is misinformed.

Even at the highest levels in organisations this is likely to be the case, and it may be that at these levels misinformation about objectives is most significant. Galbraith (1967) claims that the technostructure (the controlling executives) of an organisation usually have primary goals that are not identical with those of their employing organisation. For example, growth is more important to the technostructure than return on investment, since growth protects the executive's position.

How much more likely that at lower levels in the organisation there will be a disparate array of objectives not necessarily congruent even with those of senior management.

Thorpe (1982) also commented on the effect of a person's position in the organisational hierarchy on the objectives they perceive for the organisation, as evidenced by the productivity measures used at various levels. The higher in an organisation a person is positioned, the broader and more long term will be their planning horizon and the greater will be the need for a total and systems-orientated perspective on measures of productivity (see Chapter 3). As one descends in the organisation structure, objectives for each level are to some extent the means for achieving the objectives of the level above, and they become increasingly easier to define, measure and more short term. As a consequence partial productivity measures replace the more global measures; until at shop floor level the measures tend to be single indices of output or effort. Problems arise when the performance measures and objectives used cease to relate to the longer term needs or objectives of the company as perceived by those responsible for its direction. The process of consultation facilitates the development of a more satisfactory top management view of organisational priorities.

Consultation can also improve the understanding of what the priorities for the organisation currently are, and of how an individual's work contributes to them. This can avoid some of the problems of over-emphasis on means at the expense of goals. For example, over-reliance on labour performance indices, collected at individual or department level may fail to take account of where sales and future business is coming from. It can result in a less than optimal product mix, or too much time being devoted to work which is not of the highest priority.

Without the mechanism of communicating the organisation's requirements through extensive consultation, misunderstanding can arise with the result that out-of-date working practices, once important and easy to measure but no longer relating to the objectives the organisation may wish to pursue, become locked-in. The consultation process therefore has not only a powerful role in closing the gap of understanding and making the organisation's priorities for success better understood, but also in relating these priorities to appropriate performance measures and methods for achieving improvements. The organisation's priorities can thus be translated into objectives for a payment system and thereafter into the design of a practical scheme. It is equally important for some consensus to be achieved within an organisation about the objectives of a payment system and here again consultation has a vital role to play. It allows discussion to develop understanding and acceptance of the objectives amongst both managers and those whose work is managed. This brings in another factor: acceptance of the objectives of an incentive scheme is in part related to the success with which that incentive scheme is consistent with the individual's own objectives. And consultation is necessary to discover those objectives before any matching can take place.

The situation is complicated by two factors. Firstly, the objectives of employees have two components; role (those they share with others doing the same job) and personal. And secondly, it is possible for a payment scheme to lead to improvements in the performance of some but at the same time inhibit the performance of others. In this respect a payment system tied to carefully thought-out objectives through a process of extensive consultation can have the effect of 'lining up' the various conflicting objectives between individuals and departments.

We found that it was the lack of links provided by consultation and communication between contextual factors, strategic decisions, priorities for success, and payment system design, together with the lack of consensus and failure to marry the scheme to the objectives of key groups, that accounted for the number of scheme failures in our study.

The Importance of Consultation to Design and Implementation

'Extent of consultation' is the process by which an organisation sets about positioning itself in relation to its environment and establishing appropriate performance criteria which match the objectives set for the scheme. This process should not be considered as undertaken once, but should be a dynamic process. Should conditions change the incentive scheme and its associated performance measures should be modifed if necessary.

Judson (1982) cites an example where systematic participation in analysing the causes of poor productivity and identifying the major opportunities for improvement made it possible to make crucial trade-offs. Put another way, extensive consultation facilitated discovery of the objectives and identified their roles as constraints or tests. It was then possible to decide on trade-offs between objectives. The full consultation allowed this to be done with the minimum of conflict and the greatest likelihood of success. Judson says

> 'A credible overall productivity effort and sincere commitment from affected managers are the legs to successful implementation... commitment derives from an understanding of what must be done and why it is to be done...'

Lawler and Bullock (1978) following research into remuneration systems in the USA commented

> 'Most approaches to changing pay systems are top-down; they assume that people above those on the pay scheme should make the decisions. What about letting the people who will be affected by the plan be a fundamental part of the decision?'

Vroom and Yetton (1973) suggested that participation and cooperation in the design of payment systems lead to a greater understanding of their workings and the need for their introduction and Morse and Reimer (1956), also discussing pay, assert that if a company is becoming more participative in decisions regarding pay this is a major part of any longitudinal participation exercise.

Three distinct benefits can be identified by a consultative and participative approach:

1   Management will learn about the contingent and contextual variables that are associated with performance improvement, and can

translate these into measurable objectives for all levels in an organisation. Other researchers (e.g. Lawler and Bullock (1978)) have found that when people are involved in design, they can provide information that would have not been considered had they not been involved. In addition a great deal of useful information is learned about the organisation which can be the basis for identifying more appropriate priorities and payment system objectives.

2 Management will learn about the contingent social and behavioural variables which need to be taken into account if the design and implementation are to 'fit' the people who are to work with it. Quite often management and employee perceptions are different and what management think motivates and rewards employees may be quite different from the reality, and vice versa.

3 The very process of consultation and participation will lead to understanding and commitment. Lawler and Bullock (1978) found this to be the most important benefit of a participative approach because it substantially increased the chances of the successful implementation of a new approach. If employees and managers at middle and lower levels contribute significantly to the design they become committed to making the outcome a success. New schemes become something in which they have a vested interest in and in which they are more likely to place their trust.

The act of undertaking a systematic analysis of an organisation in this way will highlight where organisational development and organisational change is needed to meet a company's objectives. Change is far better attempted when a climate of uncertainty is dispelled.

Whyte (1978) defines information as the reduction of uncertainty. He says:

'When environmental uncertainty is high it is only by different groups or individuals pooling their own bits of information to piece together the environmental 'jigsaw' that the pattern becomes clear to any of them; that is the reduction of uncertainty is dependent on communication.'

The Benefits of Consultation for the Understanding of Contextual Variables

This part of the process involves the detailed collection and analysis of

Payment Scheme Processes

a range of data or variables within an organisation. Consultation, particularly through participation in their collection, will ensure that all perspectives are considered and will add immeasurably to the quality of the data available to management.

The process of identifying the factors and variables on which performance is contingent and then choosing a payment system which 'fits' the characteristics and circumstances of the organisation is the contingency theory approach to payment systems. Researchers such as Lupton (1966), Lupton and Bowey (1976), Lupton and Gowler (1969), and the Strathclyde team (Bowey *et al.*, 1982) established that no system is intrinsically superior to another, rather that each system should be tailored to its unique situation.

Past researchers into payment systems, in order to obtain the best 'integrating mechanism' or 'best fit scheme,' have advocated using a variety of methods of data collection. The Manchester School advocated using a number of extremely detailed measurements which profiled features of the organisation as an aid to diagnosis. Many of these proved difficult to measure in practice, for example the percentage loss in output due to work flow problems (Lupton and Bowey 1976).

White advocated the use of surveys as an integral part of the process when pay and organisation development are considered. He reported that 'change' programmes concerning worker participation, work restructuring or changes in human relations commonly incorporate the use of surveys. Lewin (1947) advocated a similar technique to 'unfreeze' the prevailing norms of a group in order to introduce change. To achieve this he used group discussion methods, so that group norms (usually unspoken) could be brought out into the open and considered afresh.

Lawler and Bullock (1978) on the other hand advocated that diagnosis should be done by small task forces of between five to nine people. Their diagnosis of the current situation would form the basis for future decisions. Decisions on future change would be on the basis of this diagnosis, together with a detailed survey undertaken by management.

The factors which are important to the design of a payment system are not necessarily the same in each organisation, but amongst those which should be considered in the process of identification of relevant factors are the following (cf. Thorpe 1982):

Payment Systems and Productivity

Technical and Organisational

Current customer requirements or dissatisfactions
The technology used now and likely developments
The nature of the work and likely changes
Prospective changes in product market segment
The aims of management in introducing the scheme
The type and level of communication and consultation
Size of the work unit and organisation
The design of jobs
The organisational structure
The interdependence of jobs
Machine breakdown and maintenance system
Availability of substitute machines and/or substitute workers
Physical characteristics of the work place
Manufacturing or servicing costs *vis-à-vis* competitors or market tolerance
Delivery performance
Pricing policy
Working conditions
Interdependence of work between sections

Social and Behavioural

Individual and collective industrial relations history
The style of management
The orientations of the workforce and management including their aims and interests
Relevant dimensions of the dominant value system in the organisation
The industrial relations climate
Fatigue
Human relations inside work
Participation
Autonomous work groups
Experience of key people with previous incentive schemes
Level of belief in the need for incentives amongst managers

Environmental

Competitiveness of product market
Product market buoyancy
Market share
The economic and political climate
The history of incentives locally and in this industry
The local culture and the traditions of the industry

Although there is now much evidence of the many benefits which can arise from an organisational diagosis prior to embarking on payments scheme design, it was clear from our research that a diagnosis was hardly ever carried out.

The few companies which we found where time was spent on diagnosis appeared to have produced better schemes as a result. For example, a steel plant which undertook a detailed diagnosis learnt many useful facts about its own operation which assisted in its payment system design. Some company managers expressed a great deal of interest in receiving feedback on the questionnaire survey because they were uncertain of the motivation and attitudes of their own employees, both generally and in relation to the newly introduced scheme.

One of the problems we found was that new schemes were being implemented by managers who were not familiar with the findings of research on payment systems and, in particular, did not appreciate the value of contingency theory, preferring instead to rely on their own convictions. It emerged from field interviews that few managers had heard of the term and were often sceptical of academics and their 'jargon'.

The complaint about jargon sometimes also hides managers' willingness to ignore Social Science findings which they dislike. For example, many managers fear that job enrichment and autonomous group working take responsibility and control away from them (Buchanan, 1979). So even though these techniques are well supported by research findings, they prefer not to accept them.

There is also an argument (Parris, 1979) and evidence from the Strathclyde Research and associated work (Keenan, 1980), (Cochrane, 1983) to suggest that even when managers do appreciate the need for a comprehensive assessment of the variables within a firm, the personnel who undertake the assessment have neither the skill nor the training to take a wide enough view; and even if they have the skill and training they are not often in a position to influence the decisions taken. This problem is particularly acute for Management Services personnel operating from traditional work study departments. The process of extensive consultation increases the likelihood that the key contextual variables will be identified by those with the power to take decisions on the payment system.

The Role of Consultation in Understanding the Motivation of the Workforce

Our research showed that many of the incentive schemes were hurriedly adopted to circumvent pay policy or because of some other pressure, and failure to research the organisation resulted in missed opportunities for concomitant change with potential for performance improvement, such as job re-design or method improvement. Extensive consultation could lead managers to understand the significance of alternative motivations to pay and take account of these in the payment system design and implementation. Gedge (1979) states that:

> 'In many cases it is often best to regard a financial incentive not as a direct spur that urges the worker to higher effort, but as a reward that he receives and deserves for achieving the task of which he is capable after management has played its part in planning, providing resources and creating the environment in which such performance is possible'.

Katz (1964) reinforces this by stating:

> 'the preferred path to the attainment of production goals is then the path of organisational controls, not the path of internalised motivation'.

Over three-quarters of the companies covered by our survey paid little attention to aspects of organisation structure or job design, preferring instead to implement 'stand alone' schemes that often failed to produce the desired results.

Table 6.1 shows replies to questions asked in the Strathclyde Survey to determine the effects which new schemes had on the way work is organised.

A second set of variables that are likely to be brought to light by an organisational diagnosis and extensive consultation are the contin-

TABLE 6.1 *Questions asked to determine the effect new schemes had on the way work is organised*

Has the introduction of the new incentive scheme caused any of the following changes?	No %	Yes %
Changes in machinery layout	75	25
Changes in the way work is organised	49	51
Changes in processes	78	22
Changes in personnel	70	30
Changes in grading	75	25
Need for new skills	88	12
Need for new machinery	52	48

gent social and behavioural variables. These are often components of the effort-reward bargain described in Chapter 1. To obtain an understanding of the components of reward and how these can be related to the various forms of effort required by management is an essential part of extensive consultation with the workforce.

Disregard of alternative motivators at work and an over-reliance on the use of money contradicts much of the research evidence which explains an individual's reactions to incentive payments (Mayo, Roy, Whyte, Ditton). Disputes regarding money are often manifestations of more complex grievances related to fairness and equity rather than always symptomatic of a lack of satisfaction with the reward for effort.

The process of consultation can often reveal aspects of motivation not possible to detect in any other way.

One example we found that illustrates the value of such analysis at the design stage of schemes was at a steel plant where an incentive scheme had been implemented with the aim of reducing operational delays in the Cinter plant. The scheme was devised on the basis that the team of operators were to have control over the process, and if the number and time of delays could be reduced, compared with a datum, then the whole workforce would enjoy a bonus. Workers would not be penalised for delays that could be attributed to poor maintenance or otherwise the fault of management. Previously, one of the aspects of work on this plant was the method of job determination. This hinged around a system of strict seniority, that is length of service, and it was this that was to be most affected, albeit unintentionally, by the bonus scheme.

Essentially, the plant was operated by a group of 'Plant Operators' divided into three shifts. Each shift had within its ranks skilled men, each man assigned to a specific job of plant operation. These jobs had attracted an informal hierarchy that was based on skill and tradition and therefore each job was paid for on a separate rate.

The system dictated that, regardless of ability or aptitude, an operator could not progress up this hierachical structure unless he had seniority over his colleagues. He was also restricted from taking over the job of a more senior colleague unless through absence.

The introduction of the incentive scheme had an impact on the everyday running of the plant for both operatives and management. The men interviewed openly admitted to jumping in on other's jobs to preserve their level of bonus. Most suggested that this was one of the better unseen benefits of the scheme. There was a much greater feeling of teamwork than ever before, and most men felt that their jobs had become more interesting as a result.

Effort, and therefore performance, had increased not through harder work, but by more effective work and greater flexibility, whereas reward had shifted from pay and seniority to an incentive bonus and job satisfaction.

Bonus earnings had not dropped below 100% since the introduction of the scheme. From the management viewpoint, where the original intention had been a reduction in delays, the scheme had also been a success. Management commented it was possible to do more with the labour, so much so that the scheme may eventually become a threat to the long-established system of seniority as men found themselves able to step into other's jobs and do the work without difficulty. It should be noted that this was one of the few incentive schemes we studied where a detailed analysis of the situation had been made as a basis for the design of the scheme.

Our in-depth study at the Coal Board also showed the value of taking careful account of employee perceptions of effort and reward. We discovered that men on different shifts were motivated as much by personal pride and the professionalism they found in the job, as by the cash bonus. The achievement of high output in the eyes of their colleagues served to maintain production at a high level. Unedited accounts from the miners' daily work diaries are included in Appendix IV.

Another factor which can be important to motivation is the quality of supervision.

During our participant observation of a high technology light engineering company we found poor supervision in many parts of the company. Management left the employees for long periods very much to their own devices. This had a very unsettling influence on the workers who realised they were not under control. Poor performance and theft of time were the most disturbing results of this inadequacy of management. The failure to plan work meant that men were often bored and our researcher, working as an employee of the company, recorded, day after day, remarks by fellow workers reflecting this boredom. Spare time had gradually been taken for granted. Once when asked to do something in a hurry he found the request to suddenly do some work very insulting as he had not done anything under pressure for days and did not see why he should simply jump to and rush then.

There is a good deal of evidence to suggest that employees would be more effectively motivated if they could find constructive outlets for using their initiative and if their work was more effectively supervised. Questionnaires to a sample of the workforce of one of the companies studied showed that 68% of the employees felt that supervision was carried out poorly, whilst no one in the company thought that it was done well.

Over half of the employees of this company thought that the management motivated poorly, whilst in a wider sample of 654 employees in 55 companies 38% thought management motivated poorly whilst only 10% thought management motivated well. When asked whether their jobs fulfilled them and whether they would like to learn new skills all employees said they would and all said they did or would like to do varied work, decide their own pace of work, have more opportunities to put forward their views, work as a team and complete more aspects of a job.

All this is evidence for the potential improvements which could be brought about through extensive consultation and the increased awareness of these issues which it would bring.

Without consultation there is a danger that impersonal change implemented by management will take no account of aspects of the work valued by the employees and will leave them with a feeling of resentment that their knowledge of the job and their points of view are not thought to be worth seeking. This can lead to a loss of goodwill.

Consultation and Commitment to Scheme Success

Our research showed that the kind of consultation that showed itself to be worthwhile, was not simply a search for contextual and behavioural variables as mentioned above or an exercise in democratic procedures, nor was it the setting up of a large number of committees or the appointment of workers to the boards of directors. A vital dimension of consultation was the expenditure of management effort in detailed discussions about features and improvement of the work and about specific changes planned. These would then be modified as a result of discussions and eventually implemented with the understanding of those to whom they were to be applied.

The process of consultation therefore achieves a number of objectives that lead to better quality decisions and smoother implementation. It should:
1 interest the workforce in change;
2 inform the workforce of the change;
3 enable employees to see how the objectives of the company can best be achieved and what are the organisation's priorities for success;
4 clarify and coordinate the objectives of different groups working within one organisation;
5 create a better climate of trust.

That successful change is brought about as much by the process as by the content of the change is something found to be important in studies undertaken at the Tavistock Institute of Human Relations (Bryant, 1979). In their change programmes there was an attempt to achieve a consensus between workforce and management from the outset, and this search for consensus was seen 'as part of a diagnostic stage'.

One important function that the consultation process achieves is the accommodation of different perceptions, for instance those of management with those of the workforce. It is clear that management and employees within the same organisation are likely to approach a given incentive payment scheme with quite different perceptions. These different perceptions may lead to considerable tension between individuals and groups within the organisation.

Management's Perception

Incentive payment schemes encourage managers to view employees as rational economic people willing to maximise their income within a given wage scheme. The perspective of many managers therefore becomes one of:

a. ensuring that the incentive payment scheme is designed to give adequate monetary reward for the required improvement in performance; and
b. ensuring that the effort–reward mechanics of the scheme are effectively communicated to employees so that the scheme induces increased performance.

Although not readily admitted, and often not even perceived, managers have power derived from their detailed knowledge and understanding of the scheme mechanics. Managers can influence the amount of information made available to employees to understand the scheme through consultation.

Management may be prepared to accept that there are many techniques for motivating employees apart from money (such as improved organisation systems, better human relations, personal development, increased decision-making involvement, job enrichment, recognised achievement, and fear of sanctions); and that payment schemes may be used for many purposes (such as recruitment and training of labour, compensation for adverse work conditions, reward for improved performance, control of costs and prices).

But when it comes to designing a payment system there is a strong tendency to think in 'scientific management' terms along the following lines (Bowey, 1978):

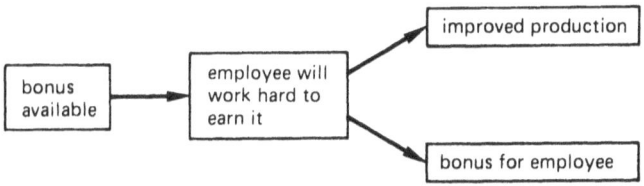

FIGURE 6.5 *Management bonus scheme perception*

Employee Perception

Employees on the other hand usually have a fragmented knowledge of organisations and types of incentive payment schemes, which they apply to their own particular work-pay situation to understand how the incentive payment scheme operates, see Figure 6.6 (Bowey, 1978).

Employees may not be concerned with the mechanics of the scheme

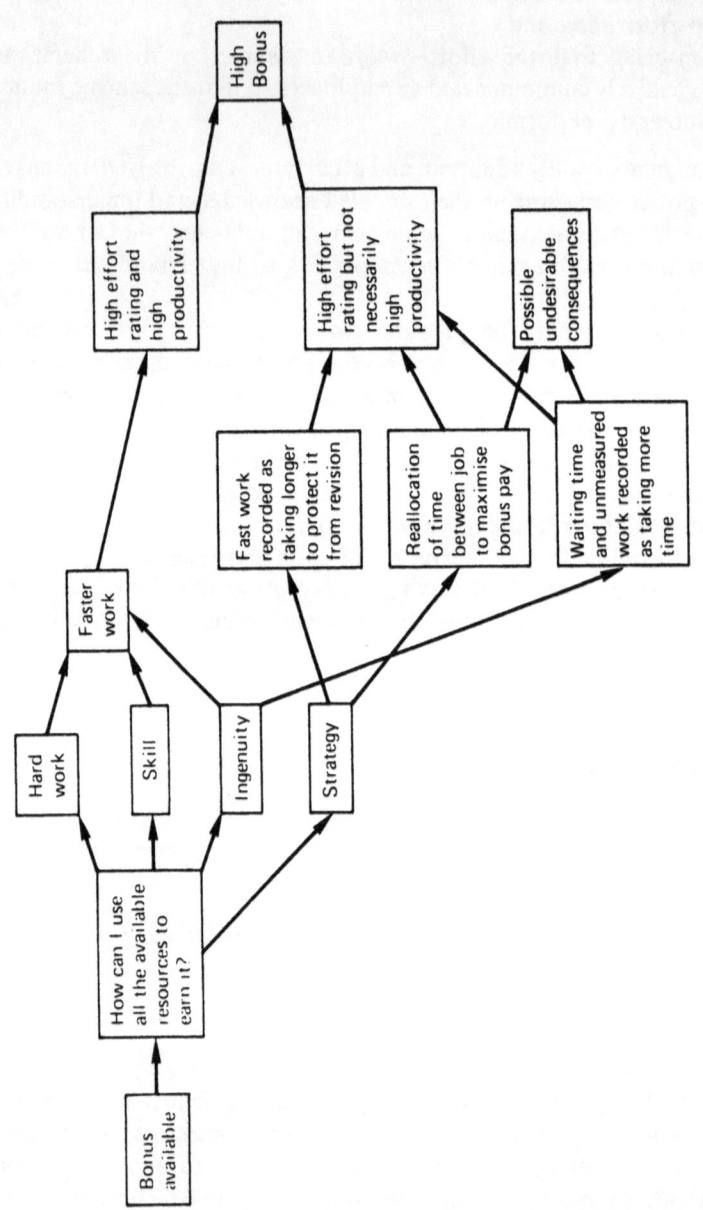

FIGURE 6.6 *Employee bonus scheme perception*

or theories of motivation. They want to know how to get a bigger bonus, what they have to do to get it, whether it is a fair reward for the work, and whether improved productivity will mean that they work themselves out of a job.

While it is unusual for an employee (or indeed a manager) to understand all of the scheme mechanics, each employee through experience develops a rule-of-thumb perception of how his pay is affected by his work. Because the employee does not have complete knowledge of the scheme calculations, and because many of the factors influencing his pay are beyond his control (such as design changes, bad planning, plant breakdowns, lack of raw materials) the operation of a scheme requires a level of employee trust of management. In a high trust situation employees are well-disposed towards cooperation with the system in spite of its uncertainties. But in a low trust situation they will take steps to defend their earnings from the vagaries of inconsistency in ways which are unlikely to assist in performance improvement. Low trust or high trust situations tend to be self-perpetuating (Fox, 1974); and extensive consultation can assist in developing a high trust situation by removing misunderstanding and the barriers to trust.

Figure 6.6 illustrates the way many employees behave in response to an incentive scheme.

Roy (1955) found in his studies that distrust of management's intentions through poor communication was a major factor in the restriction of output and the false recording of performance data under an incentive payment system.

Our own case studies suggested that in some circumstances a low level of employee understanding of a scheme could be offset by a high level of employee trust in management.

Handy (1978) also suggests in relation to delegation, why trust is hard to give as far as superiors are concerned:

1 The manager has to have confidence in the subordinate.
2 It is like a step into the unknown. It has to be given before it is received.
3 It is a breakable commodity. Like glass once shattered it is never the same again.
4 It must be reciprocal.

In most organisations supervision still plays an important role in the communication process, yet from our full sample of 620 employees we were to find 41% felt that communications were poor with only a slightly larger number (45%) thinking it was adequate. Only 14% of the total considered communications to be good.

Extensive consultation is clearly an important means by which trust and commitment may be established and maintained.

One other dimension of consultation not yet fully discussed is that of participation. It is through this process that use is made of a wide spectrum of talent and experience. As a consequence it is argued (Bowey, 1978) that this will improve the quality of decision and debate and this will in turn improve system design, cooperation and understanding. Lawler (1976) in 'New Approaches to Pay: Innovations that Work' discusses the effects of openness about salary information and how this can affect both motivation and satisfaction. Lawler (1978) later comments about his developing research 'It is not merely sufficient to consult and explain, participation appears to be desirable if not essential for success'.

Amongst the eight factors which contributed to excellence in successful American managers, Peters and Waterman (1952) listed productivity through people; a respect for the individual; 'open-door' policies by management; 'hands-on' value-driven companies; management by walking around; a culture of common attitudes and shared beliefs within the organisation.

Although Britain has a different cultural and industrial relations background to America there is evidence that participative approaches in a range of change programmes are having successes. The Work Research Unit in its *Guidelines for Successful Implementation of Change* (1982) and in *The Case for Shop Floor Participation* (Jessop, 1977) enlarged on these general points and confirmed many of the process considerations identified in our research. These were:

1 The need for managerial commitment and competence to carry through the programme, backed up by effective communication procedures to allay the fears and uncertainties of all concerned. This normally involves the participation of trade union officials and has taken the form of small conferences.
2 The desirability of a facilitator or external agent to assist the change process. This could well be a new system of reward.
3 A generally found need to be prepared to spend a fairly long gestation period, collecting information, consulting and revising plans prior to implementing changes. For this the concept of a joint steering group representing the main categories of staff to be affected by changes, is useful.
4 In the group discussions and planning, the foreman of the group should take the lead. In this way the foreman does not feel

threatened and feels committed. Prior training and briefing is often necessary both to operate in groups and fulfil rewards.

The studies not only substantiated the conditions necessary for success but also confirmed the nature of the benefits. These were:

1 The involvement did not simply encourage cooperation, but also had important effects on the way individuals helped, improved and modified plans.
2 Team spirit, through pooled knowledge, was engendered as well as a general improvement in the industrial relations climate.
3 More encouraging still was the benefit that came from the shared learning experience which induced a change mentality and promoted staff confidence in their ability to tackle future uncertainty.
4 Finally, flexibility was improved and also the individual's interest in his own job. This in turn led to a greater contribution by individuals, an improved physical environment and the opportunity for increased shared benefits.

The Role of Consultation in Achieving Organisational Change for Productivity Improvement

So far we have seen how 'extensive consultation' promotes scheme success by focusing attention on organisational objectives, on the design and implementation phases, and on the contextual and behavioural variables; and also, through the very processes of consultation, by securing employee and management commitment. One final important area where performance can be improved is organisational change.

One of the conclusions from our research is that payment systems are often central to management's thinking about improving job performance and the overall performance of an organisation. Sometimes there is little evidence of an association between poor performance and the factors which could be influenced by a payment system. On the other hand, a change of payment system permeates a large area of the organisation and requires a large amount of reorganisation and revision of procedures. Such a change provides the opportunity for changing other systems and procedures, and there is considerable scope for improving performance by combining a change of payment system with changes in communications and control procedures. Indeed, it may sometimes be the case that a new payment system improves productivity merely by facilitating the introduction of other changes, such as new technology or manning reductions.

Lawler and Bullock also advocate using the payment system in this way in order to, as they put it, 'manipulate' organisational change. They state:

'The compensation system is important to every employee and it impacts on each organisation member. Many times change programmes are limited to a sub-section of the organisation, such as a department or functional area, or to an issue that is not important to everyone. As a result change is slow and often is not very significant. Compensation provides a broad base upon which to begin organisational change...'

'Beginning with compensation can provide a model for how other problems can be dealt with. Usually organisations have no historical reference for the process of solving system-wide problems that affect the quality of working life and organisational effectiveness. These mechanisms and processes can be developed and made explicit by changing the compensation system'.

Studies designed to determine what happens when the payment system is used as a starting point for a change programme have led to improved attitudes towards pay and higher performance motivations.

Lawler and Bullock conclude 'A physicist once remarked that every time we try to separate something to study it, we find it hitched to everything else in the universe.' The same is true for organisations. It is our observation that the compensation system affects, and is affected by, virtually every other sub-system of the company. Lawler and Bullock found the most important links to be with performance appraisal, the information system, job design procedures and managerial style: one or more of these had to be changed in most of their payment scheme projects.

Some of the areas where the Strathclyde researchers found change might be required to complement a change in the payment system were:

communication and information systems
consultation and participation in decision-making
job and design layout
supervision
performance appraisal
planning and control procedures

Payment Scheme Processes

management style
chains of command and spans of control
the technical system

Our research suggested that even when schemes were designed and introduced to raise performance, it was often a redeployment of resources or working methods, installed as part of a package of change, that in fact produced the productivity improvements. In this way change in the organisation to secure productivity improvements can be said to work both ways – one way to reinforce a particular scheme to obtain maximum success by reinforcement of the incentive; the other way to modify behaviour in line with a planned change of some other component of the system. Benefits to the organisation derive from both. For example, it had long been recognised that incentive schemes can replace some of the inadequacies of weak supervision, whilst daywork schemes can exacerbate them.

Blockage to Consultation

We came across many situations in which extensive consultation had not been carried out, and the following three reasons occurred sufficiently frequently to be worthy of mention:

1 the continual search by management for a panacea solution;
2 schemes dictated by one man with influence in the organisation;
3 schemes dictated by central groups or national policy.

The continual search by management for a panacea solution. Many managers were still looking for a panacea solution to their company's payment system problems. These panacea schemes go in and out of fashion with predictable regularity. Productivity bargaining was in vogue in the mid-1960s; measured daywork was in vogue in the early 1970s in an attempt to reduce some of the disadvantages of piecework; added value was in vogue in the late 1970s; and the management fashion of the 1980s is Quality Circles.

This over-dependence on fashionable practices could reflect the quality of management education or the lack of it. To introduce something fashionable is safe. It requires little persuasive skill to have it accepted, and if it fails the failure is unlikely to be blamed on the manager who advocated it in the first place – if anyone can remember who it was.

Schemes dictated by one person with influence in the organisation. Often schemes are influenced by one person. We found that this not only had the effect of militating against the adoption of a consultative approach to scheme design, thus closing off the opportunity for wider debate, but also placed over-reliance on one individual's experience of schemes. Managers and employees alike were found to have a tendency to carry their own experience of incentive schemes – favourable, bad or indifferent – from one job to the next and from one industry to another. The lack of appreciation of the need for a careful diagnosis of the factors relating to productivity in the current situation was marked.

Schemes dictated by group or national policy. About half of the schemes implemented were in organisations which were parts of larger groups or were covered by a national policy. These schemes had been designed at head office or national level and then imposed on local management without due regard to local circumstances. Of all the schemes, the most disturbing were the directly work-measured schemes that assumed performance improvement required only one recipe: measure work, specify the method and pay bonus for standard hours produced. Schemes of this type were being introduced as a part of a national policy by health authorities, local authorities and water authorities. Many of these schemes were introduced by specialist teams in these organisations or by consultants. Most were of the same basic type with experience of implementation simply being transferred from one site to another.

In a local authority parks and burial grounds scheme, the employees commented to us that the consultants were unwilling to appreciate all the difficulties and variables in the work they undertook. The men, especially the older ones, found their targets too tight, and many feared the scheme would result in a drop in quality of which they were proud, but the 'we know best' attitude of the consultations regardless of the long experience of the employees always prevailed. The implementation of new patterns or routines with little discussion caused some consternation in this scheme. The new schedules cut directly across many of the men's ideals and satisfactions such as personal pride in their work.

The failure to take account of local variables produced many schemes that altered behaviour, but not always in the manner intended and not always for the best. Productivity increases from these schemes were usually derived from changes in the organisation of the work when the scheme was implemented, rather than subsequent improvements in effort and initiative encouraged by the offer of a bonus.

By the nature of their origins, schemes imposed from national level leave little scope for extensive consultation. However, although it was commonly so it was not necessarily so. The Coal Board, for example, devised an incentive scheme which was negotiated nationally, but which required local level consultation to agree certain features of the scheme (such as whether each face team should be paid a bonus based on its own output or on the pooled output from the whole pit).

Summary of the Processes of Consultation

This part of Chapter 5 has attempted to interpret the major finding from our research that extensive consultation was a key factor in those organisations which produced good results from their new incentive schemes. It should not be seen as a panacea in itself – as the means to employee performance improvements; but rather as a tool for facilitating the necessary stages in effective incentive scheme design – a tool which nevertheless does have many side-benefits for both managers and employees.

PART B: CASE STUDIES OF PAYMENT SYSTEM:

Design and Implementation of Schemes

This part contains details of three case studies which clearly show that the degree of effort put in by management to consultation, and the consequent modification of the proposed payment scheme prior to its introduction and during its implementation is a major factor in determining relevant measures for performance and explaining a scheme's success.

The first of these cases documents the experience of a company which changed its payment scheme from payment by results to a flat day rate, and then to a company-wide performance related bonus. The second is of a public sector organisation which introduced a short-term variable group bonus scheme on top of an existing national day wage payment system. The third details the experiences of an organisation which designed and introduced its new scheme in accordance with the findings of our research setting up a highly participative system for doing so.

Information for the first two cases was gathered by a variety of methods and from several standpoints in order to achieve as objective an account as possible. These complementary sources of data included:

a. reports prepared for the company;
b. interviews with selected organisation members;
c. questionnaires to selected organisation members;
d. company reports, accounting data and other documents;
e. the first-hand experience of employees obtained in one case from a three-months participant observation study, and in the other from diaries kept by selected organisation members for three months.

The account of these case studies follows the analytical framework outlined at the beginning of the chapter, covering:

a. Background (Figure 6.1, Cells 1 and 2 – external contextual factors, Cells 4, 5 and 6 – internal contextual factors).
b. Payment Scheme Design (Cell 3a).
c. Scheme Implementation (Cell 3b).
d. Scheme Performance (Cells 7 and 8).

The third case describes the introduction of a new payments scheme at John G Kincaid Ltd (manufacturers of slow-speed diesel marine engines) and is based on in-depth case work undertaken between 1981–83.

Coalbridge Engineering Company

Background

This large engineering company with 2000 manual employees has been established at the same site since 1910. The company originally manufactured electrical units for the medical trade. Then, in 1915, in response to a govenment need for industrial assistance, it manufactured equipment under licence for the war effort. The government is still the company's major customer.

The participant observation was carried out in the stores section of the group's main subsidiary company. In 1979 the researcher (Richard Thorpe) worked in various locations within the stores section for a period of three months. He started at the Goods Inward Section where he drove a fork-lift truck. He then progressed through Central Stores and finally worked in a sub-store, servicing final operations in the assembly section of the factory.

In addition to participant observation, a questionnaire survey of the labour force was conducted independently to gain a profile of the organisation and to obtain some attitudinal data from employees. Where additional information was required, a number of interviews were held with members of senior management, the works convenor and some shop stewards; and written documents were examined.

For manual workers, the company had granted recognition rights to six unions of the Confederation of Shipbuilding and Engineering Unions to negotiate on behalf of their members, under the leadership of a convenor. The company was affiliated to the Engineering Employers' Federation and followed its National Agreements with the Unions. There was a procedure within which disputes were resolved which conformed to a national framework.

The company's domestic agreement for handling grievances from the shop floor ensured that if a matter could not be settled between shop stewards, the convenor and the Personnel Manager, then it would be raised at a Works Committee. This committee consisted of representatives of six unions (headed by the works convenor) and the company management (headed by the works director of the subsidiary company). It was a major means of communication and met regularly once each month, as well as sitting for special matters. A brief history of the company's blue collar incentive payment schemes 1975–80 is provided in Table 6.2.

Payment by Results

In 1975, a management decision at the main subsidiary company was made to change the payment scheme as an attempt to establish a sound individual piecework system in place of the original piecework scheme which had started to drift badly. A new scheme was introduced after a five weeks strike by the employees who objected to the change.

Following this change the employees were able to make the new scheme drift quickly because of a number of failures in design. The failure of this scheme and the problems caused by the wage drift that ensued is discussed in detail in Chapter 7, as an example of an incentive scheme manipulated by the workforce.

TABLE 6.2 *Coalbridge Engineering Ltd: payment schemes, 1975–80*

1972	Piecework system drifting.
1975	New piecework payment system introduced.
1977	Major financial problems for company, related to the payment system.
	Agreement to buy-out existing piece rate scheme and place all manual workers on staff conditions.
	Agreement not ratified by group management.
	Two months of industrial action.
	The major production area, Line 1, where payment scheme drift worst, taken off scheme and paid bonus based on factory average bonus.
	Company commitment to transfer all manual workers to 40-hour week staff conditions before 15 April 1978.
	Negotiations to replace piecework scheme.
	Concept of short-term variable collective bonus introduced by management as a precondition to negotiations.
	Unions disagree with these preconditions.
1978	Short-term variable collective bonus schemes began to be introduced into many subsidiaries within the group. At Coalbridge, due to union resistance, this was modified to a fixed percentage bonus.
	Short-term fixed collective bonus introduced based on a philosophy of a participative management style.
	Lack of middle management and plant-level union support for participation or for the bonus system.
1979	Participant Observation Study.

1 The scheme was very highly geared. An improvement of only 10% in the time for jobs produced nearly 19% increase in pay.

2 Payment had drifted upwards because payments for waiting time and diversions were based on personal average bonus. It is usual in piecework schemes to pay such time at a day performance or reduced rate, to discourage cross-booking of time as a means of increasing pay.

3 The agreed incentive performance time on which the bonus was based was not derived from objective quantifiable measurement. There were no uniform work study standards applied across the site, and one result was that the rates for similar work could be different between jobs in the same area.

The switch to a new product provided the ideal opportunity for the unions and workers to 'take the scheme to the cleaners' (their own words). By holding down their rate of working on new tasks and later, after the times had been agreed, finding easier and faster ways of completing the work, they gradually slackened their rate of work at the same time as their bonus earnings increased.

Not just the unions, but some members of senior management, recognised the scheme was absurd. One said: 'It was obvious from the start that the scheme would run away. Even an army of work study engineers with a stop watch in one hand and a whip in the other wouldn't be able to control it.'

In 1977 the Chairman's report indicated that there were industrial relations problems which could be very serious in view of a fixed price contract for a new product and the high rate of inflation. Shareholders were assured that steps had been taken to remedy the situation. In 1977 the company accounts reported that there had been further drift in the piecework scheme without a corresponding increase in productivity and although there had been negotiations with the union no agreement had been reached which 'would end this absurd, damaging and intolerable situation' (Company accounts, 1977). The 1977 Annual Report indicated that productivity was expected to improve as a result of the 1977 wage deal. But on conclusion of the wage deal this improvement did not take place; in fact product line items took twice as long to complete as their target times. The production time for the first order was more than double the targetted time.

The very poor productivity and delays in settling piecework times eventually led to the complete withdrawal of the scheme from the assembly area. During the last year of its operation, only 40% of tasks in the assembly area were covered by agreed piecework times; the rest were subject to dispute. During the dispute period productivity on these jobs was less than one-third of the eventual post-dispute productivity.

As a result, there were excessive delays in delivery and very high labour costs. Since suppliers had delivered components in line with the original contract plan, there had also been a massive accumulation of stocks of parts awaiting final assembly. The interest on money tied up in those stocks trebled between 1975 and 1977. During the same period the bonus earnings for skilled manual workers had increased from £10 to £30 with no increase in performance.

And although order books for the new product were full, it was recognised that the delays were jeopardising future contracts. As a result of these problems the group made a loss for the year 1978. This was the first year the group had ever made a loss.

The Flat-Rate Scheme

The management of the company realised that something drastic needed to be done to change the deteriorating situation. An agreement was therefore concluded between the unions and senior management in April 1977 which stopped the piecework system and put the manual workers on fixed wages. It also gave them staff conditions, the main implication of which was that a manual worker could no longer be laid off without full pay during periods of temporary shortage of work.

This agreement was not ratified by the group chief executive because it was in breach of Phase II Incomes Policy then operative. In addition, the repercussive effects on other subsidiary companies had not been considered. The withdrawal of the agreement led to two months industrial action.

After the withdrawal of the original agreement a new agreement was reached later in 1977 between the unions and the company, whereby the piecework system was withdrawn from the crucial main assembly area whilst the remainder of the manual workers remained on the 1975 piecework agreement. The main assembly workers were paid factory average bonus.

Also, there was a commitment made to abandon piecework altogether in the 1978 agreement and give all manual workers staff conditions. The management felt that this was the correct course of action to enable them to introduce new working methods based on flexible teamwork, not previously possible.

Although it might be thought that there would be some reluctance on the union side to see the extremely lucrative Payments by Results (PBR) scheme taken out, change of some kind was recognised as inevitable. They saw their responsibility to ensure that a withdrawal would take place under the very best possible terms with maximum benefits to their members. With this in mind, they attempted to wring the last drops out of the dying PBR scheme between 1977 and 1978 and set about frustrating the attempts of management to remove it.

The Company-Wide Performance Related Scheme

When the time actually arrived to replace the piecework scheme with staff conditions the company struck new problems. Negotiations started in 1977. The company wished to set out certain principles before detailed negotiations took place, and one of these principles was that part of the pay should be related to company performance.

Further, the skilled manual workers' average 40-hour earnings had drifted so much over the previous few years that a differential of £1000 not only existed between employees at this subsidiary and their counterparts in the other subsidiaries of the group, but also between their counterparts in the same subsidiary on a different site. It was therefore not feasible to accommodate a buy-out with a flat rate because of the differential it would cause. A lower pay rate, 'topped up' by an incentive component paid in the form of a weekly bonus, was therefore an attractive alternative to the company.

The separate bargaining units (manual, clerical, inspection, charge hands and senior technical) would not conduct joint negotiations on the proposed scheme. The most powerful of them, notably the manual workers, did not wish to vote with the less powerful. The proposed company-wide performance based scheme was totally rejected by the unions in 1977. They were not prepared even to take part in discussions to amend the scheme. However, they were prepared to consider discussions on alternative proposals, three of which had been outlined at the beginning of the negotiations. The attitude of the trade unions to the negotiations was that the longer they could delay the change the more they would get out of the old scheme before they 'swapped it' for something else, and the better the deal they would be able to secure under some form of fixed rate of pay.

It is clear from discussions with trade unions since that they realised the scheme would have to be withdrawn and that it was only a matter of time. The works convenor also stated that so much ill-feeling had been created by the offer and the last minute withdrawal in April 1977 that they were not prepared to give management an easy time.

This attitude, the works convenor explained, was attributable to the experiences of years of mistrust and pay policy.

'People have lost the power to negotiate. You now say to management, this is what I want. You don't bother to make a proper case for it any more. The same is true of the company. They say we aren't going to pay you because we think you are in the wrong pecking order or because we can't afford it. They don't go into any details at all. A lot of frustrations are creeping into manual and staff employees alike because the management does not do enough to explain why they do things. They think we should automatically understand the company's problems irrespective of what they are. In 1977 the company could have concluded an agreement by co-operation and a ballot of the members taken. Now when it was offered again it was forced on the workforce and proved to be far more costly to the company than the first deal would have been'.

The company, after making a few amendments to their scheme, mainly concerned with the attendance factor, stated their intention to implement the scheme, whether the unions were in agreement or not.

Payment Scheme Design

As the holding company was a public company answerable to shareholders, one of the primary objectives at the time of the study (1979) was to return to a situation of profit. There was an urgent need to improve the industrial relations climate which had been destroyed by piecework disputes, mistrust and ill-feeling.

The Bullock Report on industrial democracy had been recently published, which encouraged larger companies to seriously consider employee participation. The new payment scheme based on company performance, which was devised by senior management, also aimed to introduce a participative management style. The payment scheme was introduced in conjunction with:

a. improved methods of communicating within the subsidiary company;
b. a proposed joint union committee to discuss the scheme;
c. the publication of an annual review.

The chief executive was keen on participation and constantly made reference to the need to consult, communicate and involve individuals more. 'Participation', he said 'was the reality of today.'

Three factors made up the performance figure that was used for calculating the bonus. The first was a turnover performance factor based on actual turnover compared with budget turnover. The second was employee costs indexed against budgeted payroll costs and the third was a combined index of both against an overall budget of company performance for the period. Appendix V contains further details concerning the bonus calculations.

The company's senior executive sincerely believed that this performance-related scheme would change the behaviour of the workforce and improve their effort at work. In the conclusion to his 1978 review of the company, the Chairman laid great emphasis on the scheme. The need for flexibility and effective work was stressed. He stated that a scheme which relates pay to performance month by month in a manner that is intelligible and acceptable to the average person was the realistic way to proceed.

In spite of the long-term aim to increase employee participation, management (particularly middle management) had a short-term strategy to regain control over the workplace. Under the piecework system, with continual bargaining over rates, much of the production control rested with the unions and the workforce. Control had been lost and surrendered to the men who knew the job and who kept all initiative and short cuts for their own remunerative benefit. A senior production manager commented, 'The shop floor and the job ran itself largely with management running behind.'

Senior management felt very strongly that the removal of piecework and the adoption of a participative approach would enable the company to obtain commitment to a common objective. Although it was never the specific objective to win back control a climate was created whereby the removal of piecework gave management the opportunity to obtain increased control over the production process. Supervisors and managers alike were encouraged to correct bad working practices, correct poor layouts, carry out better production planning and to motivate and improve operator effort.

Differences in perception as to the reasons for the participatory approach depended largely on the level in the organisation from which it was viewed. Whereas senior management and union officials had spent nine months seriously discussing participation and were committed to it, middle management and local union representatives were not so committed and failed in the task. This in turn created at shop floor level, a still different perception of the scheme, its workings and purpose; usually one of disinterest and non-comprehension.

Scheme Implementation

An explanatory leaflet to employees. The incentive scheme was explained in a twelve-page leaflet distributed to all employees. It stated that the company believed that employees performed best as a team, and the more they understood the scheme the more they would see how to increase performance.

The better the performance, the better the payment. The booklet explained 'that it is real co-operation between us that will make the scheme work. More effort and closer co-operation are necessary to improve performance'.

It encouraged employees to act in the following ways:

'Produce more – give your job your best effort.
Work together – teamwork always produces more.
Keep an open mind to change – always be on the lookout for ways to improve performance and reduce costs.
Be on time every day – lost time reduces performance.
Cut out mistakes – every error increases costs and reduces performance.
Talk things over – if you are not sure about something, ask your supervisor'.
[Company Performance Relation Payment Scheme, 1978]

Modification of the stated policy. When the enterprise-wide scheme was introduced there was considerable distortion of the underlying policy as it was interpreted and applied through the two major communications systems, unions and management. The degree of distortion can be judged from the way in which the policy was interpreted by the employees who worked under the new payment system. The participative philosophy behind the scheme was almost undetectable and universally misunderstood by employees. Taking each communication channel separately it is possible to identify the pressures accounting for modification.

Management. The policy was misunderstood by middle and lower management. There had previously been an individual piecework scheme and the change required drastic revision in the approach to industrial relations by many managers. This was not always possible to achieve quickly because of their past education and experience. Many who were interviewed were not in full agreement with the new approach. Some openly thought it was a 'load of rubbish' which hardly suggests that it would be implemented with a commitment to its success.

In this particular company, because of its size and range of specialist departments, there were several layers to the hierarchy. As the policy was explained, agreed and modified at each level, each lower level of management perceived it slightly differently. They, in turn, modified it in the light of their own understanding and experience. The degree of this misunderstanding could certainly be detected in the stores area where the participant observer worked. Discussions with a chargehand and foreman indicated that they thought the scheme was simply a way to pay more money and they had no comprehension of its wider implications, particularly the participative style which was still a major objective of the company. They thus communicated and consulted as they had always done and judged success by the old standards and criteria.

When it came to the choice between quick ways of obtaining short term objectives and the longer term participative approach, the former won through. After the withdrawal of piecework there was a massive programme of cost reductions, productivity improvement and supervisory development to set the organisation on a sound footing. However, although it can be said the controls were much needed, the mechanisms used in their implementation were not in line with a participatory approach.

Almost totally neglected were job design considerations and organisational changes to improve shopfloor involvement. One senior manager compiled a check list for supervisors which actually reduced the opportunities for employee involvement. Whether these operating plans were drawn up because of lack of understanding of the policy or because of management disagreement with it is difficult to detect. What is certain is that middle and supervisory levels of management had little opportunity to incorporate a participative style and employee's perception of the policy was modified by the way control was administered.

Modification also took place in some cases as a result of individual managers wishing to retain control of all the factors of production. For these managers, a participative approach was viewed as a loss of management control (rather than an increase in the scope of the function) and a threat to their authority and status.

Union power had, in the past, succeeded in undermining the authority of supervisors, as was manifested in many ways. For example, men transferred by the supervisor from one job to another to assist the production process were moved back after intervention by the union. This reduced the credibility of the supervisor in the eyes of the men, especially when it was to senior management that the unions went to complain and when it was senior management that reversed the decisions of a supervisor. Both unions and senior management bypassed the supervisor.

The dilemma of the supervisor is illustrated in Figure 6.7. The participant observer when commenting on this situation wrote,

'... supervisors in all the ... departments I visited played little part in the daily work of the employees. All had a strange detachment from the men. I found that one talked to the foreman out of politeness, not because he affected very much what one did or could help to do it

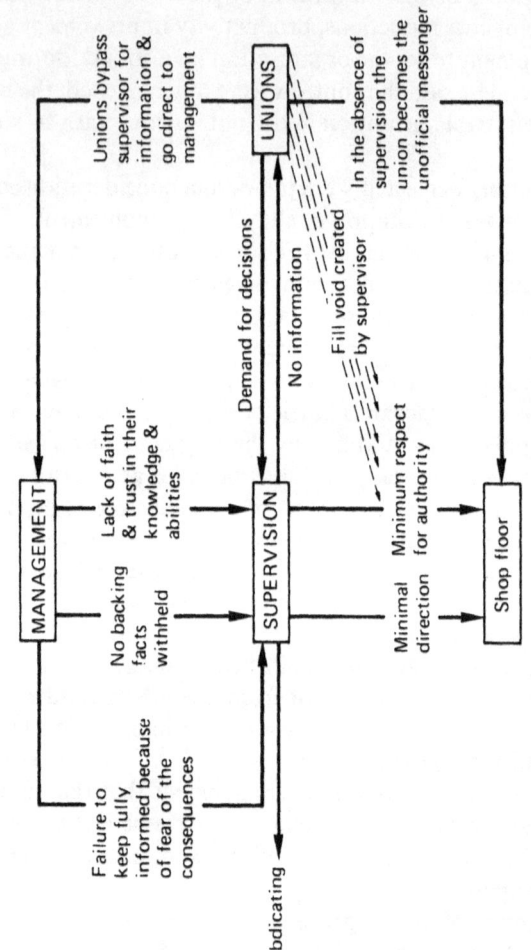

FIGURE 6.7 *Model of the supervisor's dilemma*

better. The foremen in all departments gave the impression of having been sent to work with the men as a punishment. They worked independently for the majority of the day. In one section, I had the distinct impression that the foreman was trying to shame his men into working harder, so hard would he work himself; yet he would never try to organise the men under his control. Often he could be found unloading vehicles himself... I formed the opinion that by working harder they were trying to compensate for their weakness in the management functions of their job'.

Unions. Fear of losing control of their traditional historic role was an important reason for the distortion of policy by the unions. They did not wish to see their power and role diminished by a participative scheme. In this organisation the unions were well established and powerful, they had moved into the vacuum at supervisor level to become the dominant communicators of information.

They were in a unique position to act as brokers rather than as messengers in communicating the workings and reasons for the payment scheme. In fact, the trade unions saw the participative scheme as one way management could directly talk to the workforce, thus by-passing the trade union.

They did not consider it to be in their long term interests and the unions proclaimed their opposition to the scheme from the outset. No reinforcement of the workings of the scheme or its merits were undertaken by the union and it was portrayed as worthless and irrelevant. The production workers did not agree to the proposed plan and did not encourage it to work. The unions had little expectation that improved performance would be rewarded by increased wages, for the bonus calculation was based on accounting data compiled by senior management.

The production workers' union opposed the scheme and had no interest in operating it effectively. Faced with this kind of opposition from the strongest bargaining unit within the company, other unions were reluctant to support the scheme either. The official union view expressed by the works convenor was that, if the management wanted to throw away money on a scheme, then they would welcome it.

The failure to make the necessary organisational changes to accommodate the new payment system was also responsible for the scheme's subsequent modification.

Organisation. Apart from changes in some methods of communication, there was very little evidence to suggest that the policy was reinforced by changes to any of the operating procedures. Change was essential if employees were to be able to make a realistic contribution to the organisation. Changes were necessary in both communications and consultation chains of command, training and additional education programmes for all employees were necessary modifications to the organisation structure in order to facilitate the implementation of an effective enterprise-wide incentive scheme and the participative policy of which it was part.

As a consequence of these structures being left as they were the scheme was badly communicated. In some cases it was hardly ever heard of and most supervisors interviewed did not understand its aims or underlying philosophy. There were no formal consultation procedures at management level within the company. As stated earlier, supervision was weak and by-passed by the trade unions which made formal consultation difficult, even if the supervisors had the skill and knowledge and backing from higher management to undertake this task.

The discussions with employees that did exist were carried out by the trade unions and were notably one way communications which did not provide an opportunity for employees to express their views and have them taken into account. As a result there was no forum where employees could learn and discuss exactly how their contribution could be more meaningfully related to the benefit of the company and themselves.

The interpretation of the policy was modified by the reality the employees experienced in their work situation. They weighed what they were told in the company's published material with what they were told by the local management and unions and how they saw the effects in practice. In addition, they had their own experience of previous ways of working and their knowledge of past company performance from which to generate their interpretation.

Figure 6.8. provides an outline of the influences affecting payment scheme modification within the Coalbridge Engineering Company.

Responsibility for the scheme's modification ultimately lay with senior management who did not recognise or reinforce the implications of their policy, or develop and publish monitors of scheme performance.

Scheme Performance

Before the company based incentive scheme was introduced (1978) the

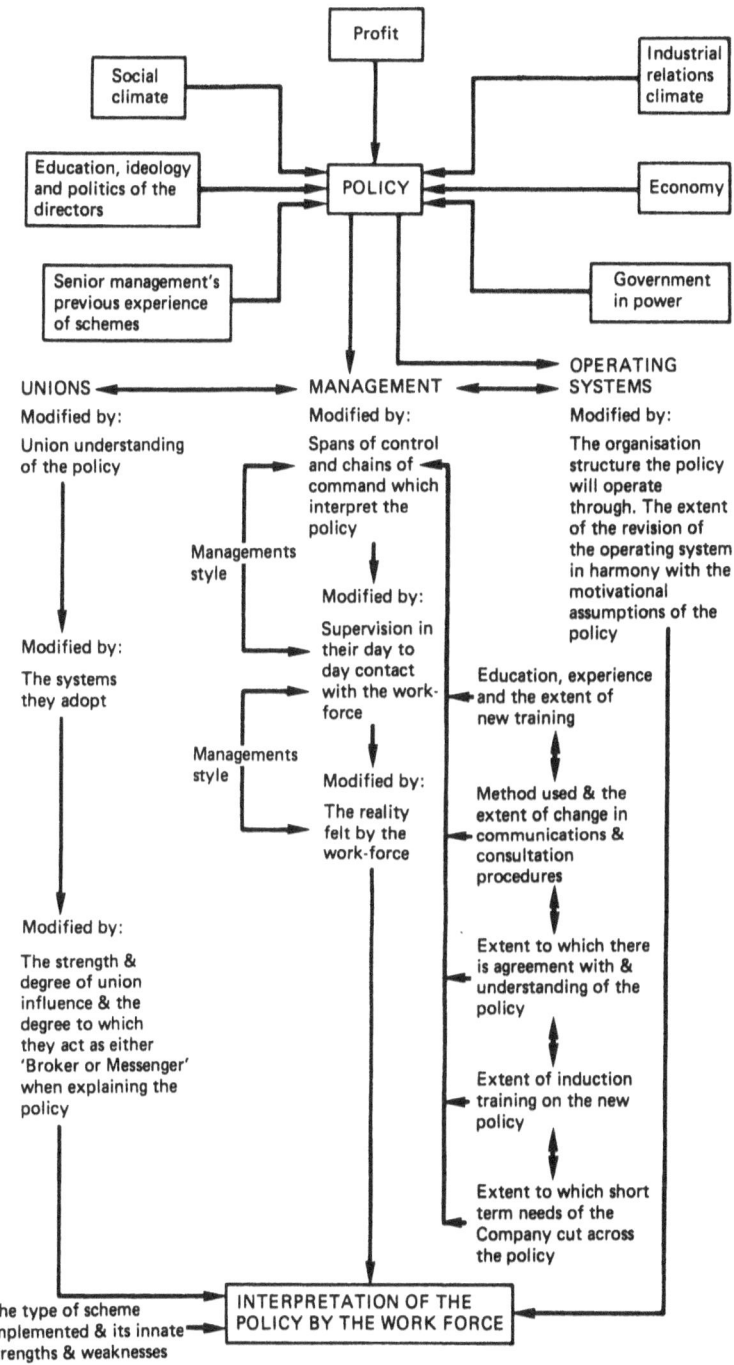

FIGURE 6.8 *Modification and interpretation of policy in the main subsidiary company*

production workers union at Coalbridge succeeded in having the variable bonus converted to a fixed rate bonus. (They did not trust the management's financial calculations which suggested workers could earn a variable 10% bonus).

Subsequent to the introduction of the company based incentive scheme for the manual labour force, there was a fall in performance. Output fell from 105% under payment by results to 65% under the new scheme (measured on the standard BSI rating scale).

In one shop, where it was well-known that the management was weak, production hours per unit increased from 400 to 1000. However the fall was temporary. The average performance rose from 55% for the first 13 weeks after the change to 72% for the next 13 weeks on product line 1; and a slightly smaller increase on product line 2, from 65% performance in the first 13 weeks to 76% performance for the second 13 weeks. However, these better results were mainly brought about by improved production control rather than the new payment scheme.

In early 1979 with the change of government the shadow of compulsory participation evaporated. Following the company's attainment of good trading results for the first time in two years, the strength of the participatory policy and the board's commitment to it weakened. Although participation was still the chief executive's aim, little new evidence of it appeared in practice or in print. The procedures for tightening control adopted by management did produce sufficiently improved organisational performance for the company to move to a profitable position. However, this had little to do with the payment scheme. Most employees did not understand the scheme and several did not even know there was a scheme. Also, participant observation revealed that there was extreme inefficiency in the use of shop floor labour and the potential for improvement was enormous. The participant observer wrote:

> 'On one occasion I noticed that the work had begun to back up on the conveyor. Asking why this was, I was informed by one of my colleagues that it was Wednesday and that was quite usual. Apparently inspectors would create an artificial backlog to enable overtime working at the weekend. Overtime had to be arranged in advance with the supervisor so the backlog would disappear and overtime workers would have a relatively easy time on Saturday morning or an enhanced premium. After observing the performance of these

employees during the week one might have been forgiven for saying management were being taken for a ride.

One employee told me 'Supervision isn't part of management, they just carry out management's wishes'. Another, from a different department, said 'Management are soft these days. They will neither tell you to do something that needs doing, nor stop you doing something you shouldn't.'

This attitude to work that had developed could have been remedied. Extensive interviewing and discussion revealed an extremely loyal workforce. One person volunteered, 'This company is a lazy company. How they survive and make a profit I'll never know'. On another occasion, the researcher asked a fellow worker why he did not feel guilty idling the day away. 'Yes', he said, 'I do feel guilty, but it's management's fault. We should be controlled better.'

Management did not appear to manage and left the employees for long periods very much to their own devices. This had a very unsettling influence on the workers who realised they were not under control and could do what they liked all day. Poor performance and theft of time were most disturbing results of this inadequacy of management. The failure to plan work meant men were often bored and our researcher's diary records day after day remarks about being bored.

He reported:

'Boredom for the workers in the stores took on two forms. One was boredom that comes from having nothing to do, the second is the monotony that comes from doing repetitive and futile jobs. Working in the stores, I undertook my fair share of both. Often the two would combine, for example, where the job was repetitive, futile and endless, the workers would manufacture breaks and stoppages to relieve the strain. In these circumstances, one of the main reasons for lack of motivation was the complete absence of a target or indicator of performance. Satisfaction was not intrinsic to the job and workers relied very much on their own conscience when setting their pace of work'.

In one department to alleviate the boredom, the team had developed a pattern of working where they worked for the first hour or so and then took a break, had a wash and a walk outside. On certain days they changed their overalls in the laundry, which involved a walk of about 600 yards and a break of about half-an-hour. After mid-morning, the pace became much slower and after lunchtime very little work was done at all.

Summary

The above case study shows that without two very important aspects of payment scheme design and implementation poor results can be expected. The first is the extent and nature of consultation and negotiation, to identify the contingent, contextual and behavioural variables which the scheme design needs to take account of and to obtain the understanding and commitment of employees to the proposed new system.

The second aspect is the extent to which the organisational structure, work features, behaviour and operating systems are adjusted to take account of the new payment system so that when it is introduced it can operate effectively.

The contribution of the case studies to an understanding of payment scheme dynamics can be illustrated by the analytical model: Figure 6.9.

In the case of Coalbridge Engineering it was the lack of effective consultation about design and implementation and the lack of complementary operating procedures that made the scheme such an unmitigated failure.

Due to extreme pressure resulting from lack of profit, failure to meet orders, and inefficiency caused by the former payment-by-results incentive scheme, the senior management negotiated-out the old scheme and sought to introduce a new one. The new scheme was to be a company-wide performance-related bonus scheme supported by a new participative management approach based on greater employee involvement and commitment to the organisation.

This philosophy was quite contradictory to the prevailing management style and procedures that operated within the organisation at middle and lower management levels and from the outset it was implemented in a manner consistent with a strong faith in managerial prerogative and control and with little evidence of participation. At senior management level there was a genuine commitment to the policy and consultation and discussion had taken place about the design and implementation over a period of 6 to 9 months. But below this level consultation had been minimal and the scheme was imposed under the threat of dismissal notices.

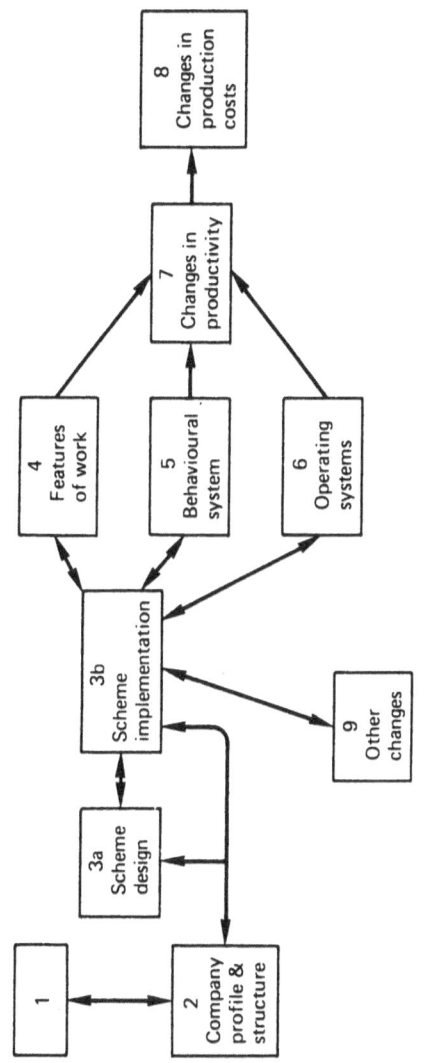

FIGURE 6.9 *The dynamics of payment scheme implementation*

At employee level there was little or no consultation about the payment scheme design and introduction and no changes were made in the operating procedures by management or union to enable it to work effectively when introduced. In addition there was little or no attempt to monitor and provide feedback information on its results.

One of the reasons for failure was that the strong unions did not welcome the new scheme because it had been imposed and they wanted it to fail. They communicated their views about the worthlessness of the scheme to their membership. Their anger extended as much to their full-time officials who had been party to the agreement as it did to the management and they were keen to re-establish their independence. In their anxiety to regain control they quickly negotiated a 5% fixed bonus to replace the 10% variable bonus, partly because they were distrustful of management.

The absence of a downward flow of information from management was the other major reason for the failure of the scheme. The number of levels in the organisation doubtless militated against good communications; but other factors were identified such as managers' failure to understand the new 'participative philosophy' fully; lack of management training and ability of middle and lower management; and the fact that many managers also questioned the benefits of the new scheme. Some managers wrongly believed it to be simply a device to win back control. These were all reasons why middle management did not promote the scheme or change the operating systems of the company, and consequently devoted no time to consulting with the unions or the various levels and specialisms within the organisation about the design and implementation of the scheme. As the scheme and its accompanying philosophy were not adequately communicated or understood it had no impact on the way employees and their managers went about their jobs.

The scheme was ineffective from the beginning, even though commitment at senior management level was strong. The failure of the payments scheme was clearly associated with the lack of management time and effort devoted to communication about its design and implementation and the subsequent lack of effort to monitor its performance.

The company's financial performance did improve, but this was largely the result of improved management control and removal of impediments to efficiency (Cell 9, Figure 6.9) when the old piecework bonus was taken out.

The National Coal Board: Hillend Colliery

Background

A detailed case study of the National Coal Board (NCB) incentive scheme at a colliery in the North West of England was conducted over a twelve week period (1980).

Eleven employees and managers who worked together at the colliery were shown how to write their own accounts of their day-to-day working lives and the ways in which the bonus scheme affected them. In addition, one researcher spent the majority of his time for three months monitoring these diaries, liaising with the diary writers and collecting further data from company records and interviews with key staff.

Economic and wage environment. This incentive scheme was introduced in 1978 to supplement the non-incentive wage system (called the National Power Loading Agreement) which had been introduced in 1971 to replace the previous system of local piece rates.

As far back as 1972, the Coal Board had suggested to the Wilberforce Court of Inquiry that incentives should be looked at as a way of raising efficiency and production and pay, and the report recommended that a productivity payment scheme should be agreed at national level by September of 1972. At that time, the National Union of Mineworkers (NUM) had little interest in such a scheme, and the miners themselves did not welcome the proposal to reintroduce incentives. It was six years before an incentive scheme was finally introduced in 1978. However, plans for an incentive scheme had been underway since 1972, and were actively discussed with the unions at many stages thereafter. In terms of time spent on consultations and negotiations, this was undoubtedly the longest in the research project sample.

Acceptance of the incentive payment scheme. The incentive scheme had been planned by the management for a very long period, and preparations and negotiations took place intermittently over six years. The majority of trade union delegates, particularly in the militant and 'left wing' areas, opposed its introduction. They were overruled by the right wing majority on the NUM executive when the 1977 Incomes Policy made an incentive scheme the only way to obtain a pay increase within 12 months of the last one. There had been extensive consultations, working parties of the union, and negotiations about the incentive scheme when it was finally introduced in January 1978.

The Coal Board wanted a productivity scheme largely as a way of increasing productivity and also as a way of avoiding a national strike over the current and future wage negotiations.

Once the NUM executive had given its approval for areas to go ahead with productivity schemes, those that were originally in favour of them did so very quickly. The National Coal Board emphasised its willingness to discuss local productivity schemes where there was union agreement to do so and remained enthusiastic about their introduction. Although areas opposing incentive schemes tried to take out an injunction halting their introduction and threatened industrial action, the substantial bonuses being earned in areas immediately implementing the scheme made it increasingly difficult for area leaders to maintain their opposition. By the end of January 1978 nearly all areas had accepted the scheme.

Payment Scheme Design

Management objectives. The incentive scheme was part of a major change in the policy of the Coal Board, who wished to raise productivity and the output of coal. Motivation under the former system was believed to be inadequate and further incentives were believed to be needed.

A White Paper, 'The Attack on Inflation after 31st July 1977' permitted self-financing productivity schemes to be negotiated provided they complied with the Department of Employment's interim rules, namely that they could lead to no increase in unit costs, no resultant increase in prices, and that they would increase efficiency.

Many NUM negotiators regarded the National Coal Board scheme as primarily a way of increasing wages. The Government and the Treasury feared it might be a way of getting round the constraints of incomes policy and needed a considerable amount of convincing by management before they accepted it as self-financing. The scheme was designed to become self-financing after a certain level of output was exceeded. Beyond this point the Coal Board would start to increase profitability while simultaneously paying a higher bonus. (This breakeven point was exceeded almost immediately the scheme was introduced.)

The scheme was designed in such a way as to give more autonomy to local management and local union officials. It was realised that local management sometimes used unofficial incentives under the old system.

Payment Scheme Processes 195

The new scheme would enable them to use their own judgement and initiative more widely. Although the scheme was a national one several aspects of it were negotiable at local level. It was also thought that by consulting with local union officials on an area basis disputes would only break out locally, at which level they would be easier to resolve and have only a minimum adverse effect on total output.

Table 6.3. shows the effect on output of the national disputes in 1972 and 1974. The Coal Board particularly wanted to avoid any future national dispute with its consequent severe effect on total output.

TABLE 6.3 *Coal output per year, 1970–76*

Year ending March	Deep mined output (million tonnes)
1970	142.0
1971	135.4
1972	111.0
1973	129.0
1974	98.7
1975	116.8
1976	114.4

NOTE
1972/73 figures were adjusted to new definitions introduced in 1973/74.

SOURCE: NCB Report

The mechanics of the scheme. The principle of the scheme was that tonnes of coal cut per week per coal face (adjusted to take account of manning and coal face conditions) was expressed as a ratio of target performance (similarly adjusted) and this ratio used to calculate incentive payment. The bonus payable to other workers was a percentage of that paid to the men on the coal face and in other direct production areas where the work achieved was directly measured.

The method study team would set a standard level of manning that they considered necessary to perform the standard task to arrive at a standard task per manshift, bearing in mind the working conditions at the time. This was then expressed as linear metres at an expected depth of strip, i.e.,

$$\frac{\text{standard task per shift}}{\text{number of men}} = \text{standard task per manshift (in metres at expected depth of strip).}$$

The basic task per manshift was taken as 75% of the standard. The incentive payment was made for each percentage point above 75%. Adjustments were made to this calculation to take account of variations in the depth of strip mined. If the average depth of strip exceeded the expected depth of strip or was more than 5% less, the linear yards of coal face cut were increased or reduced accordingly. If work was interrupted by a breakdown of machinery or other difficulties for more than 20 minutes, the task achieved was adjusted to take account of this.

Incentive was not paid for weekend work. However if it was measured work it did affect the incentive, as it contributed to the task actually achieved per manshift in the weekly calculation. The adjusted task per manshift was related to the standard task per manshift, to arrive at a percentage performance level. That is

$$\frac{\text{adjusted task achieved per manshift}}{\text{standard task per manshift}} \times 100 \text{ performance level}$$

The incentive was paid weekly. When it was introduced each pit was able to decide if it wanted the incentive paid separately to each face team or if it preferred the payments to be averaged over the faces at the pit. A pit was originally only able to change its option of face or pooled incentive pay once.

Men who were not working under the incentive agreement were paid a bonus which was a percentage of the incentive payments. The union at colliery or area level could opt for bonus payments based on the average incentive payment at the individual pit, or over the area. This option could only be taken once. Where some collieries in the area opted for a bonus calculated on an individual basis, and others opted for one on an area basis, the latter were deemed to have opted for a calculation based only on those collieries which exercised the same option. Men who worked on the coal face but were not eligible for incentive pay (because they are not members of a face team, such as mechanics, and men who were normally eligible for incentive pay but were on authorised absence, received 65% of the incentive. Craftsmen on the face, who were not members of a face team, received 100%. Other underground workers received 50% of the appropriate average incentive pay per manshift. Surface workers received 40% as did other workers who were not attached to a colliery. Workers eligible for incentive pay, but who earned less than the 65% rate of colliery or area bonus were eligible for that rate as a fall back. All workers in the industry therefore received either incentive or bonus payments. The following example is for a pit with three installations. The average incentive pay per manshift was calculated for the week. For each installation the total incentive pay per week was calculated by multiplying the incentive pay per shift by the number of manshifts worked each week.

Installation	Incentive pay calculated per shift	Manshifts worked per week	Total incentive pay (per week)
A Face	£4.90	200	£980
N Drivage	£6.00	150	£900
S Drivage	Nil	50	Nil
		400	£1880

Average incentive pay $= \dfrac{£1880}{400} = £4.70$ per manshift.

The different levels of colliery bonus could then be calculated:

Average incentive pay = £4.70
65% rate = £3.055 per shift (£15.28 per 5 shift week)
50% rate = £2.35 per shift (£11.75 per 5 shift week)
40% rate = £1.88 per shift (£ 9.40 per 5 shift week)

Bonus on an area basis was calculated in the same way.

When considering this incentive scheme it is important to make a clear distinction between incentive pay, which was paid to men on measured work, and bonus, which was paid to other men in the industry. This was an idiosyncratic distinction, not typical of the way other industries use the words, and indeed in their diaries the men used the word 'bonus' to refer to both payments.

Management were also paid by the bonus scheme. Their payment was calculated on an area basis and was made every three months. Members of the National Association of Colliery Overmen, Deputies and Shotfirers (NACODS) agreed to a productivity deal that gave its members the same payments as the men they supervised. This agreement was reached in March 1978, two or three months after most pits had adopted the incentive scheme. Members of NACODS received their bonus payments two weeks in arrears, as did men on incentive. Bonus payments of NACODS members were based on what the men under them had earned, but were calculated in a slightly different way and related to a four-week period rather than just one week. The Coal Mines Act states that officials cannot be paid on the mineral gained. Although the major purpose of the agreement was to increase output, for legal reasons this was not technically the governing variable in management's bonus calculation.

The payment of bonus to so many employees meant that for every £1 paid in incentive pay, the NCB had to pay £7 altogether. The high ratio of performance level to total payments made any drift particularly significant. Thus at $82\frac{1}{2}$% performance on incentive agreements £7.05 would be earned on 5 shifts by one face worker. A face team of 10 men would earn £70.50, but total payments under the agreement would be £493.50.

Incentive payments, but not bonus payments, were made on overtime, and incentive payments were not made on weekend work. There was no upper limit to the amount of incentive that could be earned. Incentive payments were not made to men who took a day off without authorisation, thus discouraging absenteeism.

Scheme Implementation

The individual or pool face option. Once an area had decided to adopt the incentive scheme the individual pits had to decide how they would like to operate it. Very few pits (those in North Derbyshire) decided to be paid on an area basis. The majority decided that within their pit they would prefer the incentive payments to be pooled between the faces, rather than paid on an individual face basis. Table 6.4 illustrates the situation in April 1978 and in June 1980. There was some pressure from the NUM to opt for the pooled system as it might be more conducive to union solidarity – and there was a slight tendency for large pits to opt for the individual system and small ones for the pooled one.

The exercising of this choice by each individual pit had the effect of involving the local union officials and all the miners in the scheme right from its inception. This early active participation at a local level turned

TABLE 6.4 *Face incentive option*

Area	April 1978		June 1980	
	individual	pooled	individual	pooled
Scotland	1	18	4	15
N. East	6	22	10	18
N. Yorks	2	15	4	13
Doncaster	0	10	4	6
Barnsley	6	13	13	6
S. Yorks	1	17	6	12
N. Derby	1	10	1	10
N. Notts	6	9	6	9
S. Notts	6	6	7	5
S. Midlands	2	16	3	15
Western	6	15	11	10
S. Wales	10	28	13	25
TOTAL	47	179	82	144

SOURCE: NCB.

out to be a good feature in the design of the scheme. Discussions over which option to adopt generated interest in the scheme and encouraged men to try to understand how it worked. In fact, at many pits discussion continued after implementation as men considered which option was the most favourable. In practice the only changes of option involved moves from a pooled to an individual face system. Experience showed that men tended to earn more money and output was higher under the face option.

Union involvement in method study. At each pit some method study was carried out, which took one or two months. However, the method study engineers already had a considerable amount of data about the work and synthetic values were used in several cases. If the face conditions had altered substantially since the data was collected, a new study was carried out of the whole face or drivage, but if just some new machinery had been introduced, the job done by the machine would be the only one to be remeasured. Close involvement of the union in method study was a distinctive feature of this incentive scheme; one frequently absent in others.

The method study department gave its assessment of the standard task and the men required to achieve it to the colliery manager. The colliery manager might wish to revise the amount of work that could be done in a shift or the number of men required to do it. Negotiations would then take place which involved the colliery manager, the deputy colliery manager, an NUM official, the chargehand and a worker from each shift on the face whose standard task level was being negotiated. The negotiations would concern the amount of work to be done or the number of men working on a face, but in either case the agreement had to be reached within a certain range of standard task levels. Thus the manager of the colliery was brought fully into the implementation of the scheme and his particular knowledge of conditions in his own pit was called upon to supplement the data at area level.

Local flexibility and involvement. Although it was a national scheme and the same design was applied at all pits, as much local flexibility and involvement was incorporated into it as possible. This allowed account to be taken of local conditions and the active participation of local managers, union officials and miners made them feel that they had contributed to the formulation of the scheme at their own pit.

If conditions on a face changed, such that re-negotiation of standards was required, no incentive was paid while negotiations were going on, but payments based on the subsequent agreement were backdated over the period of the negotiations up to six weeks. Thus the men on that face would start to lose incentive entirely for each week in excess of six over which negotiations were conducted and were encouraged to settle within that period. Furthermore, after six weeks, the shifts worked by the men in dispute were put into the divisor in the calculation of task actually performed per manshift over the whole pit, and thus the payments of all the workers at the pit were reduced, apart from face workers on individual face incentive agreements. Thus pressure was exerted on the men to reach an agreement within six weeks.

The participation of the chargehand and a worker from each shift during the negotiations ensured that the other men who worked on the face whose standard task per manshift was being decided were kept well informed of negotiations.

As in all method study, it was likely that the men did not work at their top performance level while they were being studied. Some of the men from Hillend commented on this and the NCB thought that there was holding back of effort in August 1977, but viewed as part of the long-term trend in output per manshift, it was not of major significance.

Management and supervisor understanding. Before the scheme was introduced, all managers, deputy managers, under-managers and assistant managers went to a conference for all of their area, at which the incentive bonus scheme was explained. Literature explaining the scheme and emphasising important aspects of it was produced for local managers by the NCB head office in London. The scheme was explained on courses for deputies and overmen by area officials. The NUM local officials were told about the scheme by the union and the NACODS official at Hillend learnt about it on an NCB course. Thus there was overall a reasonable level of understanding of the scheme and this was actively encouraged by the NCB.

Employee work satisfaction. The incentive payment scheme appeared to positively assist the men to achieve satisfaction at work. The miners' diaries provided a rich source of information about patterns of work satisfaction and reactions to the payment scheme.

The *first* source of satisfaction, and one which was held by all the men, was money. But it was of varying importance to different people. Face teams who were predominantly composed of men highly motivated by money responded best to the incentive. B88 face was very often the face which performed best during the week. The colliery manager attributed their high performance level to the fact that they were 'a very young team and they like the money'. Another miner commented that some men were 'just plain greedy'.

Money was clearly important to men like Peter, who had made a decision to enter mining from another industry. He would usually work an hour overtime between 6.00 a.m. and 7.00 a.m. to obtain extra money. He had two children to support. On 25th February (1980) he wrote, 'I hope I can make it for 6.00 a.m. all week, as the overtime will help towards my holidays, but I have a habit of oversleeping.' However the money did not appear to be sufficient to induce many men to work weekends. Peter, '... Barry came around again and was asking the men who wanted to work weekend, and it was the same old faces that told him they wanted to work, and the rest of the men are always joking about them and saying that they must have a lot of things on H.P. and cannot afford to have a weekend off, and in some cases I think it is true.' Peter did work weekends.

The *second* source of satisfaction identified at Hillend Colliery was that of target attainment. Most men were aware of the 'norm', the number of cuts to achieve the standard level of task per shift, on their face. Satisfaction was gained from achieving this number of cuts for its own sake.

For example, on 20th February (1980) Robert remarked that the shift had done $2\frac{1}{2}$ cuts: 'That is the first time this week we even reached our norm, but I checked our face advance rate for this week so far... our weekly norm cannot be reached this week.' And again the following week, '... no doubts about reaching our norm, by 12.30 a.m. the cutter starts on the 3rd strip'. Also Jim, 'This made just over 2 full cuts for 18 men (and myself) which is a very good day.' The incentive scheme offered the miners a target level of performance that they did not have before.

A *third* motivator detected at Hillend was that of respect derived from achievement. This was related to targets, as it was gained by being a member of, or particularly the overman of, the face team which had made the highest contribution to the pooled incentive each week. Although the incentive payments were pooled between the faces at Hillend the performance of each individual face, and hence its contribution to the pool, was recorded on a board. This board was displayed near the lamp room which every incentive worker had to pass during the day. The satisfaction of knowing that his face team had made the biggest contribution to the pool was very important.

The importance of achievement as a motivator is reflected in the diary of Jim, the overman of F3 face. On Friday some men went home early. 'Even so, the face had an average advance of 12.75 metres, which was over 3 metres more than any other face at Hillend, and this gave me the Yellow Jersey.' The Yellow Jersey was a fictitious item that the overmen at the pit strove to get. It was copied from the Milk Race and meant your face had the best advance of the week. 'It's all about honour you know.' The working of the 'bonus board' on which each face's performance was displayed also created a sense of rivalry. Jim, '88's have been doing OK, but not as good as they (F3) did. F3 did the best advance it's ever done, 12+ metres, and it was great to go around 88's and rib them and tell them to get their fingers out.'

The men on different shifts were motivated as much by personal pride and the professionalism they found in the job, as by the cash incentive. The achievement of high output in the eyes of their colleagues also served to maintain production at a high level.

A *fourth* source of satisfaction, of particular importance to overmen and deputies, was simply the knowledge that they had done their job well. The norm might not have been reached and the incentive pay might not be high, but men walked away from their job at the end of the day pleased that it had been done well. The concern with doing a job well was closely related to the particular dangers encountered in mining. It was especially important that the overmen were more concerned with safety than with the bonus, as this ensured that safety was not disregarded for the sake of more money.

Jim: 'Yesterday I came out of my district (F3) with some degree of satisfaction. It had been a particularly good day for a number of reasons. Firstly we had done two full cuts for the first time for several weeks. Although this is one third of a cut down on the norm set by the manager it is still good performance on what I consider a very difficult face to work.'

Safety was a major priority of all the men. As Andy wrote: 'While tackling a difficult job, I was seriously injured a few years ago and this was at the back of my mind all the time. I was off work on crutches for 8 months and all the bonus in the world is not worth being injured again.'

A *fifth* source of satisfaction, and one that was mainly of importance to managers, was the regard in which they were held by their superiors in the Coal Board. The NCB used management by objectives, and the management at Hillend were given certain targets to reach by the area officials at Staffordshire House. While management did have a sense of achievement and pride in reaching the targets, they were particularly concerned to satisfy the area officials.

A *sixth* satisfaction of great importance to the miners in general was that gained by leaving work. On Friday afternoons the men would often leave early, even though their pay was reduced by this. It would happen to a greater extent on the day preceding a holiday.

The men were only supposed to leave the pit at 7.30 p.m. on Friday. The early leaving was described by Jim on F3. 'When the cutter gets to the end of the face on Friday afternoon the men won't start cutting again for love nor money ... When they stop at 6.00 it grieves me but unless you go around bawling at everybody there is little else I can do.' As Andy put it, 'Friday today, thank God. It seems that the life of a coal miner is all darkness and dust. All week long I have been looking forward to Friday. It's a pity that it's not Friday more often.'

All our daily work diaries were well written, providing interesting and rich insights into the work and motivation of the miners under study. Examples of the information from the diaries are included in Appendix V.

Scheme Performance

The scheme, as has been shown, succeeded in motivating the men. It encouraged the face men to use more of their own initiative in their work. Several respondents commented on this, but it was also thought that this incentive effect had worn off to some degree since the scheme had been in operation. Fred said, 'When the incentive came in men did take more initiative, but not so much now.' The overmen thought that the scheme had made it much easier for them to supervise the men. When an overman wanted a man to do something he would frequently refer to the effect it would have on the incentive bonus if the job was, or was not, done.

Although the scheme was designed around money as an incentive it had also enabled satisfaction to be obtained from target attainment and achievement. Another result had been that the workforce had put more pressure on management to organise the pit well; it made them less tolerant of management inefficiencies that were seen to lose them pay. But in some respects, the scheme had not had a dramatic impact: men still left early or went absent, even though they lost pay in consequence.

In the year up to March 1980, the pit produced a record output of 845,000 tons at a record output per manshift of 2.39 tonnes. Incentive pay, output per manshift and output had all risen between March 1979 and March 1980. There had been no major changes in machinery used or organisation of the pit so the figures suggest that the scheme had motivated men to work harder.'

TABLE 6.5 *Output and bonus at Hillend Colliery*

	March 1979	March 1980
Total shifts worked	309 833	304 205
Total incentive and bonus paid*	£993 823	£1 088 655
Average bonus per shift	£3.20	£3.58

NOTE The total paid includes that at the 100%, 50% and 40% rate.

The men at Hillend did not seem to think that the scheme had had an adverse effect on safety. To many men, safety was considered to be of much greater importance than any bonus. This was particularly true of overmen, who were motivated much more by personal satisfaction gained from doing the job well, especially maintaining safety standards.

The overmen on G69 face described the concern for safety in difficult conditions, '... the men have settled down to working in these appalling conditions. There have been further falls of ground from the left-hand side of the rip and there is very little we can do to avoid this, only try to make things as safe as possible. Today they have set two completed arches. Nobody can complain about their efforts. On this type of work under these conditions incentive bonus is not thought of at all. The only thought on this type of work is the safety of men working in the area'.

However, there were some examples in the diaries of safety rules being disregarded in order to enable more incentive to be made. The conveyor belts that carried coal along the face were called panzers. Officially they should be stopped whenever men had to do a job that involved leaning over them, but on B88 face these jobs were often done without switching them off, in order to make incentive pay.

Another example, again from B88, was reported: 'Later on in the shift a red light came on the top motor panel, which means the cable to the top motor was snagged. They found out where it was damaged, but instead of changing it, it was decided to run the face with just the bottom motor, a bit risky but at least another full cut was wanted to make it three for today and seven for the two shifts, which is going good.'

The accident figures for Hillend comparing the three years ending March 1978, 1979 and 1980 showed little change in the number of accidents except perhaps in the category 'handling supplies' which had increased.

Summary

This case study demonstrated that when the implementation process is done well an incentive scheme is more likely to be successful. Not only was design and implementation carefully considered, (Cells 3a and 3b Figure 6.9) but adjustments were made to the organisation and work situation to accommodate the scheme (Cells 4, 5, 6, 9 and 12), for example, early feedback of performance and the provision of a bonus board.

The significance of consultation and negotiation. The implementation of the scheme involved the active participation of all the workforce, if only in casting a vote for an option of payment. This participation in the implementation of the scheme provoked interest in understanding. Although the workforce were far from having a complete understanding of the scheme, they were a lot nearer than other groups of workers studied. Furthermore, the motivation of the men was improved by the generally good industrial relations. The level of mutual trust between management and workforce and the level of understanding of the scheme by the workforce was high; in some other organisations studied, these were substitutes for one another. The degree of local flexibility allowed by head office also stood in contrast to that in other large organisations examined. To an extent it was made necessary by the variable local conditions, but it certainly helped to overcome local problems of industrial relations and motivation. The greater autonomy was welcomed by local management and local union officials as a satisfaction in itself.

The Hillend Colliery scheme succeeded in motivating men initially by money because of its careful implementation. It also succeeded in motivating them in other ways by providing opportunity for meeting targets, earning respect for achievement and rivalry over performance.

It showed the importance of changing other parts of the organisation as well as the payment system, to facilitate the working through of the influences on motivation.

The importance of organisational change. Even though the Hillend payment scheme was initially successful, it did draw attention to the need for adequate and timely organisational change. Bunkering problems for example (as described below) meant constraints on productivity and considerable worker frustration.

At Hillend there were a larger number of faces than at most other pits. This was because the particularly difficult geological conditions were always likely to stop one or two of the faces producing, but if this happened the remainder of the faces working would ensure that the pit was still producing coal. However, if all the faces were working simultaneously the pit did not have the winding capacity necessary to get the coal up the pit as fast as it was cut. Some of the coal could be stored in underground bunkers, to be wound up later. If all the faces were producing coal, the bunkers were soon filled and faces had to be stopped. A stoppage for this reason was known as bunkering.

When the bunkers were full the decision on which face to stop was taken by the colliery manager or the man in charge of the control room. Bunkering was a source of considerable frustration to the men, especially as it always tended to happen when they were doing well.

Fred, 26 February (1980): 'This bunkering went on all day, stopping and starting in 20 minute intervals. At the end of the shift when I went to the panels checking up on stoppages, I found that we had six 20 minute and three 25 minute stoppages. This was a very bad day for cutting coal, also for making our bonus up.' When a face was stopped for this reason it was even more frustrating for them to know that other faces in the pit were still running. David commented on the reactions of the men in this situation. 'Bunker was reported full on four occasions during the shift, causing long delays. They (the men) appeared edgy all shift, thinking that whilst our bunker was reported full the south side was still running.'

Bunkering led to bad feelings between men and the management, and some suspicion. '... we were stopped again with the bunker at the pit bottom. It seems that when we are doing well this always happens. Some of us think it is fixed by the management to stop us getting a better bonus and we are getting fed-up with it. It seems that if all the faces are doing well they cannot get the coal up pit, and this is depriving us of making more bonus. Again, we had done just above our norm for the shift when we were stopped'.

The problem with bunkering illustrates a more general aspect of the operation of bonus schemes that have attempted to motivate employees. If such schemes are to work it is necessary not only to motivate employees but also to facilitate the working through of those motivations by other changes in the organisation in addition to the payment system. In this case the men were motivated to cut more coal but if they did and it was not possible to get it all up the pit, they were frustrated. At Hillend there was talk of constructing a bigger bunker so that this problem might be solved.

John G. Kincaid Ltd*

This case study relates to work undertaken after the results of the Strathclyde research had been publicised, and it shows what happened when advice based on the findings was put into operation.

John G. Kincaid Ltd, a subsidiary of British Shipbuilders, at Greenock on the Clyde, has been manufacturing marine engines since 1868. Like many other parts of the shipbuilding industry world-wide it has faced great difficulties in recent years. The position was particularly serious in 1981 when the company embarked on a programme to improve performance over its whole range of activities.

---

*This account is based on a paper written by John Taylor (Production Director, John G. Kincaid Ltd) and Angela Bowey.

Features of the position in 1981 included:
1. a very poor delivery reputation such that customers had lost confidence in delivery promises;
2. lack of cost competitiveness with orders being lost; productivity was low, workflow was affected by a poor layout and there was a practice of high systematic overtime;
3. heavy criticism came from the auditors and from British Shipbuilders for lack of financial and production control which was exacerbated by the absence of experience and training in systems at all levels;
4. there had been a commitment since 1976 to close down a section of the business with a consequent loss of 400 jobs (one third of the total); with the approaching end of the last contracts for this work in this section the problem of reducing the numbers employed had become urgent;
5. and most significant of all, there was widespread doubt over the company's survival and recurring rumours of impending closure which produced despondency within the works.

At that time Bowey was approached to advise the company on the design and introduction of self-financing productivity schemes. She had just completed the survey of newly introduced incentive payment systems, and advised that the key to success with an incentive scheme lay not in the kind of scheme, nor in the matching of the scheme to the company, but in the amount of time that the management were prepared to spend discussing it before its introduction and the range of people who were brought into these discussions within the company.

Bowey advised that success with a new payment system would only come about if it was designed and introduced in a participative way and a programme was developed for achieving this participation. The aim was to ensure that the management at all levels and in all departments, together with the trade union representatives and the shop floor and office workers, were involved in the discussions in preparation for a new payment scheme designed to achieve improved company performance.

Although the programme was initially established to bring about a change in the payment system it was recognised that this kind of programme was entirely consistent with the preferred management style of John Taylor, the production director and Bill Scott the new managing director, and therefore should not be compartmentalised and isolated from the many other developments in the company. Productivity Circles have thus been developed as an integral part of the new approach to management at Kincaids.

Productivity Circles and the Involvement Structure

The first stage involved a management group identifying the priority areas for improving company performance; the second stage was the establishment of a set of channels for participation in the process of payment system design and productivity improvement; the third stage was the training for effective participation; and the fourth the operation of the participatory system.

There are four main elements in the involvement arrangements which have been set up at Kincaids. The first is the formal representative structure dealing with terms and conditions of employment which the company supports; second is an open style of management characterised by a determination to discuss problems with employees as early and as fully as possible; third is the structure of Productivity Circles; and fourth is the Production Council, a representative body of managers and employee representatives which advises the company on business issues. Thus Productivity Circles are one part of a system for involvement.

Productivity Circles

As the name implies, Productivity Circles are groups concerned with improving performance. They are designed around types of work and physical proximity. Examples are the Fabrication Department; the Plumbers Shop; Light, Medium and Heavy Machine Shops; Drawing Office; Commercial Staff; Maintenance Department.

The terms of reference of the Circles are to:

1 draw up ways in which their deparment's performance can be measured and advise on how this information can be collected;
2 consider ways in which departmental performance can be improved and put them into effect;
3 monitor results and try to improve both the means of measurement and the results;
4 report regularly to a central group on their department's progress and the reasons for it.

Each circle has joint chairmen: a supervisor and an employee representative. Chairmanship alternates with meetings. Joint chairmanship is important symbolically, demonstrating that this is not a management structure. It is also important that the foreman is seen in this role as the responsible manager and that the representation structure is recognised. There are usually two or three employees in the circle at any time, with membership changing. It is important that there should be no coercion to set up or take part in any circle.

Results

We are concerned to avoid giving the impression that whatever the success there has been at Kincaids on various fronts has followed solely from the introduction of Productivity Circles, inviting the conclusion that if other companies follow the same pattern productivity improvement and beneficial change will automatically result: nor indeed do we wish to suggest that the work is complete and the final conclusions drawn. There have been improvements at Kincaids and Productivity Circles are a part of the process of change; discussion within the Circles has led to changes in workshop organisation and methods of working. The overall participative structure is leading to closer and more effective co-operation in bringing about much needed changes. Let us look at some of the things Kincaids achieved over the first eighteen months of Productivity Circles:

a. the outfitting section has completed its contracts and been closed, with all the trauma involved;
b. the work force has been reduced by five hundred, one third of the total;
c. a new management structure has been introduced;
d. a range of control and information systems have been installed, many computer based and often where no system previously existed;
e. new engine types which the company had never made before, have been built;
f. engine building methods have been changed;
g. new safety and quality procedures have been introduced;
h. a new bonus scheme has been designed and agreed, but shelved by agreement until such time as the company is in a more favourable position for orders;
i. the company's quality and delivery reputation has been greatly improved;
j. its trading loss has been reduced.

These changes were not bought with money; no payments were made beyond those under National Agreements.

For those who see some relevance of Productivity Circles to their own organisation, we would offer the following words of caution:
1   Productivity Circles are still being developed at Kincaids. Their design was based on research and considerable experience, but they are new in the sense that this particular form of participation did not, to our knowledge, exist previously;
2   Productivity Circles are not Quality Circles, nor are they Briefing Groups nor any other popular off-the-peg management technique. They have the following four distinguishing features:
    a. They are a joint management and union endeavour. The role of the representative structure is recognised, supported and integral to the concept of the circles;
    b. The work of Productivity Circles embraces all aspects of work and organisation, there is no restriction to quality and it is not a communication nor an industrial relations exercise;
    c. Productivity Circles are concerned quite explicitly with involving the work force and the management in the really important issues which affect company performance, with identifying the means of measurement and improvement, and with linking rewards to these factors;
    d. Productivity Circles are not consistent with managers making all the important decisions, they require the workforce to play a real part in decisions about layout, equipment and methods of operating at the shopfloor level.

There are a number of pre-conditions which we think need to be met before a programme of this kind can be successful, and recent joint work between the University and the company has been directed towards producing guidance for other companies wishing to implement Productivity Circles.

These pre-conditions are listed here:

Top management are committed and involved. Top management must demonstrate in all aspects of their working practices that they believe in participation in the full sense of sharing decisions with employees and are prepared to give this conviction practical form through the circles.

There is an accredited programme for survival and prosperity. The company must be able to convince its employees that it has a programme which can lead to reasonable continuity of employment for significant numbers and that the top management and unions are committed to the success of the company. This then makes it possible for open discussion of strategic matters.

Priorities for improvement are known and accepted. There is little point in setting up groups of people with the aim of improving company performance if they do not know what the priority issues are and understand why they are priorities. Two requirements follow: that the priorities are identified and accepted and that employees understand both the analysis involved and the conclusions drawn.

Unions are committed. Productivity Circles are a joint endeavour. The comments above with respect to management commitment and investment are equally true of senior union officials.

There is good communication. A vital element in Productivity Circles is sound communications by which we mean the establishment of a body of shared knowledge and information about the business, its day to day operation, the roles, responsibilities, expectations and attitudes of its people, and a common language in which this information is expressed and discussed.

Circles tackle the real work. Productivity Circles are not, and must never be, associated with some vague idea of industrial democracy. To set up sham circles and then make the real decisions elsewhere misses a great opportunity. Managers must have the courage and conviction to put the real issues to the circles, be prepared to trust the people and support actions recommended.

There is a structured system for circles. Meetings should never be talking shops, they should always have a clear structure and purpose with clear allocation of responsibilities and a commitment to successful discussion and to the changes resulting from the discussion. This means an agenda, papers prepared and distributed well in advance, good chairmanship, clear responsibility for action on decisions, mechanisms for liaison with specialists and other parts of the company, mechanisms for reviewing progress on decisions taken, procedures for collecting, analysing and presenting information on which to base the discussions, preparation of minutes and generally good administration. To achieve effective meetings it is very likely that some training will be needed.

There is a continuous process of review and change. No programme of change ever goes exactly according to plan, and the introduction of Productivity Circles requires that adaptations be made to cope with contingencies as they arise (for example, responding to a change in senior personnel or union leadership; or changes in the business situation; or policy directives such as those from head office). Not only does the programme need to be reviewed so that such contingencies are coped with but also it needs regular re-appraisal to ensure that the programme has not moved away from its primary aims.

The following quotations are from the people most directly involved with Productivity Circles.

'When the idea of Productivity Circles was first made known by Management to the work force at Kincaid's the general feeling was that the views of the shop floor would either not be heard, or if heard, then ignored. ... Initially ideas coming from the shop floor did not get very far. This was put down to the entrenched management view that they knew best, when it came to production. This point was put to Senior Management in no uncertain terms by the Convenor and thereafter a gradual change took place. Senior Management made Circles aware that it was not the case of Management only putting points on the Agenda. Time has shown that there is a place for Productivity Circles and that the Shop Floor has much to contribute to the running of a modern factory.'

From a statement by the Chairman of Shop Stewards, William Boyle and the Convenor of Shop Stewards, Robert Jackson.

'Productivity Circles in my opinion can lead to considerable improvements in both Productivity and Industrial Relations if they are organised properly and based on total and honest commitment from Management and Trade Unions co-operation.'

The Personnel and Industrial Relations Manager, Bob McCann.

'I was involved in Productivity Circles at the very beginning, first as a shop steward. ... In speaking to a lot of people throughout the factory the most common opinion was, why in our present climate of little work could we possibly talk about having Productivity Circles. It was explained that this could probably be the best time for setting up Circles as it gave us the chance to sort out the teething problems. ... Their ideas are put into practice, giving people a sense of achievement and satisfaction in what they are doing.... If this is a sign of things to come then it is very encouraging but we still have a long way to go ....'

The Productivity Circles Co-ordinator, Jim Dorrian.

'Having been involved with the formulation of Quality Circles before restructuring at John G Kincaid Ltd, I was extremely sceptical about the success of the formation of Productivity Circles.... one year later I am both impressed and encouraged with the response we have received and I am convinced they can play a major role in other companies.... provided they are organised properly and with genuine commitment from senior management.'

Works Manager, Bill McCready.

'Productivity Circles are really a vehicle which allows/encourages involvement, they are not the answer to all of a company's problems. At John G Kincaid they act as a catalyst helping effective action to take place. It must be stated that participation does not mean abdication of decision making on the part of management: Productivity Circles are not a means of offloading responsibility.'

Managing Director, Bill Scott.

The case shows the advantages which may be derived from a participative approach to the design of an incentive scheme. It lends substantial further support to the findings from the earlier work.

Payment Schemes as Agents for Change

The potential for increased productivity relates to the ability and opportunity taken to use the payment scheme to make wider changes in the organisation. When firms instal schemes they often fail to carry through the motivational assumptions underlying the incentive scheme to all facets of the organisation. They miss the opportunity to make wider changes that would reinforce the scheme or yield other benefits to the organisation, such as the introduction of new technology or a change in operating systems. The Coalbridge case illustrates a situation where this opportunity was missed and together with the lack of consultation, this contributed to the failure of the scheme. The Hillend case shows how a payment system change can, through consultation and management attention to ways of making the system work, act as a facilitator of complementary changes. And the Kincaid case takes this a stage further: changes which were made initially to facilitate the design and implementation of a new payment system became part of a much broader change in management style and procedures.

It is hoped that the three case studies will provide insight into the processes which may take place when a payment system is changed. The next chapter considers another kind of payment system process, namely, the changes which take place once a scheme is in operation.

7 Degeneration of Payment Systems

A perennial problem facing managers, payment system administrators, consultants and academics in this field is the understanding of the processes by which incentive schemes degenerate over time.

As we have seen, when implented and used well payment systems can be effective in assisting change. Used in the wrong circumstances, poorly maintained and without a full understanding of payment system dynamics they can drift in such a way as to have serious consequences for the organisation in which they operate. Much research evidence and many case examples relate to the symptoms exhibited by decayed schemes, but few identify the processes of degeneration which can inflict such great costs on an organisation. It is particularly important to identify the circumstances in which a payment system can lead to improved and sustained productivity levels, and differentiate these from the circumstances in which degeneration occurs. What are the changes in behaviour through which the process of degeneration may come about? And what might be done about them? These are the questions addressed in this chapter.

Payment scheme degeneration is here defined as the process by which the work performance of employees paid under incentive conditions either declines or fails to increase in proportion to increases in the pay derived from the scheme.

If this process remains unchecked it can result in the payment scheme reaching a state of decay: the scheme becomes so debilitated that any improvement in organisational performance is of less value than the continuing cost of the incentive scheme.

For the purpose of illustration, assume that the real value of the increase in organisational performance per month can be expressed as a monetary figure 'V'; and that the total monthly costs of operating the incentive scheme (including direct administrative costs which would not otherwise be necessary plus all payments to staff and employees resulting from the incentive scheme) can be expressed as a sum of money 'C'. Then three stages of payment scheme effectiveness can be identified by the coefficient V/C (the ratio of organisation performance to total continuing costs resulting from the scheme). These are Robust ($V/C > 1$); Static ($V/C = 1$); and Decay ($V/C < 1$) (See Table 7.1.).

Note that the calculation for Table 7.1 does not take account of the initial costs to the organisation of introducing the incentive scheme. A successful scheme would need to remain robust for a long enough period to recover at least these initial costs.

TABLE 7.1 Stages of payment system effectiveness

Stage	Explanation	performance/cost coefficient V/C
ROBUST	Work performance increase is of greater value than the operating costs plus incentive payments made.	> 1
STATIC	The increase in performance is more or less equal to the costs plus incentive payments	$= 1$
DECAY	The increase in performance is of less value (or even negative) than the costs plus incentive payments	< 1

Payment scheme degeneration is the persistent decline in magnitude of the performance/cost coefficient, and if not overcome will lead to a state of decay with consequent net losses to the organisation (See Figure 7.1). It may be a continuing process, or it may occur in fits and starts, or a scheme may be in a state of decay as a result of earlier degeneration which has since ended.

The processes by which an incentive scheme degenerates are very subtle and difficult to detect. Even with no outside influences performance and attitudes may 'creep' downwards. Were the degeneration processes more obvious, managerial effort to avoid them might be more successful. It should be recognised that managers who have recently introduced an apparently successful incentive scheme will be unlikely to seek out evidence of its degeneration for dissemination. It is also unlikely that employees will broadcast information about the work procedures through which an incentive scheme may be degenerating. So unless a researcher has established a high degree of trust and credibility in an organisation they are unlikely to learn more

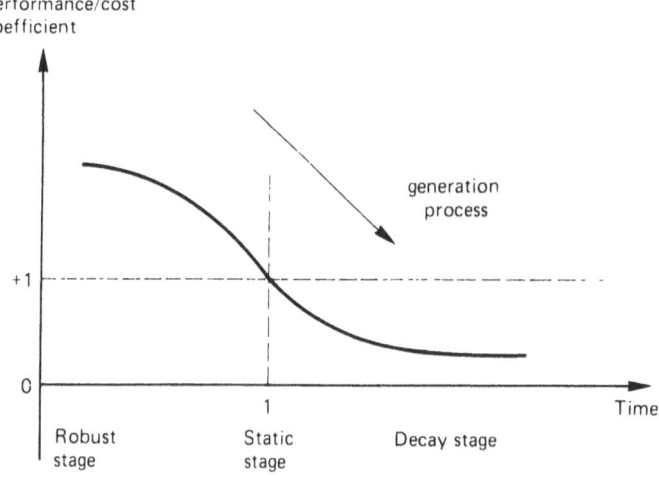

FIGURE 7.1 *The degeneration process*

than the superficial story of its surface operation. It is only in situations where researchers have been very close to the workers (such as in participant observation) and had a continuing close relationship with them that they have been able to identify the process of degeneration (Roy, 1952; Ditton, 1979; Lupton, 1963; Wilson, 1953; Thorpe, 1980).

EVIDENCE OF DEGENERATION

Some of the classic processes whereby payment systems degenerate are:

The Proliferation of Special Allowances

These usually take the form of allowances for waiting time and/or for unmeasured work. Deliberate or accidental performance/cost drift could also occur through shift premiums, conditions allowances, process control allowances, learning allowances; difficult work allowances, etc. A large number of such components in pay serve to complicate the pay packet and reflect an over-dependence on pay in an endeavour to achieve control, rather than control by better management. Imposing one layer of 'influencing worker behaviour through pay' upon another limits the effectiveness of either by confusing the supposed motivational message. The result is increased cost for no additional improvement in performance. This kind of degeneration can be identified by monitoring the number of allowances being paid, the proportion of employees who receive each one, and the total cost of these allowances. If either of the first two of these indices plus the last are increasing then the scheme is degenerating through this process.

Manipulation of Allowances

The allowances just discussed are very often the source of manipulation to increase the incentive or bonus payments. Manipulation can be effected by increasing the period for which an allowance is payable; by claiming an allowance which is not strictly justified; by – and this is not uncommon – recording additional time spent waiting or working on tasks for which average bonus is payable and so less time on the bonus-generating activities (which therefore accrue more bonus by being completed in a supposedly shorter time). By these devices it is possible to increase incentive/bonus earnings per hour. As we will demonstrate in our case examples, this manipulation is usually done by employees; but it is sometimes done by supervisors who wish to see a fairer allocation of earnings or to favour a particularly helpful employee; and it is sometimes done by work study staff or payment system administrators who wish to see a more acceptable outcome from an incentive scheme. When the manipulation is done by employees, it usually results in more pay and is referred to very often as 'making bonus with the pencil'. When the figures are altered by supervisors, managers or administrators this may be to increase or decrease an individual's (or group's) pay, usually with the aim of achieving a better match between effort and reward than would otherwise occur; but sometimes also to resolve industrial relations or motivational difficulties.

The process of degeneration may occur through the increasing use of the above methods of determining pay. They can be identified by monitoring the levels of allowances paid month by month (collectively and separately). If these are increasing, or if they intermittently increase and subsequently remain high, then the scheme is degenerating through this process, unless some objective and external change – such as a fall in market demand – can incontrovertibly account for the whole of the increase.

Slackening Performance Standards

An incentive scheme can degenerate because the performance standards to which pay is related may become less stringent over a period of time. This can be caused by a number of factors, from operators simply becoming more skilled to a change in the criteria used to establish performance standards.

Cross-Booking Time Between Easy and Difficult Tasks

This type of degeneration has been recognised since Donald Roy's study of an engineering machine shop in the 1940s (Roy, 1952; 1954). It has turned up many times since, and can still be found in many engineering workshops. It arises because from some tasks it is easier to earn bonus than from others, due to the impossibility of setting a uniform performance standard where there are many tasks which an employee can be asked to work on (there is always an element of error in setting such standards and variation between different work study practitioners). And it is a particularly common source of payment scheme degeneration where there is a 'fall back rate' or basic rate of pay which is earned however low the performance level. In such circumstances there is a tendency for employees to cross-book time from medium speed jobs on to slow jobs and fast jobs. This higher incentive payment rate for a shorter period for the medium speed job, and no change in the rate of pay (because it is below the threshhold for bonus payment) but a longer period for the slow jobs. Whether or not this increases overall pay will depend on the slope of the line relating pay to performance (with a marked improvement in pay where the scheme has an upper limit to pay or a lower benefit from improved performance at fast speeds of working); and on the extent to which jobs which would have fallen below the threshold for bonus payment are brought into the bonus-earning range by manipulations. Donald Roy's study, which was described in chapter one, shows how this can operate in practice (Roy, 1952).

Even where employees are not benefiting financially from the manipulation (as in the case study by Yetton, 1979), they may still choose to cross-book time in this way in order to protect the easy jobs from management's notice (Roy, 1954).

It should also be noted that even without a fall-back rate employees could benefit through increased pay by cross-booking time wherever the relationship between performance and pay is not uniform for all levels of performance. It could apply, for example, if salesmen's commission varied with total sales for a period, resulting in cross-booking sales from one period to the next.

This process of degeneration can be identified, as Donald Roy identified it, by plotting the frequency with which tasks completed by a workforce (or section of a workforce) are recorded at each performance level in the appropriate range [zero to the maximum recorded level]. A large sample would need to be taken covering all the tasks completed by the group in a selected period of time. The performance range should then be divided into equal segments and a tally made of the number of completed tasks falling into each segment. If the segments are small enough and the number of tasks large enough a graph or histogram of the results may then be drawn. If this histogram approximates to the shape in Figure 7.2, it is reasonable to assume that the employees are applying a fairly uniform rate of effort to tasks which vary in their degree of difficulty but tend towards a mean represented by the performance at point A. There is nothing in such a pattern to suggest cross-booking of time between tasks.

If the pattern approximates to the shape in Figure 7.3, with a higher proportion of jobs above the peak (B) than below it, then it is reasonable to assume that the employees are motivated by the higher bonus payments from easy jobs to put in more effort on those jobs and

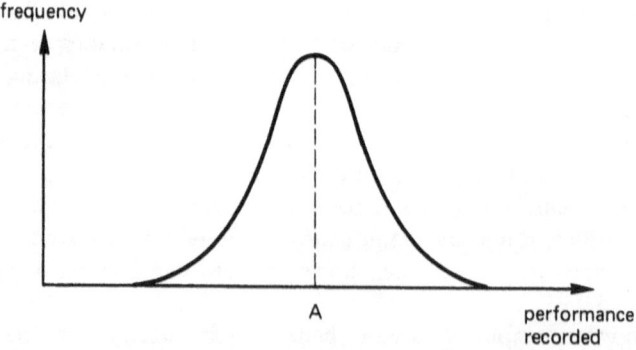

FIGURE 7.2 *Normal distribution of performance; no evidence of cross-booking*

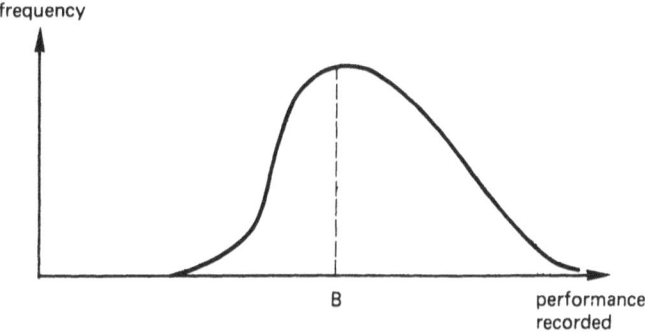

FIGURE 7.3 *Performance skewed towards easy jobs; no evidence of cross-booking*

so raise them into a higher performance category; but that on the whole they are not manipulating the recording of performance.

Figure 7.4 shows one possible shape for a frequency curve showing evidence of cross-booking. The relative size of the peaks is not important, nor the number of them. The key indicators are the marked trough between peaks (which does not, however, have to be this low) and the more or less sharp cut-off point at the top end (which may, however, have been exceeded by a few non-conformist individuals, but always the same ones).

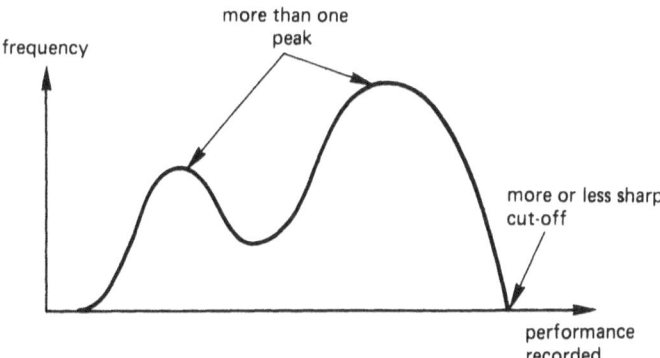

FIGURE 7.4 *Possible shape showing evidence of cross-booking*

Further Evidence of Degeneration

In addition to the above methods of identifying the main processes of degeneration, there are other symptoms which may indicate that the payment system is degenerating. These include:

Fixed Levels of Performance

An incentive scheme is designed to reward additional effort from employees, but it is well known that performance standards vary between tasks and so achievement should vary between tasks and show a general trend upwards as skill improves. An incentive scheme that is constantly 'stuck' at one level of performance will usually indicate a need for further investigation. Either the scheme is being manipulated to give a steady income (which may or may not be a problem depending on the kind of manipulation); or it has so little motivational impact that employees are maintaining a steady but low level of performance.

Loss of Control by Middle Management and Supervision

Because pay is vitally important to employees, they usually seek to control those factors which they know can affect their bonus/incentive earnings. This may result in the workforce dictating (directly or indirectly) aspects of the production schedule or even the production plan, so that work which pays well is allocated to the beginning of the week, shared out between individuals or teams, and/or given preference over the other types of work. It does not follow that this is the best allocation of production effort from the company's point of view. It may well result in inefficient use of materials and machinery (for example, rolling different steels in a sequence which safeguards bonus payments but requires excessive changes of rollers) or in a less profitable product mix. Managers and supervisors frequently accede to these pressures in order to avoid other problems which the workforce might create.

Frequent Disputes About Pay

Claims for regrading, arguments about differentials, disputes over performance standards, etc., can result from a degenerating bonus/incentive scheme. These can lead to poor industrial relations and overall poor company performance.

PROBLEMS ASSOCIATED WITH DEGENERATION

A degenerating payment system has the obvious disadvantage that unit costs will be increased as it degenerates. However, that is not the end of the story. Other problems which accompany degeneration are often more damaging to an organisation and can bring it to the point of collapse as will be discussed in the case examples later in this chapter. A brief summary of these problems is:

a. Increased unit costs as a direct result of relatively higher labour costs.
b. Sub-optimal production scheduling as a direct effort to improve the motivational impact of the incentive scheme.
c. Inaccurate pricing as a result of extra labour costs being cross-booked to some products and possibly lower labour costs recorded for others. This can result in sales failure for products with an excess labour cost component in price because they are dearer than competitors; and successful sales of products which are underpriced and on which profits are lower than required.
d. Inappropriate tenders for similar reasons to (c) above, namely inaccurate recording of labour costs and manufacturing times.
e. Sub-optimal production scheduling as a result of inaccurate records of manufacturing times.
f. Sub-optimal product mix as a result of incorrect information about labour costs and time required, or other inaccurate performance information, or because of inflexibility of workforce due to feared loss of earnings from change.
g. Low productivity on aspects of the work with relatively less financial reward.
h. Low productivity during periods of negotiation about rates of performance.
i. Low productivity due to workforce efforts to conceal how quickly certain tasks can be completed.
j. Resistance or slow acceptance of new technology because of its less attractive incentive/bonus payments compared to a degenerating or decayed incentive system.

EXTENSIVE CONSULTATION AND LONG-TERM PERFORMANCE OF A PAYMENT SYSTEM

The link between 'extensive consultation' and the long-term effectiveness of a payment scheme is an important one. Too many schemes have been considered, introduced and then forgotten. The need for effective consultation at both the design and the implementation stage has been emphasised, but the need is just as important once a scheme has been installed. In order to ensure that a scheme remains relevant and effective, consultation amongst management and between managers, trade union representatives and employees should continue. The trust so developed and the communications channels formed can provide a very important part of the 'early warning system' to detect signs of degeneration.

Marchington [1977] has identified seven factors in the context of industrial relations which have a significant influence in bringing about change. One such change could be the onset of problems with a payment scheme. The factors are:

1. Product market
2. Technological environment
3. Institutional influences external to the plant
4. Organisation structure
5. History and nature of unionism
6. Labour context – markets, region, and sex
7. Organisation culture.

Through the passage of time any one of these factors or a combination of them could change in such a way as to make the payment system less appropriate than it was when it was first introduced. Or they can change in such a way that degeneration of the scheme through one of the processes discussed above is facilitated. It is one thing to consider that the payment scheme may require modification throughout its life; it is another to have such modifications accepted by employees and their trade union representatives. Lack of consultation is likely to produce a situation where the changes proposed are all put forward by management to resolve management problems. But payment systems may cause problems for employees and trade union representatives; they, also, may wish to see changes but not so much that they would risk the benefits of a decayed old system for the uncertainties of something new. Only through continuous consultation can such fears be allayed and fair adjustments made to a payment system to solve the problems of all the parties affected.

CASE EXAMPLES ILLUSTRATING DEGENERATION PROCESSES

In order to illustrate the processes of degeneration six cases have been described in the next section of this chapter, all drawn from the Strathclyde Survey of Incentive Payment Systems (Bowey *et al.*, 1982) and including two which were considered in detail from a different perspective in Chapter 6. Although one of these, Hillend Colliery, started off very well, it began to show signs of degeneration after a fairly short time. Each of the six shows a different pattern of degeneration as summarised in Table 7.2.

Case 1: Coalbridge Engineering Ltd

The background to this company has already been explained in Chapter 6.

The company had until 1975 been operating a traditional payment-by-results scheme, but rate drift had become a feature of the system and in that year the new deputy managing director established what was termed a piecework system on what he thought was a sounder basis. This new scheme which had worked well at the subsidiary company for which he had previously been responsible was, in fact, more highly geared than the previous scheme and it, too, soon became subject to drift, as indicated by Table 7.3.

In 1977 the deputy managing director tried unsuccessfully to remove the scheme – he was prevented by the prevailing Incomes Policy from buying it out – and the ensuing bad feeling following the attempt provoked the employees to set out to prove the absurdities of the piecework scheme in order to encourage management to buy it out. The reasons why employees were able to make the scheme drift so quickly and the consequences of their actions are set out below.

Gearing

Firstly the highly geared nature of the scheme meant that a small

TABLE 7.2 Aspects of the degeneration of payment systems in 6 organisations

	Types of degeneration				Further evidence of degeneration			
	(a) Proliferation or extension of allowances	(b) Manipulation of allowances by employees / by other staff	(c) Slackening performance standards	(d) Cross-booking time between easy and difficult jobs	(a) Fixed levels of performance control	(b) Loss of management control	(c) Frequent disputes about pay	(d) Increased unit costs
Coalbridge Engineering	✓		✓			✓	✓	✓
Government Engineering Workshop	✓	✓				✓		✓
Longshore Dock Company					✓			✓
Domestic Appliances Ltd			✓		✓			✓
Hillend Colliery		✓ (by other staff)						✓
Latex Fabricators	✓		✓		✓			✓

TABLE 7.3 *Annual averages for bonus payments from old and new incentive schemes at Coalbridge*

Scheme	Date	Average weekly bonus earnings
Old Scheme	May 1974	14.5
Old Scheme	May 1975	20.06
New Scheme (new base)	July 1975	10.00
New Scheme	July 1976	16.99
New Scheme	May 1977	22.66

SOURCE Sowdon (1979).

adjustment either of the estimate of time required for a task or in the performance achieved (the time taken) resulted in a large increase in earnings. An improvement of only 10% in the time for jobs produced nearly 19% increase in pay. This is unusual for this type of incentive scheme.

Negotiating Rates

As is common with piecework agreements of this type, times for jobs had to be agreed between the company and the employees doing the job (through their Union) and once established they would not be altered unless for reasons relating to changes in the method of work. This is laid down by the 1931 National Agreement of the Engineering Industry relating to piecework prices and bonuses and in any case is subject to custom and practice. Times would therefore be fixed by mutual agreement between employer and the worker who would perform the job, thus providing scope for negotiation of time rates to take place and also protecting them from alteration or revision.

In addition the agreed 'incentive performance' time on which bonus was paid had no objective quantifiable measure. Although this was the tradition in the industry, the system lacked accuracy, objectivity and equity and was prone to reflecting differing bonus payments for the same work content. Additionally, no uniform work study standards were applied throughout the site. If the company proposed 6 minutes for a job and the union put in a counter request for 8 minutes, a compromise settlement might be made of 7 minutes. The implications of this can be seen below.

In a 40-hour week, 400 six-minute jobs could be completed.

However, in our example the union had negotiated an extra minute for each job representing 400 minutes or 6.66 hours per week. If the jobs were completed each in six minutes, and if the bonus payment for completing the job in the allowed time was 30% above basic pay of 83.3 pence per hour, then the difference between the original proposal and the negotiated settlement works out as follows:

Original proposal: number of jobs completed = 400. At an allowed time of 6 minutes each this represents 40 hours work at 30% extra on basic pay = 40 × 1.3 × £0.833 = £43.32.

Settlement: number of jobs completed = 400. At an allowed time of 7 minutes each this represents 46.66 hours worth of work at 30% extra on basic pay = 46.66 × 1.3 × £0.833 = £50.53.

If the company's original proposal was accurate then £7.21 was gained in additional remuneration, representing a 'negotiated' drift of 72%, i.e. £17.21 as against a bonus of £10 (40 × 0.3 × £0.833) on the basis of six-minute jobs. (Source: Sowden 1979). It should be noted that although incentive bonus schemes were originally conceived as a premium payment on top of basic pay, as calculated above, it has become common practice for the bonus rate of pay (which is used to pay for 'hours saved' from the time allowed to complete a weekly workload) to differ from the basic rate of pay (the actual rate of pay for hours worked before any bonus or allowances are added). This had the benefit of allowing employers and unions to negotiate a larger increase in basic pay at their annual negotiations, because it did not flow through on to the bonus rate. Equally, it acted as a counter to the process of degeneration, in the sense that the bonus payments were eroded in value relative to basic pay through the various processes of degeneration of the performance/cost ratio. There is, however, very little to be said in favour of such a random method of preventing bonus payments from increasing. At best it is a means of cutting back on losses caused by deficiencies in managerial control.

Returning to the implications of this separation of the bonus rate from the basic rate of pay, the calculation shown above for bonus earnings of the original proposal, would actually have been made in the following manner. 400 six-minute jobs = 40 hours of work at Piecework Rate (the rate to complete the jobs in the allowed times) which is multiplied by the Factor for Daywork Performance of 1.3 (i.e. the factor by which it is assumed that piecework exceeds daywork or non-incentive working) to yield an expectation of 52 hours worth of work for a daywork performance.

Degeneration of Payment Systems

The actual time taken to complete the work (40 hours) is subtracted from the time expected to complete this work at daywork rates (52 hours) to yield 12 hours of bonus pay at 83.3 pence per hour = £10.

Subdivided Jobs

A third method of increasing the performance figures for a job and thus increasing bonus is by breaking large jobs down into smaller ones. For example, a 40-hour job could be split into 4 sub-jobs and the time actually achieved for each sub-job could vary, as shown in the following example:

Sub-jobs	Hours allowed	Factor for daywork performance	Allowed daywork time	Actual time taken (hours)	Bonus hours earned
(a)	10 ×	1.3 =	13	6	7
(b)	10 ×	1.3 =	13	16	zero
(c)	10 ×	1.3 =	13	7	6
(d)	10 ×	1.3 =	13	17	zero
	40			46	13

Thus by actually taking longer (i.e. 46 hours instead of 40) yet achieving bonus hours of 13, earnings could be increased to 13 × £0.833 = £10.83. Note that this could occur without any manipulation of the figures by the employee; but there is obviously considerable scope for such manipulation. Also note that part of the problem lies in the lack of any mechanism for balancing very poor performance on one task against good performance on another.

'Personal Average' Payments

A fourth reason that times could become slack in this company was because personal average bonus was the basis of payments for waiting time and diversions (to work which did not count for incentive bonus calculations because it was not yet measured, or the *measured* rate was not yet agreed, or the work was unmeasurable). This was not a true average because it related only to the time spent on bonus-earning work. It is more usual in piecework schemes to pay for diverted time or waiting time at a daywork performance or a reduced bonus rate (e.g.

230   *Payment Systems and Productivity*

seven-eighths) to ensure that the employee is discouraged from spending more time than is strictly necessary on such tasks or from cross-booking time to these tasks and so increasing his average bonus by reducing the time taken to complete his 'measured' work.

The Opportunity and the Consequences of Degeneration

The switch to the manufacture of a new product provided the ideal opportunity for employees to exacerbate the situation. They negotiated more generous times for the new tasks in the manner described above and later found easier ways of completing the specified tasks. Further, only 40% of the manual work in the company on that site was carried out under 'piecework'. Other manual workers had their pay established by reference to piecework earnings. Therefore, not all the workforce needed to 'drift' the scheme for all employees to benefit and affect the wages bill of the company.

Degeneration of the piecework scheme took place primarily in one of the subsidiary companies of the group and in that company it was confined largely to one of the operating sites – but this was by far the largest of the four sites covered by this subsidiary, and the subsidiary company produced 73% of the group's turnover. The impact of its problems were therefore serious for the whole group.

As a result of the manipulation of the incentive payment scheme product manufacturing times increased so much that when the new product line was introduced into the factory the first one produced took 50,900 hours to complete although its target time had been 16,000 hours including an allowance built in for the extra time needed for new work. Table 7.4 shows the shortfalls in target production times for the new product.

One of the main reasons for this was the number of disputes that arose over the piecework rates. Because the product was new there was a potential to dispute all the times and negotiate each one separately. This proved to be an extremely long and costly exercise. Figure 7.5 shows a typical range of assembly line tasks that were subject to disputes; there were hundreds of these, and their graphs all show the same pattern. Columns A show the times which the company proposed for completing the task. Columns B show the times which the workforce claimed were needed, and these were always considerably higher than the targets, usually about twice as much. The disputes always resulted in compromise and Columns C show the times which were

TABLE 7.4 *Coalbridge Engineering: shortfalls in target production hours – new product line*

Product	Actual hours compared to target hours home market		
	Target hours	Actual hours	Excess hours
1	16 000	50 900	34 900
2	12 600	42 600	30 000
3	10 300	20 700	10 400
4	9 600	19 900	10 300
5	9 000	19 400	10 400
6	8 200	17 500	9 300
7	8 000	15 500	7 500
8	7 700	14 900	7 200
9	7 500	12 600	5 100
10	7 300	14 000	6 700
11	6 800	14 300	7 500
12	7 100	10 500	3 400
13	6 600	13 700	7 100
14	6 500	13 700	7 200
15	6 300	13 700	7 400
16	6 000	11 600	5 600
17	5 800	7 800	2 000
18	5 600	10 200	4 600
19	5 500	7 300	1 800
20	5 400	5 800	400
21	4 800	7 500	2 700
22	4 600	7 000	2 400
TOTAL	167 200	351 100	183 900

eventually agreed – usually slightly nearer the workforce claims than the company's targets. When the times had been agreed the workers would settle down to production taking the times indicated by Columns D, which were always remarkably similar to the company's original figures (Columns A). But the really devastating aspect of the situation was that the times taken during the period of dispute were those shown in Columns E – enormously higher than even the claims of the workforce.

Productivity during the dispute period was typically less than one third of the eventual post-dispute rate of working. The pressure from delay in settling these piecework times was one of the main causes of the eventual withdrawal of the scheme. When it was withdrawn from

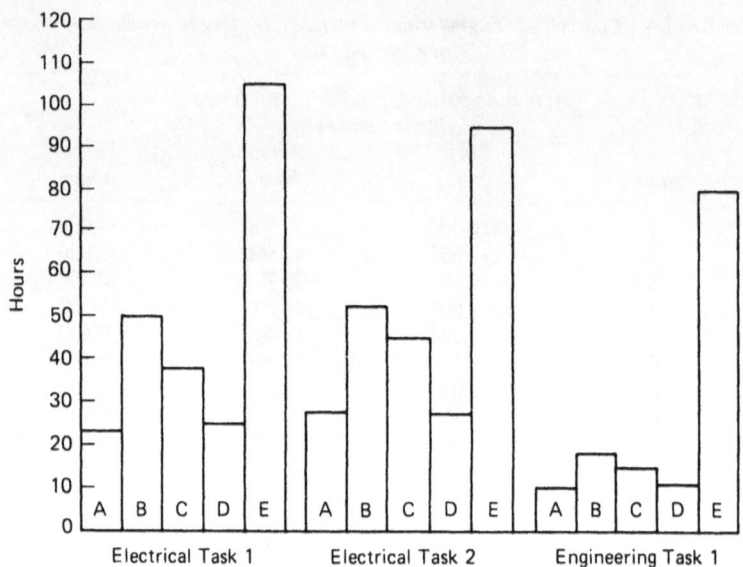

FIGURE 7.5 *Coalbridge Engineering: comparison between times set by rate fixers (A), times claimed by employees (B), times eventually agreed after dispute (C), times achieved by workforce after agreement (D) and times achieved during period of dispute (E)*

the assembly area in June 1977, only 40% of the assembly piecework times had been agreed and the patterns shown in Figure 7.5. were typical of the many jobs which were examined. By the end of 1977, 26 items had been delivered against 70 which had been planned. By February 1978, with a re-negotiated production plan in force, 32 items were delivered against a planned 115. All contracts for the company were fixed price contracts and delay in delivery meant not only lost revenue at a time of very high inflation, but also penalty clauses and large sums of money tied up in expensive stocks for the targetted production plan. The interest on money tied up in those stocks trebled from 1975 to 1977. All items had to be paid for yet very little revenue was coming in from sales. Throughout the period order books for the product were full, yet it was not possible to meet orders. Poor delivery performance, it was recognised, would prejudice future contracts.

Analysis of the group accounts shows that even allowing for inflation the company was in a sound position until 1977.

Losses on the affected new product line amounted to £13 million in 1978 which was only reduced to £6 m by profits on other lines and to £2.8 m when offset against the Group's other profitable subsidiaries.

This was the first overall loss the company had ever made. Table 7.5 shows the financial performance for the Group over five years 1974–78.

In addition to the direct effect of poor productivity on company profits, caused by the employees' tactics of very slow work on tasks for which piecework times had not yet been negotiated to their satisfaction, there were other problems arising from this payment system especially in the industrial relations area. The major cause of these difficulties was the effect on differentials between different types of employee of the company, including some managers.

TABLE 7.5 *Group financial performance over 5 years (£m)*

	1974	1975	1976	1977	1978
Turnover	82.4	108.4	131.2	138.9	166.6
Profit/loss before Tax	6.6	7.2	9.3	5.8	(2.8)

The bonus pay for skilled manual workers had increased from an average of £10 to an average of £30 between June 1976 and the beginning of 1978, although performance, in fact, had declined. Figure 7.6 shows the gradual drift of earnings against what should have been paid during the periods of incomes policy in those years. The increase in bonus pay occurred largely through the degeneration of the payment system and not through annual negotiated increases. The latter were kept in line with Government Incomes Policy requirements because the company depended on Government purchases of their products. The drift in the bonus element itself was not of great concern although it had risen substantially. However, its effect on differentials within the subsidiary company and within the Group had produced severe tensions that were manifest in the number of disputes experienced between 1975 and 1978, further disrupting production and adding to costs.

Two important differentials which were eroded by skilled manual workers' bonus earnings were those between these workers and their supervisors and inspectors, who because of the government policy of wage restraint had their salary increases kept in line with the statutory norms. Figure 7.7 shows the comparison of pay for these three groups from 1975–77, a situation which led to continual industrial relations problems as foremen and inspectors strove to restore their former differentials. During 1976 and 1977 there was little that could be done,

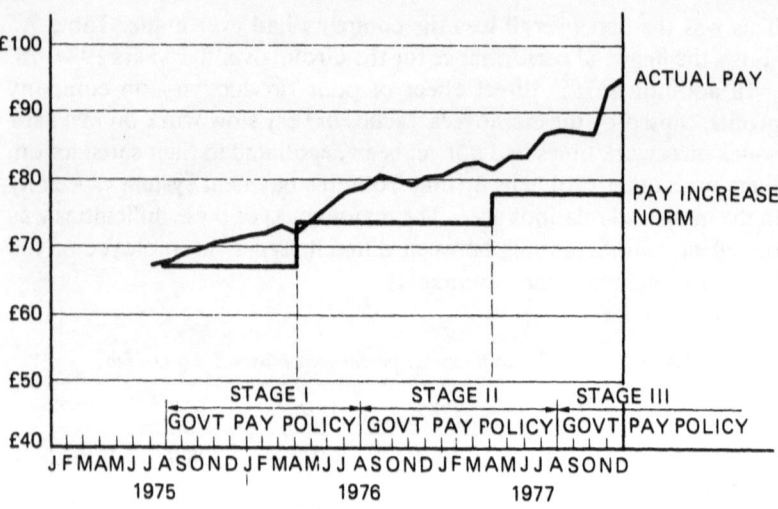

FIGURE 7.6 *Coalbridge Engineering: earnings levels for skilled manual workers for 40 hours compared to pay norms in force at the time*

but Stage III allowed additional pay increases through self-financing productivity deals and there was pressure on the company to restore differentials by introducing such a scheme.

The major problem was that the inspectors had traditionally enjoyed staff conditions along with pay parity with the factory average for skilled workers. In the engineering industry inspectors are important and a high calibre of employee is required. A situation was reached due to piecework drift where the differential of factory average over inspectors was as much as £20. It was generally considered by inspectors and management that the staff conditions were only worth £10 and pressure was placed on management by a strategy of non-cooperation by the inspectors in order to change the situation.

A self-financing productivity deal was devised to restore the differential, but once arranged for the inspectors it was demanded by all other groups in the factory. The inspectors had been an easy group with which to arrange a deal because their productivity was low with plenty of scope for improvement. Management were reported to be quite happy that this deal was genuinely self-financing and to have said that it would have withstood Department of Employment scrutiny. However, a deal for the supervisors to enable them to earn £20 to maintain their differential was justified by the number of completed assemblies leaving the factory. When these targets were found not to be attainable

Degeneration of Payment Systems 235

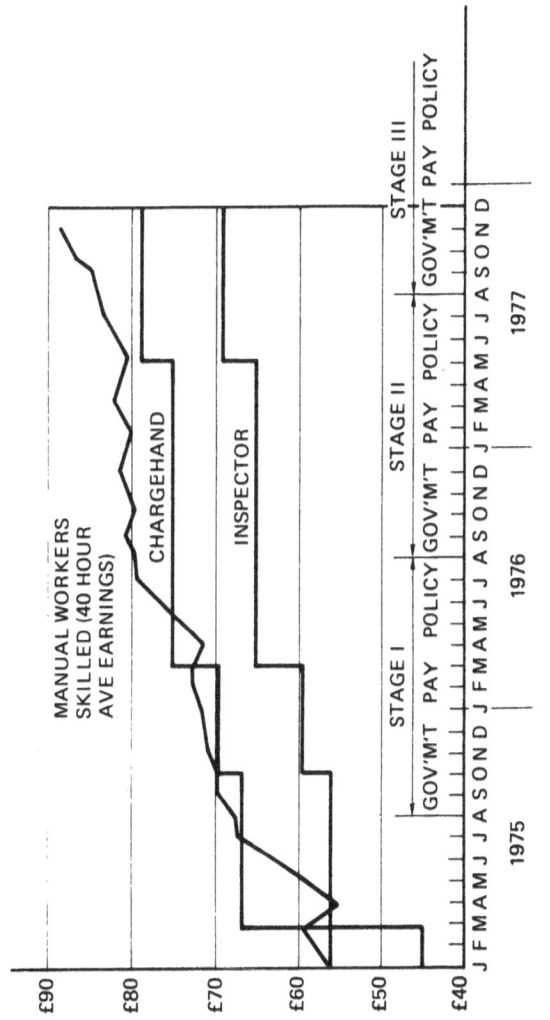

FIGURE 7.7 *Coalbridge Engineering: wage movements for three groups of employees 1975–77*

it was changed to the number of sub-assemblies made, purely to enable the £20 to be paid.

Another problem discovered with the bonus scheme for supervisors and inspectors was that parties could connive to increase their bonus payments. For example the works convenor indicated that inspectors, in order to achieve their £20, would continually fail work for small faults so that they could re-check them again later, thus claiming two inspections on the same part and enhancing their bonus earnings. He also pointed out that supervisors would think of reasons why assemblies would not be ready or could not be done in a particular way so that allowances would be added to their bonus.

In addition, during the period when there was an acute problem with differentials and a manifestly inequitable payment system, not only were costs very high, but also it became more difficult to attract and promote high calibre staff to the supervisor and inspector positions and to other white collar and technical grades. These were serious problems for a company with heavy dependence on the quality and advanced technology of its products. It should also be noted that the escalating incomes of employees at this site also caused problems for the Group as a whole, due to parity claims from other sites.

Even more important was the fact that new technology itself was being effectively impeded by the workforce through their efforts to negotiate better piecework times for themselves. Improved technology was the cornerstone of all the markets in which the company competed, and yet when new techniques were required they were simply seen by most employees as opportunities of gaining more money. There are two schools of thought on this issue. The National Board for Prices and Incomes in its guide to payments-by-results schemes (NBPI, 1968) states that these schemes help to overcome resistance to change in technology because of the opportunity the system gives workers to raise their earnings. However, in this case, where workers were confident of their negotiating strength, changes were welcomed only as opportunities for prolonged negotiations to push up wages. In an earlier study Bowey found a company so afraid of the delays in production that their employees would impose on a new product produced with new machinery, that they ran the machine in their laboratory to meet initial orders.

Coalbridge Engineering – Summary

The degeneration of the incentive payment system at Coalbridge is a frightening example of the serious effects on a company's finances and prospects. The degeneration initially took the form of slackening performance standards through pressure from the workforce. There were greatly increased bonus/incentive payments through a period when productivity actually declined, with consequent additions to labour costs and difficulties about differentials. The most serious problems which were caused arose because of the decline in productivity, especially from the artificially low performance on the new product line. Falling dramatically behind on its production targets for this product, the company lost millions of pounds through late deliveries, penalty payments, and money tied up in expensive stocks.

Only when the 'piecework' incentive payment system was taken out in July 1977 did these problems with the new product line begin to be resolved. Even though overall factory productivity fell by almost 50%, the ending of delays and bottlenecks on the new product line meant that the company returned to a profit-making situation in the following year. Overall productivity was steadily increased as a result of improved management control and information systems which were more easily introduced without the resistance to change which had become endemic with the 'piecework' payment system.

Case 2: Government Engineering

In this second example of a degenerating payment system the incentive payment scheme was applied to 243 equipment maintenance employees, whose work was highly varied and included the repair of a wide range of items. The bonus was calculated over 12 week periods by relating credits for work done to the total attendance time. The scheme was introduced in March 1979 after negotiations which had lasted from November 1978 to February 1979. Very comprehensive information was obtained covering the first 12 months operation of this scheme.

There was a fair degree of consensus about the objectives of the scheme between the different groups who were interviewed, indicating a primary objective of increasing earnings and recruiting more staff, and a secondary one of improving productivity. Although the workshop was in an area of high unemployment and working conditions were good, poor levels of pay had caused several skilled men to leave and it had been very difficult to replace them. Thus recruitment, relativities and increasing earnings were all seen as major objectives of the scheme.

During the twelve months that the scheme was studied (March 1979–February 1980) the number of employees fell steadily from 243 to

238 Payment Systems and Productivity

229. It thus failed to resolve one of the major problems, that of recruiting and retaining skilled men, although it was not possible to tell whether the problem might have been worse without the additional earnings offered by the incentive scheme.

Figure 7.8 shows the graph of performance over the monitoring period. Performance fell in the first two months and then showed an overall increase with various peaks and troughs.

These figures show a considerable rise in performance in the fourth month of the scheme (June 1979) about the time when the follow-up interviews were carried out. In this month both man-hours worked by direct workers and total productive hours rose, while standard man-hours of work produced fell (Figure 7.9). These movements would normally be expected to produce a fall in performance. The opposite effect could result from an increase in allowances for such things as diversions, waiting for work, shortage of materials, unmeasured tasks. This would have the effect of increasing the credits counted towards the performance and thereby increasing the bonus. Comparing total productive hours and time spent on measured work (Figure 7.9), there was a substantial increase in the difference between the two figures after

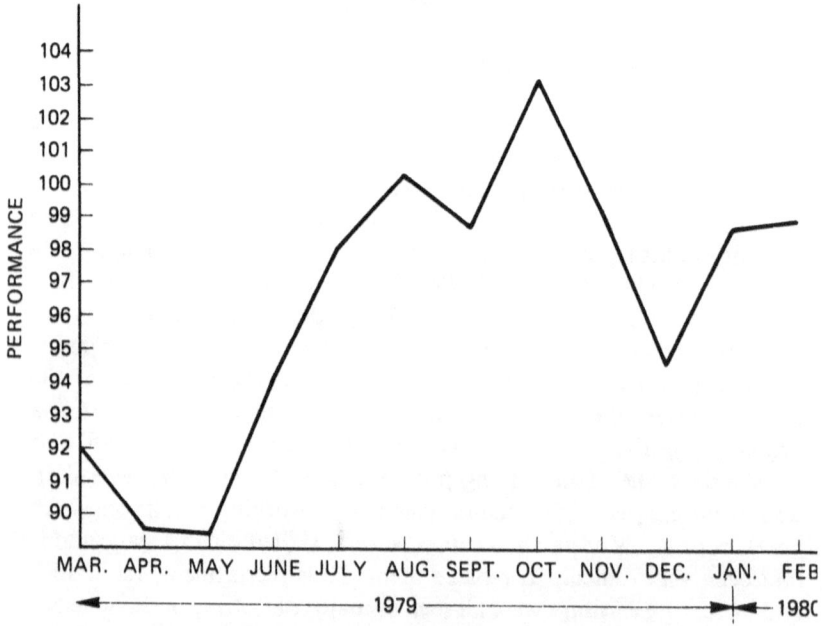

FIGURE 7.8 *Government Engineering Workshop: average performance (BSI Scale)*

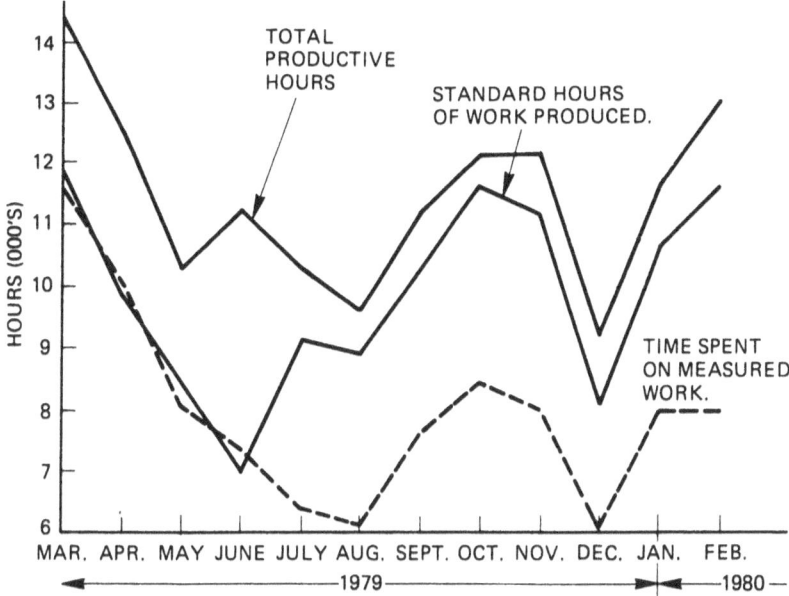

FIGURE 7.9 *Government Engineering Workshop: comparisons of total productive hours, standard hours of work produced and time spent on measured work*

May 1979. In other words, there had been a major increase in the hours spent on work to which time standards had not yet been applied (i.e. it was unmeasured) during June 1979 and the allowances given for this probably accounted for the major part of the increase in performance that month. This is more clearly shown in Figure 7.10 which shows total man-hours spent on measured work expressed as a percentage of total productive hours for direct workers. In the fourth and fifth month there was a sharp drop in the percentage of productive hours spent on measured work. Although it then increased for two months, the trend continued to be downwards, and a new norm in the region of 65% persisted instead of the original 80%.

The degeneration of this payment system could be an example of the manipulation of allowances, a process which has been documented elsewhere (e.g. Turner and Leech, 1982; Roy, 1954) as a means of increasing recorded performance and therefore bonus/incentive pay. If an employee increases the proportion of his time recorded as spent on unmeasured work, he thereby shortens the time recorded as taken to complete the measured work he has done, which has the effect of

240   *Payment Systems and Productivity*

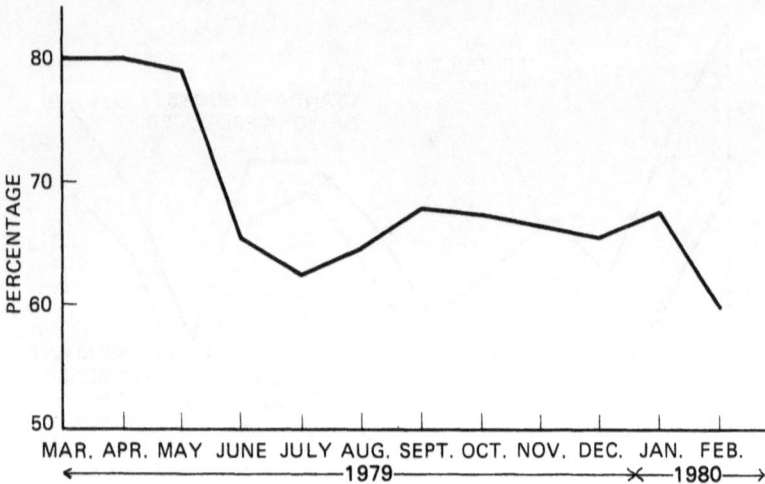

FIGURE 7.10 *Government Engineering Workshop: total man hours spent on measured work as a percentage of total productive hours (direct workers only)*

making it appear that he worked faster, and increases his effort rating and his bonus. It cannot be certain that this was happening in this organisation. The alternative explanation is that for some reason the kind of work undertaken changed in such a way that far more of it was unmeasured, and the respite which the employees obtained when working without pressure on this unmeasured work allowed them to work very much faster on the measured work, which alone counted towards the calculation of their performance level for bonus purposes. It would seem that some combination of these two factors is the most likely explanation for the outcome, and it should be remembered that the latter represents only another form of degeneration of a payment system, in which the use of allowances – in this case for unmeasured work – has been extended.

Further evidence of this degeneration can be seen by comparing total man-hours spent on measured work with standard man-hours of work produced. These moved in parallel up to the fourth month of the scheme, then diverged sharply. In other words, the amount of work produced during the 'measured' working period suddenly increased, as it would if time was being cross-booked from one heading to another.

There was mention in some of the interviews that more time was being allowed for 'diversions' and even that the times had been slackened, and it is reasonable to conclude that this incentive scheme had degenerated. Since it had not succeeded in improving productivity to any significant extent in the first place, this is a classic case of an incentive scheme in decay.

Case 3: Longshore Dock Company

At the time of the study Longshore Dock was only equipped to handle non-containerised cargoes and suffered strong competition from its rivals in what is a decreasing section of the shipping market.

The directly work-measured incentive scheme which it had introduced in February 1979 covered 18 blue collar harbour maintenance employees. 13 of these workers were skilled employees covering eight major trades.

The variable individual bonus scheme was introduced at the request of the employees, who had been wanting an incentive payment scheme for some time and finally threatened industrial action. Prior to the scheme maintenance men were paid a basic rate which they believed compared unfavourably with other groups of workers at the harbour, such as dockers, who were on bonus schemes.

The research team monitored this scheme from its introduction in February 1979 until January 1980. Over this period the scheme had little discernible effect on hours worked, overtime, manning or the amount of work contracted out see Figure 7.11). Although the scheme paid a variable bonus based on individual performance, the average performance each month was remarkably consistent (between 93–97 BSI) and the bonus paid to each employee only varied between £8 and £10 per week.

Employee interviews conducted in November 1979 suggested that foremen carefully allocated work and adjusted allowances for unmeasured work to ensure that each worker earned a bonus and that bonus payments were equitable between employees. Since more than a quarter of the work remained unmeasured and foremen were able to adjust times recorded for unmeasured work, there was ample scope within the scheme for such manipulation to occur.

In practice, the bonus scheme operated more like a measured day work scheme and was sometimes referred to as such. The personnel manager thought that the bonus could be incorporated into the basic rate in the future. He was of the opinion that the scheme had been instrumental in establishing new work patterns, (such as increased labour flexibility and reduced demarcation problems), which would not have occurred under a flat basic rate increase.

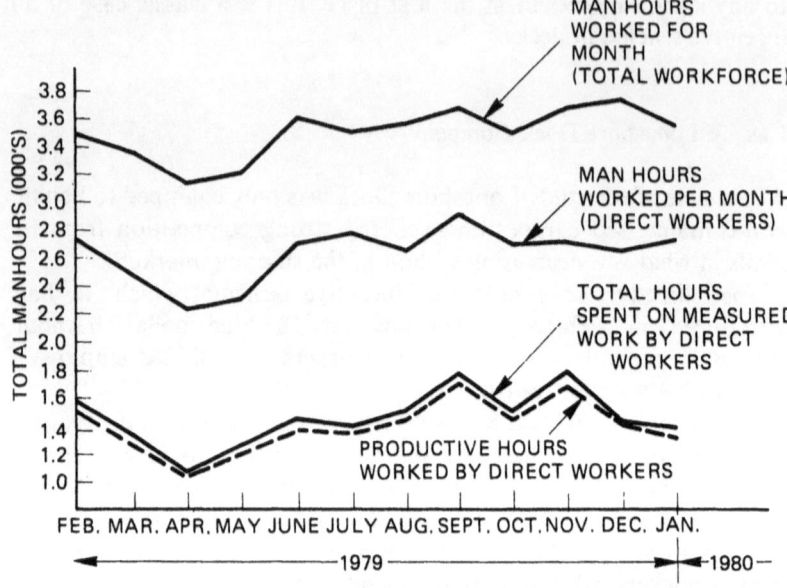

FIGURE 7.11 Longshore Dock Company: performance figures

This example of a degenerated payment system – in the sense that there were no discernible improvements in performance related to the incentive payments – illustrates the point that it is not always the employees who manipulate allowances to control bonus payments; in this case it was the supervisors. The result was an incentive scheme which amounted to little more than a pay increase, except that it strengthened management's hand in securing some changes in working practices, because of its discretionary nature. Such arrangements are not usually accepted so placidly by a workforce.

Case 4: Domestic Appliances Limited

This company was a United Kingdom domestic appliance division of an international electrical manufacturing enterprise. It operated in a stable market but was required to respond to rapid technological change. It employed approximately 1450 workers.

It had introduced a plant-wide profit sharing scheme in 1975, not as a direct work incentive scheme, but as part of a package of policies designed to increase employee flexibility, commitment and identification to the company. The bonus was calculated as a fixed percentage of product profit margin and was allocated twice a year as a percentage of basic pay to all employees and managers. Monitoring of the payment scheme was undertaken during 1979 and 1980, some three and a half years after the scheme's introduction. As the parent organisation maintained a policy of not revealing the profits or mark-ups of any of its member companies, it was difficult to evaluate the performance of the scheme. From the data received three trends could be discerned over the monitoring period (Figure 7.12):

1 the value of output and man-hours worked per month (direct workers) fluctuated about an upward trend;
2 there was a close positive relationship between man-hours worked by direct labour and the value of output;
3 output expressed as a proportion of the company's programme fluctuated about the 95% level over the period, and in only one month was it better than the specified company programme.

During the monitoring period there had been some change in the

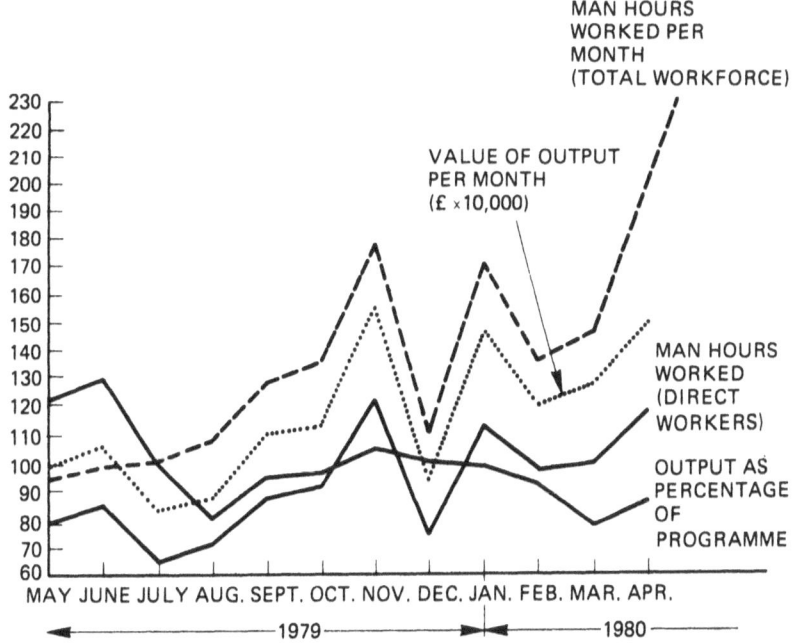

FIGURE 7.12 *Domestic Appliance Ltd: performance figures*

244   *Payment Systems and Productivity*

products manufactured and new equipment and a factory extension had been brought into operation. These factors may have contributed to the upward trend in the value of output and direct man-hours worked.

Management interviews conducted midway through the monitoring period revealed that for the first two years of the payment scheme there was insufficient profit to justify a bonus payment, but the company paid the bonus in spite of this in order to increase employee–management trust, to gain commitment to improving product quality and to ensure co-operation with work systems from an individual to a group-based approach to make it easier to introduce new technology in the future. Although the company expressed satisfaction with the scheme, the original standards for performance in terms of profit improvement were not achieved, and in this sense the scheme represents degeneration through the slackening of performance standards. On the other hand the scheme was not continuing to degenerate and was not apparently causing problems for the company.

Case 5: Hillend Colliery

This nationalised colliery employed 970 workers and introduced an incentive scheme in April 1978 which related target output per man-shift (after taking account of the manning level of the team and difficulties in extracting the coal) to actual output. The background to this incentive scheme was given in Chapter 6.

Figure 7.13 shows national data for the incentive payments per shift for direct workers and the output per man-shift for face workers and all employees. The data cover the first 28 months of the national incentive payment scheme. It can be seen that the incentive bonus per man-shift was closely related to the overall output per man-shift between April and October 1978, but after that date the gap between the two widened. The extent to which incentive pay and output per man-shift diverged varied between pits; and at Hillend Colliery it was less marked than at many others. Nevertheless, any such diversion indicates degeneration of the scheme and this scheme appeared to begin degenerating after about seven months of operation.

Because detailed work diaries were completed by men and their managers at Hillend it was possible to understand how this degeneration was occurring. After a time of working under the scheme the miners and their overmen learned that certain ways of recording the

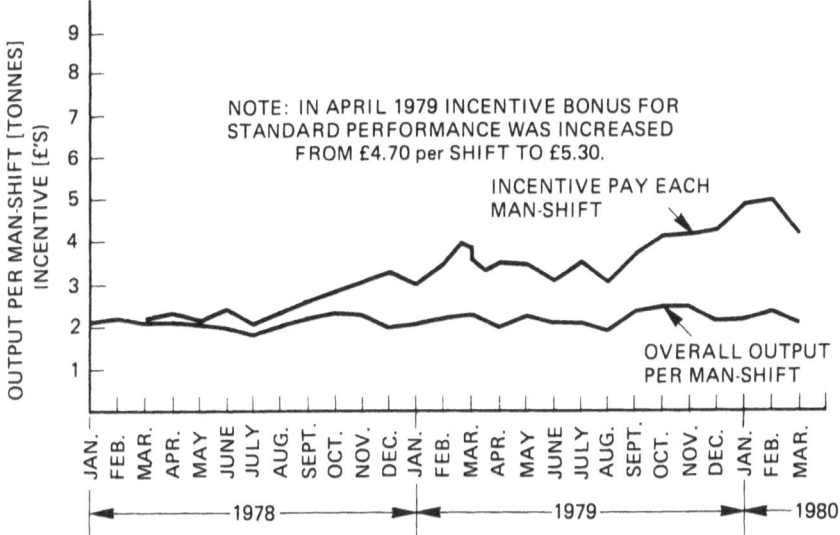

FIGURE 7.13 *Hillend Colliery – national data: incentive pay per man-shift; and overall output per man-shift*

information about their work produced better performance figures and higher bonus/incentive payments than others. Sometimes unadjusted recording produced lower bonus payments than normal and this was regarded as unfair when it did not relate to effort. To the miners the logic of this situation was that a limited amount of manipulation was justifiable; and their managers, they believed, turned a blind eye to such practices provided they were kept within limits.

The processes which produced the degeneration were all versions of manipulating allowances. There were allowances made in the calculation of performance for the time which men from a face team spent on work other than that directly related to extracting the coal. There were allowances made for the geological and physical problems of extracting coal from a particular seam. And there were allowances made when the work was interrupted for more than 20 minutes for a reason which was not the fault of the face team. All of these allowances could be, and to varying extents were manipulated.

By recording fewer men working on the production of coal than was actually the case and more men on other activities which did not count towards the target, it was possible to make output per man shift appear higher. As one employee said, '... it was not long after the scheme was introduced that we realised that by reducing the amount of men on the scheme on paper and keeping up our norm (standard level of production), the bonus payments started to climb'.

If the mining equipment was unable to work for over 20 minutes, the men were able to claim an adjustment in the bonus calculation. The reason for the interruption to work had to be recorded on a timesheet by the overman and then approved by the colliery management. Management would not approve an allowance made for an interruption of work if the employees were at fault. For example, if insufficient supplies had caused the equipment to lie idle, then this was regarded as the responsibility of the overman and other men in the work group. Overmen had learnt how to phrase the report on interruptions in such a way as to make it more likely that they would pass managerial scrutiny. They learnt that 'electrical fault' was likely to be considered a valid reason for work stoppage due to machine failure, whereas 'shortage of supplies' was not.

When a breakdown occurred to a machine the group would assess how long it would take to repair it. If it was clearly going to take less than 20 minutes, and therefore could not be claimed as an allowance in the bonus calculation, the mechanics would be urged to repair the machine as quickly as possible. On the other hand, if the repair was likely to take a significant time the mechanics would not be urged to hurry and the team would be happier if it took over twenty minutes.

Although there were clear instances where management was in conflict with employees over claims related to the bonus/incentive payments there were others where they gave the impression of condoning the manipulation. For example one employee commented '... (the deputy manager) knows but keeps only one eye open'. And another wrote, '... there is a limit to how much you can do this and it must be kept away from management, although the deputy manager knows of this and is willing to co-operate as long as it is kept within reason'.

There was also evidence that members of staff concerned with the administration of the incentive/bonus scheme sometimes made adjustments of their own to ensure that the results did show a close correlation between tonnes of coal produced and payments made. A fairly senior manager said that he and his colleagues would make adjustments to the allowances if it appeared that a large yield of coal had been produced, but the unadjusted calculations warranted a less than proportionately high payment. This is not an unusual practice amongst managers or payment system administrators who wish to maintain the credibility of a payment system by keeping payments in line with what they believe the employees will regard as fair. It cannot be proved that this happened at Hillend.

In general, the Hillend incentive payment system had favourable results at colliery level for at least the first seven months, but thereafter it began to degenerate. There were however, some national effects which were not apparent at local level. Wide differences in incentive/ bonus earnings between some pits developed and caused dissatisfaction where the payments were low. And the ability of the National Union of Mineworkers to find common ground on which to mobilise its members was affected by the decentralised nature of the scheme. To some extent this latter result appears to have been a conscious intention of the management negotiators so that the probability of any future national strike of mineworkers might be reduced.

One of the assumptions of this book has been that incentive payment systems are intended to motivate improved performance. But we do recognise that there are times when they are introduced for quite different reasons, which will be discussed further in the concluding chapter. Fragmenting pay bargaining had been one of the Coal Board's objectives in introducing the incentive scheme. It should be remembered, however, that any such alternative objective in no way detracts from the need to ensure that a payment system is as effective as it possibly can be and does not degenerate into a major source of problems.

Case 6: Latex Fabricators

This company was an industrial rubber division of an international enterprise which produced rubber sheeting and hose for commercial use. Its incentive payment system applied to 80 manual process workers and paid an incentive bonus based on individual performance measured against standards set by work study. There was an upper limit of £23 per week which a worker could earn from the scheme.

The original scheme had been introduced in 1974 after 12 months negotiation with the unions involved; and in March 1979 it had been adjusted to take account of loose rates which had developed. The revised scheme was based on new times for some of the jobs. Information was collected covering the period January to December 1979, and a selection of employees and management were interviewed in June of that year.

Over the period of the study demand for the firm's product had fallen and market competition had increased. Output, man-hours worked, and output per man-hour (direct workers) had all declined by 30% or more during 1979. This should have led to a reduced bonus to the employees, but the average effort rating upon which bonus was calculated had increased from 106 to 109 on the BSI scale, and so had bonus payments.

An error frequently made by managers and others is to regard the average performance as an indicator of productivity. This is not the case. It indicates only the net result of the various recording procedures which have gone into the calculation of the performance figure. And in a situation where there is a shortage of work and workers receive allowances for time spent waiting, the performance figures on which bonus is calculated may well increase due to their better performance on the work that is available, at the same time as their productivity in terms of output produced goes down. This is an example of degeneration as a result of more extensive use of allowances.

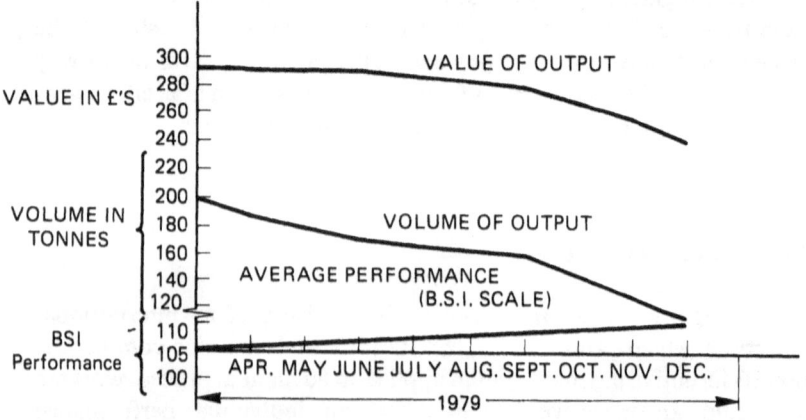

FIGURE 7.14 *Latex Fabricators: value and volume of output per month, compared to average performance (based on work measurement data)*

An alternative explanation would be that the workforce was manipulating claims for various kinds of allowances. Interview responses indicated that although several new pieces of machinery had recently been installed, most of the equipment was old, and required increasing amounts of time for maintenance and repair. The conditions appeared to exist for employees to increase their claims for allowances or for management to make such adjustments. The more likely explanation was that waiting time had increased as demand for the factory's products had decreased; and that allowances made for this waiting time had maintained the almost steady bonus payments.

Another point about this payment system was that several workers indicated that the bonus limit of £23 could be readily attained and provided little real incentive. Workers were content, perhaps because of group work norms, to earn a bonus of £18 to £19 per week, and maintained a steady pace of working in order to do so. This suggests slack performance standards and that the incentive payment system was not effectively motivating high levels of effort.

SUMMARY

In this chapter we have classified the types of symptoms of the degeneration of payment systems (Table 7.2) and discussed with reference to case examples how each of these may be detected in an existing system. This should facilitate a more systematic approach to the management of payment systems and contribute to a more rigorous approach to the study of pay.

By identifying the nature of degeneration and its extent in any given payment system, those responsible for its management can devise suitable strategies for improvement. By calculating the performance-value/cost coefficient (Table 7.1) it should be possible to determine whether a payment system has reached a state of decay. In our experience there is little that can be done about a decayed payment system, and the organisation will benefit from taking it out and replacing it either with a totally different incentive scheme or with a flat-rate wage system coupled with improved management practice. Without the latter there would usually be a further fall in performance on removal of a scheme; though this is not inevitable and there should not be a permanent drop unless the management failed to respond to the challenge of motivating the workforce in other ways.

A scheme which is degenerating but has not yet reached a state of decay may be worth saving, and the following comments relate to each of the different types of degeneration.

Proliferation or Extension of Allowances

Where there has been an increase in the number of allowances in use or the extent to which they are used, the reasons for the increase should be sought. It may be simply that the market demand has changed, creating more waiting time; or that new technology is being introduced, creating more unmeasured work; or that the product characterisctics have changed, creating more production difficulties. In each of these cases, provided the reasons are genuine and the scheme has not yet reached a state of decay where costs exceed benefits and is not causing other problems for the organisation (such as slow adoption of new technology), it is possible to retain the scheme whilst monitoring carefully any further degeneration. We are not aware of any cases where a process of serious degeneration has been reversed, although theoretically a well-informed management should be able to reduce the use of allowances once the circumstances change, e.g. the market demand picks up, the technological change is completed, or the work returns to a less difficult state.

Manipulation of Allowances by Employees

Where a payment system has been degenerating due to an increase in allowances claimed by the workforce without an objective/external justification for such increase, whether this occurs through cross-booking time from production onto waiting time or unmeasured work or simply from extra claims for conditions, allowances etc., the extent of the problem should be considered by calculating the performance – value/cost coefficient. If this shows that the scheme has already reached a state of decay it is better to take it out than to persist with it. If this stage has not been reached, it may be worth attempting to control the degeneration. One way of achieving this would be to set upper limits to the amounts of the specific allowances which any individual or group is allowed to claim in a period. Another would be to require an investigation into the causes of the highest claims for allowances until such time as the former levels of claim were restored. And a third would be to restrict allowances to the maximum level which prevailed before degeneration became evident. Each of these strategies carries the possibility of creating hostility; it may also prove impossible to show that the allowances were not justified because there is no recorded evidence to prove otherwise. And experience has shown (Roy 1954) that attempts to put controls on payment system fiddles very often fail because of the ingenuity of the workforce. They are motivated by the financial benefits of beating the system', collectively they have a great deal of time to practise their ingenuity. Careful monitoring of any such attempts will show whether they are having the desired effects or merely exacerbating the problem.

If degeneration is occurring and cannot be brought under control, then preparations should be made for taking the scheme out, preferably while there is still time to consult widely and extensively about a suitable replacement system before the existing system reaches a state of decay.

Manipulation of Allowances by Management

Where there is evidence of managers manipulating a payment system and this is causing either degeneration of the scheme or other problems such as resistance to new technology or sub-optimal and wasteful production scheduling, then examination of the scale of the problems is needed before a decision can be reached as to whether the scheme is worth retaining or not. Manipulation by staff or management is not something which can be openly discussed without undermining the credibility of the individuals concerned. Their motives for making such adjustments may well be in the best interests of the organisation, if somewhat misguided in some cases. It is very difficult to identify management manipulation of an incentive scheme, and even more difficult to remedy. If the scheme is not degenerating towards a state of decay and if there is no evidence of other serious problems caused by the manipulation, then there is no major cause for concern. But if there are such problems, then the scheme will be best removed and replaced by something sufficiently different to avoid the same kind of practices being retained.

Slackening Performance Standards

If a scheme has degenerated because of slackening performance standards this is likely to cause problems not only of additional labour costs, but also of discrepancies in pay between jobs with differing degrees of slackness and problems inherent in the process of producing slacker standards (such as exceptionally low productivity during the process of bargaining for standards on new tasks).

In the past the solution to this type of degeneration was sought through a programme of re-timing all the jobs. This usually resulted in a long period during which some jobs were timed at the original standard (with widely disparate degrees of slackness), some were not timed at all, and others were timed at the new standard. There would be all kinds of allowances and variations in payment entitlement attaching to the different jobs – a situation ripe for manipulation. We have studied schemes where one wave of re-timing has followed another, each taking a year or more to complete and none getting fully implemented before the next round of re-timing. Clearly this approach offers no solution to the degeneration problem.

More recently companies have tried to solve the problems of slack standards by bringing in a consultancy company with the capability of conducting a blitz programme of work study and using pre-determined times for the application of new standards in a few weeks or months. This works better than the old method, but it is only tackling the symptoms of the problem. The causes of the slackness of standards will not usually have been removed, and so the new standards also become slack. By analysing the rate of degeneration and the estimated time before a state of decay will occur, it is possible to assess how long it will be before a replacement payment system will be needed and make preparations well in advance for such a change. If the degeneration is a continuing process then a complete change to a different kind of scheme is recommended.

It should be remembered that the rate of degeneration of an incentive scheme through the slackening of standards can accelerate and the time-scale for bringing in something different may foreshorten quite suddenly.

Cross-Booking Time Between Easy and Difficult Jobs

This is probably the most difficult source of degeneration to detect, and careful consideration should be given as to whether the problem is serious before remedial action is taken. If the cross-booking has produced a state of decay, or if the system is rapidly moving in that direction, then a change to a different kind of payment system is indicated. For such cross-booking to occur the employees must be engaged on several tasks and must have developed an attitude towards the incentive scheme which rationalises or appears to justify the practice. Any system based on times allowed for different tasks compared to time actually involved in the completion of those tasks is likely to encounter this, so another type of scheme would be needed.

Payment Systems Which Are Not Degenerating

Before leaving this chapter we should point out that there were more schemes in our survey of 63 companies which were not degenerating than those which were. These non-degenerating schemes were identified by the fact that the graphs for overall output, recorded employee performance, and bonus/incentive payments all showed a similar pattern, rising together or falling together and bearing a fairly constant relationship one to the other.

8 Conclusions

This book substantiates many behavioural science findings of the past that have remained largely ignored by British managers. In the 1920s the Industrial Fatigue Research Board in Britain and Mayo's research colleagues at Harvard in the US began to uncover the complex issues involved in productivity and motivation. These and later studies showed that understanding worker motivation required them to go outside the boundaries of logical and rational models based on responses to financial incentives which were in vogue at the time. What was found then and substantiated many times since, is that people have multiple needs, feelings and personal goals that are not always consistent or compatible with those ascribed to them by incentive scheme designers.

The majority of research studies of industrial behaviour in recent years have led to conclusions consistent with a 'contingency theory' or 'best fit' approach, where the technique or system with the best chance of success is recognised to be the one tailored to fit the particular circumstances.

We expected to find managers adopting a contingency approach. This would have involved making a diagnosis of:

Environmental conditions
Structures
Features of the work
The behavioural system
The operating system

But we found no evidence to suggest that managers selected or designed new payment systems in this way, nor even that the approach would have worked had they done so.

Throughout our research we made the assumption that managers *should* be seeking to improve their employee work performance when they introduced an incentive scheme. Logically this is a reasonable assumption, since incentive schemes deliberately link work performance to extra pay; and it has certainly been the assumption behind advice available to managers in the literature.

However, we came across many organisations where an incentive scheme was being introduced for reasons which were quite separate from motivating improved work performance. These included making a pay increase appear smaller than it actually was (because part of it was payment for supposed productivity improvements); fragmenting pay bargaining to reduce the likelihood of a national strike; restoring to some extent former differentials between groups of employees (such as white collar–blue collar); complying with National Incomes Policy; complying with an internal policy directive. If a major aim of introducing an incentive scheme is something other than performance improvement, then it should be no surprise when performance does not improve. However, we take the view that it is a mistake to introduce an incentive payment scheme without a primary aim of influencing performance. There are many problems which can arise from a poor incentive scheme, and the adverse effects on costs and industrial relations are not worth risking for aims which can better be achieved with other means.

HOW CAN COMPANIES BE MORE SUCCESSFUL?

Extend the Information That Is Taken Into Account

We found that with careful and competent preparation in terms of consultations and discussions about the design and implementation of a new incentive scheme, a good management team can achieve results with many different types of scheme. This is not to say that the incentive scheme itself is totally unimportant. However the process of matching a payment scheme to an organisation is one that demands considerable time and effort. Achieving a match between the payment system and the expectations, motivations, patterns of inter-personal relationships and past history, and understanding the people in the system, is more important than matching the type of payment to non-social characteristics of the organisation and its environment (such as new technology, market, location and size), even though some of these structural contextual factors do have an effect on results.

The importance of the way the incentive scheme is designed and implemented is crucial to its success; and success is associated with the extent of consultation about the design and implementation of a scheme.

Ensure the Scheme Is Not Modified or Subverted in Its Implementation

Our in depth study of Coalbridge Engineering demonstrated how a company's strategic policy could be modified or subverted by lower level of management pursuing other goals and objectives. This process has been observed when other change interventions have been made, for example, the introduction of new technology. The gradual weakening of a policy by individuals or groups pursuing other objectives at this important operational level can be further exacerbated by the failure to install adequate operating or control systems along with the introduction of the scheme. The effects at shopfloor level of what was originally a firm commitment at senior level to a policy or objective is governed by how it is seen and experienced by those lower down the organisation. It can differ greatly from what was intended.

Be Participative

Research and the experience of companies who have tried it have shown that consulting and involving employees in making decisions which affect the way they do their work leads to the best results, and indeed can lead to dramatic improvements in company performance (e.g. Jaguar cars; John G Kincaid; and the Strathclyde payment systems research). It has been shown that a company facing possible closure can rally its staff and workforce through a system of involvement and consultation and turn the company around from one with poor quality, unreliable delivery, high costs and poor reputation. With an already successful company the results may be just as substantial because these principles of good decision-making still hold.

The PROCESS of involvement and consultation at the design and implementation stages of a new payment system can:

1 Provide a better understanding of the contextual structural variables.
2 Provide a better understanding of the contextual behavioural variables. Many of these are just not understood by managers who rely instead on their firmly rooted beliefs and prejudices.

Conclusions 257

3 Lead to greater trust, understanding, motivation and commitment. This helps to line up the efforts of all to the priority objectives of the company as well as indicating how these objectives can best be measured.
4 Alert management to many areas where performance can be improved and satisfaction increased, irrespective of the incentive scheme.
5 Minimise drift and decay of the scheme.

PRACTICAL STEPS TO A PARTICIPATIVE APPROACH

The first requirement is for commitment to a programme of change to be made at the top of the organisation. The next is to develop a team of managers who know what is required of them and have the enthusiasm to make it work. And the third is for the rest of the workforce concerned to be convinced that the project is worthy of their support, to be shown how to make it work, and to be assisted in its operation.

The programme could follow a schedule such as:

1 Discussions amongst senior managers about the programme and identification of a management team to develop it further. It should be recognised that participation is difficult to restrict to just one set of decisions, and that achieving a participative approach to designing a payment system requires a change of management style and the establishment of a structure of participation.

   Since the aim of an incentive scheme is to improve productivity, a key focus of attention in the participative process should be ways of improving productivity. This should be linked to a payment system capable of paying increased rewards when these improvements are achieved. It is not the payment system which will lead to improved productivity. A payment system can only reward productivity improvement and make it easier to gain cooperation with efforts to improve productivity.

2 A participative structure can be established by setting up a series of small groups of 6 to 10 people from different levels of an organisation (such as shopfloor workers, supervisors and managers) whose work is closely interdependent because they are from the same section or department or function of the company. They would need to meet fairly regularly to discuss ways of tackling particular problems related to productivity improvement. These problems are

of two kinds. Those which the group puts forward as ways of improving productivity; and those which management feed into the group as tasks. It is important for both types of problem to be sorted out and the decisions implemented.

Decisions should be reached by discussion based on full information until a consensus or best compromise is reached. The manager still has his authority and responsibility for the decision in the end; but the team will have influenced the decision and agreed that it is the best decision as a result of the discussions. They will each have had the opportunity to contribute their ideas and knowledge towards making it work when it is implemented. Issues about which management and the workforce are likely to disagree fundamentally are better left for the normal channels of negotiation, and care should be taken to recognise any such issues and transfer them as soon as possible or avoid bringing them into team discussions.

The area of operation for the participative approach includes all the issues associated with getting the work done more effectively — such as methods of working, ways of organising the work, systems for increasing efficiency, changes in technology, etc. There is no satisfaction for anyone in a company in seeing these things done ineffectively, and participative teams can tap the common interest of everyone in doing the job better.

This kind of participative approach requires essentially a change in management style. For the range of issues just mentioned, instead of managers taking decisions independently, based on their own judgement, they will deliberately involve the people whose work is to be affected by the decision, in making that decision. For some people this is not a major departure from their present style, and for them the approach is a way of ensuring that the style is applied reasonably consistently by management and the maximum benefit for the company and its employees is obtained. For others it may be a very different way of reaching decisions, and some supervisors and managers will find it difficult to understand. They will need advice and encouragement until such time as they can see for themselves how effective a style of management this is.

A participative team may sometimes be set up drawing together people from different sections of the company, where the traditional departmental boundaries may themselves have to change in the future to meet some change in the work or in the technology, or where a project affects several different sections of the company.

Such a team could be temporary if the project is one which does not require a permanent realignment of responsibilities and change of organisation structure; that is, if things will return to normal more or less when the project is completed. However, teams would usually be permanent groups. It is advisable to change membership periodically to give other people the chance to take part, for example by replacing two members annually.

It is desirable to have a managers' team to consider changes in the way managers do their work, and the same for white collar sections of the staff. It follows from this that a managers' team is an essential first step to introducing this kind of participative approach since they are being asked to change their way of reaching decisions, and if their commitment to making the exercise a success is to be there, they need to be involved in the decisions about how to set up the system in the first place.

3 *Programme of work for the management team*
   a. Discussions of how to operate through Participative Teams; what difference it will make to their own decision-making responsibilities; why they *should* open up their decisions for prior discussion with those affected; how the approach differs from what they do already; and the effects on their authority.
   b. Discussions of how to cope with proposals which arise from the teams; the need to respond and show that things get done; the need for flexibility and willingness to alter things to suit others; the need to encourage team members to prepare and research their proposals adequately; the need to review how much change has been made in response to team proposals.
   c. Identifying the areas of the company which each team will represent, and some initial ideas as to which to start first.
   d. Identification of suitable tasks for the management to give to the teams. This should involve analysis of company priorities and future plans and from those to pick out one or preferably two tasks for *each* team. These tasks should be matters which require a reasonable amount of work and discussion, with a time scale in the range of one to six months. Longer projects could be divided into stages if this were possible.

   Each manager should play a large part in identifying the tasks for the teams in his areas. These managers should prepare suitable remits for the task, with back-up information needed to get on with the project.

4   *Discussions with staff/workers for whom participative teams are intended*
    a. The first step is to convince them that they wish to take part in the exercise. Since it will give them the opportunity to influence the decisions which affect their work, a good presentation of the proposals should win their support. There is nothing in the approach which runs counter to the aims of trade union representatives, and if the employees are unionised the representatives' support for the exercise will greatly assist in its acceptance by their members. It is wise to ensure at this stage that such representatives know what the project is about, how it has worked elsewhere, and how they can play a vital role in its operation.
    b. The next step is to invite the workforce or staff to nominate or volunteer to make up a team for their area (say six for each team) and ask them to select one of these people as *their* joint chairman. The management team should nominate the supervisor joint chairman and check that he is willing to accept this role, plus any other management and support staff thought to be needed in each individual team.
    c. The next stage is to hold discussions with all the joint chairmen about the matters they will need to know in order to operate the teams. These will include more information on what the team should do; its procedures, remit, etc; how to chair a meeting; how to write a report; efficient administration of meetings; effective communications within the team and outside it; understanding how the company operates (systems, procedures, manufacturing methods, economics etc.); and any other issues which the management team feel should be discussed and/or the joint chairmen request.
5   *Recruitment of a full-time coordinator*
    By this time most people in the company will understand the exercise and will know how much interest they have in it and how much commitment the company is giving it. This is a suitable time to call for a volunteer to be seconded for one or two years to the post of full time Participative Team coordinator. This job involves ensuring that the teams operate smoothly and are adequately serviced.
6   *Pilot teams followed by extension to other areas*
    The teams can then be set into operation.

7 *Six-monthly review*
It is necessary to review achievements and progress to a date on a regular basis in order to resolve difficulties which will arise, answer questions, provide greater impetus where necessary, etc. The first review should take place about six months after the teams begin to operate, and should take the form of presentation of the relevant information to a group consisting of all the joint chairmen of existing teams plus members of management and, where relevant, trade union representatives.

8 *Co-ordinating sub-committee*
A very small group of 4 or 5 people is needed to meet the joint chairmen of each team for about an hour each month, to discuss how their team is progressing, what problems it has run into, and what it has achieved.

And finally...
We recognise that the blueprint outlined above is very different from the traditional work study approach to designing incentive schemes. We believe the evidence is overwhelming that it is a more effective approach. But to make it succeed requires a change in attitudes which are very deep rooted in some sections of British management. We hope those who doubt our advice will re-examine the evidence very carefully before deciding that they have nothing to learn from it.

Appendix I Details of the Study Reported in Chapters 4 and 5

TABLE A1.1 *Organisations which were included in the study, classified by industry*

SIC order no.	Label	Firms no.	%	Employees* no.	%
2	Mining	2	3	29	4
3	Food	5	8	57	9
5	Chemicals	3	5	26	4
6	Metal manufacture	6	9	90	14
7	Mechanical engineering	4	6	35	5
8	Instrument engineering	2	3	13	2
9	Electrical engineering	7	11	78	12
11	Vehicles	1	2	19	3
12	Other metal goods	1	2	3	—
13	Textiles	3	5	15	2
15	Clothing	2	3	28	4
16	Bricks – cement	3	5	38	6
17	Timber furniture	1	2	12	2
18	Paper – printing	2	3	28	4
19	Other manufacturing	2	3	15	2
20	Construction	2	3	5	1
21	Gas electric water	6	9	55	8
22	Transport – communic.	3	5	39	6
23	Distribution	1	2	10	1
25	Professional service	2	3	30	5
27	Public admin. – defence	5	8	37	6
Total		63	100	662	100

NOTE
*Employees = labour force (including management).

Appendix I

TABLE A1.2 *Organisations which were included in the study, classified by sector*

	Firms no.	%	Employees no.	%
Production	44	(70)*	484	(73)
Service	19	(30)	178	(27)

NOTE
* Figures in parenthesis indicate percentages. Percentages in tables may not always total to 100 due to non-responses.

TABLE A1.3 *Organisations which were included in the study, classified by region*

	Firms		Employees	
Scotland	33	(52)*	355	(54)
London S.E.	9	(14)	108	(16)
N.W. & Midlands	4	(6)	38	(6)
Elsewhere	17	(27)	161	(24)

* Figures in parenthesis indicate percentages. Percentages in tables may not always total to 100 due to non-responses.

TABLE A1.4 Characteristics of questionnaire sample

	No. of responses	No. of companies providing one or more response
Number of senior managers	62	57
Number of personnel managers	54	53
Number of finance managers	52	52
Number of management services	50	50
Number of supervisors	68	53
Number of shop stewards	58	49
Number of sales managers	34	33
Number of employees	662	61
Total	1040 questionnaires	63 companies

TABLE A1.5 *Age distribution of sample*

	no.
Under 21 years	48
21 – 19 years	147
30 – 44 years	237
45 – 60 years	186
Over 60 years	30
Question not answered	14
	662

TABLE A1.6 *Union membership of employees in sample*

	no.
AUEW	105
GMWU	47
TGWU	105
26 other unions	234
No union or answer not clear	171
Total	662

TABLE A1.7 *Calendar of main stages of research*

1978	June	Research proposal accepted and Pay and Reward Research Centre established
	July.	Literature Survey.
	Aug.	
	Sept.	Company Recruitment Commenced.
	Oct.	
	Nov.	Questionnaires designed.
	Dec.	Productivity Indices designed for monitoring questionnaire.
1979	Mar.	Additional funding granted for outside survey research assistance.
		Questionnaire survey pilot completed.
	Apr.	Design of coding frame for questionnaires.
		Questionnaire survey distributed.
	May	Questionnaire coding started.
	June	Interview pilot completed.
		Interviews commenced.
	July	First in-depth study commenced.

Appendix I

	Aug.	
	Sept.	Company summaries written up.
	Oct.	First in-depth study completed.
	Nov.	Company summaries write ups completed.
	Dec.	Content analysis frame developed and analysis started. Questionnaire survey ended.
1980	Feb.	Second in-depth study commenced.
	Mar.	Monitoring questionnaire distributed.
	Apr.	Various visits to coal mine.
	May	
	June	Second in-depth study completed.
	July	Content Analysis completed.
	Aug.	Last monitoring questionnaire returned.
	Sept.	Monitoring questionnaires coded.
	Oct.	Data analysis commenced.
	Nov.	Preliminary analysis and feedback to companies.
	Dec.	
1981	Jan	
	Feb.	Detailed analysis and writing up commenced.
	Mar.	
	Apr.	
	May	Final report submitted to sponsors.
	June	Main team dispersed.
	July	
	Aug.	
	Sept.	
	Oct.	
	Nov.	Revised Final Report submitted to sponsors for publication.

Appendix II Questionnaire on Incentives

QUESTIONNAIRE AS DISTRIBUTED TO EMPLOYEES

List No.
Serial No.

UNIVERSITY OF STRATHCLYDE

QUESTIONNAIRE ON INCENTIVE SCHEMES

DO NOT PUT YOUR NAME ON THIS QUESTIONNAIRE

This questionnaire is part of a large scale study of productivity schemes and incentives being carried out by the Pay and Rewards Research Centre at the Strathclyde Business School, University of Strathclyde.

The study in your company is concerned with the ....
scheme introduced on.................... in the ....
section.

This questionnaire is *strictly confidential:* its results will only be used in such a way as to ensure the anonymity of yourself and your company.

We would greatly appreciate your help.

Instructions:
    Please tick the appropriate boxes and return the questionnaire *within a week* in the stamped addressed envelope.

For office use
C1–3
339
C4–6
C7–8
C9
C10
C11–13
C14–16
C17

Appendix II

QUESTIONNAIRE ON INCENTIVES

Deck I

1. How long have you worked for this company? Please tick appropriate box. [C18]
   - Under 6 months ☐
   - 6 months–1 year ☐
   - 1–3 years ☐
   - Over 3 years ☐

2. Are you a member of a trade union? [C19]
   - Yes ☐
   - No ☐

   2a. If 'YES', which trade union? [C20]
   ....

3. Who represents you in discussions/negotiations with management? [C22]
   - Self ☐
   - Anybody speaking up ☐
   - Nominated spokesman ☐
   - Shop steward ☐

4. Does a grievance procedure exist in your company? [C23]
   - Yes ☐
   - No ☐

5. Were employees involved in discussions about the change to the new scheme? [C24]
   - Yes ☐
   - No ☐

   5a. If 'YES', with whom did these discussions take place? Please tick all relevant boxes.

   [C25]
   - Senior management ☐
   - Junior management ☐
   - Unions ☐
   - ....Other (SPECIFY) ☐

6. Were claims about differentials a source of difficulty *between groups of workers in the company* before the new scheme was introduced? [C26]
   - Yes ☐
   - No ☐
   - Don't know ☐

   6a. If 'YES', do you think that this scheme will help to overcome them? [C27]
   - Yes ☐
   - No ☐

7. Were claims about differentials a source of difficulty *compared with workers in other companies* before the new scheme was introduced?
 	
    Yes ☐
    No ☐
    Don't know ☐
	C28

7a. If 'YES',
        do you think that this scheme will help to overcome them?
 	
    Yes ☐
    No ☐
	C29

8. How much control does a worker have over his/her output in this section?
 	
    Complete control ☐
    Some control ☐
    No control ☐
	C30

9. In your section how often are work methods and standards checked?
 	
    Regularly ☐
    Occasionally ☐
    Never ☐
	C31

10. Do you consider that under the new incentive scheme to earn a bonus you have to work?
 	
    Too hard ☐
    About right ☐
    Not very hard ☐
	C32

11. Does your scheme require work study?
 	
    Yes ☐
    No ☐
	C33

11a. If 'YES',
        are contingencies and relaxation allowances
 	
    More than adequate ☐
    Adequate ☐
    Less than adequate ☐
	C34

12. In your job have there been problems relating to work allocation?
 	
    Yes ☐
    No ☐
	C35

12a. If 'YES',
        has the new scheme improved this?
 	
    Yes ☐
    No ☐
	C36

Appendix II

13. What do you think accounts for hold-ups in the work flow? Please tick *a maximum of three* of the following. — C37–38

    - 01 Shortages of work ☐
    - 02 Equipment breakdown/faults ☐
    - 03 Special work ☐
    - 04 Supply problems ☐
    - 05 Bottle-necks ☐
    - 06 Low employee performance ☐ — C39–40
    - 07 Poor time keeping ☐
    - 08 Labour shortages ☐
    - 09 Inadequacies of supervision ☐
    - 10 Inability to adapt to market/demand changes quickly ☐ — C41–42
    - 11 Poor training—low skill ☐
    - ....Some other (SPECIFY) ☐

14. What is the breakdown of your average weekly wage? Please fill in (in the relevant boxes) the amounts *to the nearest pound*—both *before* and *after* the introduction of the scheme.

    C43–44

    C49–52

	Before scheme	After scheme	
Basic	£☐	£☐	C53–56
Shift allowance	£☐	£☐	C57–60
Overtime pay	£☐	£☐	C61–64
Bonus pay—weekly	£☐	£☐	C65–68
Bonus pay—monthly or longer	£☐	£☐	C69–74
Other (SPECIFY)	£☐	£☐	
	TOTAL £☐	TOTAL £☐	

    C80
    1
    Deck I
    C1–3
    339
    C4–8

15. How many hours overtime do you work *on average* per week? — C9–10

    .... hours

    15a. From your point of view, is this amount of overtime— — C11

    - Too much ☐
    - The right amount ☐
    - Too little ☐

Appendix II

16. For *each* of the following, please tick the appropriate column according to whether it is true now, whether you would like it to be true, or whether you are not interested. — C12–13

	True now	Would like	Not interested
1 Learn new things and develop skills			
2 Do varied and interesting work			
3 Decide own pace of work			
4 Encourage my views and opinions			
5 Follow through tasks to completion			
6 Work well as a group in my section			

C14–15
C16–17

17. What effect do you think that the new scheme will have on each of the following? Please tick each line. — C18–20

	Increase	No effect	Decrease
1 Skill/proficiency			
2 Quality/worth			
3 Safety			
4 Output			
5 Take home pay			
6 Differentials			
7 Morale			
8 Co-operation with management			
9 Co-operation between employees			

C21–22
C23–24
C25–26

18. Has the introduction of the incentive scheme caused any of the following changes? Please tick all relevant boxes. — C27–28

    1 Changes in the way work is organized ☐
    2 Changes in machinery/equipment layout ☐
    3 Process changes ☐
    4 Personnel changes ☐
    5 Grading changes ☐
    6 The introduction of new skills ☐
    7 The need for new machinery ☐

C29–30
C31–32
C33

19. Do you think that the new scheme will lead to a fall in manpower? — C34

    Yes—now ☐
    Yes—later ☐
    No ☐

20. How would *you* describe the reactions of each of the following to the scheme to date? Please tick *each* line. — C35–36

	Favourable	Indifferent	Discontented
1 Senior management			
2 Middle management			
3 Supervisors			
4 Employees			
5 Yourself			
6 Shop stewards or workers representatives			
7 Local union officials			
8 Union leadership			

C37–38
C39–40
C41–42

Appendix II

21. If the incentive payment were made sooner after it is earned, would this affect your attitudes to the scheme?
 	
    Yes ☐
    No ☐
	C43

22. What do you think were the company's main objectives in introducing the scheme? Please tick a *maximum of five*.
 	
    01 To increase earnings for employees ☐
    02 To increase output ☐
    03 To reduce wastage ☐
    04 To improve quality of product/service ☐
    05 To improve labour mobility or flexibility ☐
    06 To reduce stoppages or industrial action ☐
    07 To reduce absenteeism ☐
    08 To reduce labour turnover ☐
    09 To reduce overtime working ☐
    10 To reduce manpower ☐
    11 To decrease lead time on order deliveries ☐
    12 To improve recruitment ☐
    13 To adjust differentials between groups in this plant ☐
    14 To motivate and provide more employee commitment ☐
    15 To increase company profits ☐
	C44–45
	
	C46–47
	
	C48–49
	
	C50–51
	
	C52–53

23. How well do you think *each* of the following functions of management are carried out in relation to your work?	C54–55

	Very well	Adequately	Poorly	
01 Communications				C56–57
02 Supervision				
03 Quality control				C58–59
04 Production planning and control				
05 Inventory control				C60–61
06 Maintenance				
07 Recruitment and selection				
08 Training				C62–63
09 Method study/work measurement				
10 Employee motivation				

Appendix II

24. Which of the following factors are most important to your job satisfaction? Please read the whole list carefully and then tick a *maximum of three*.

C64–65

- Regular increases in wages ☐
- Guaranteed job security ☐
- Opportunity for promotion ☐
- Fringe benefits, e.g. subsidized meals, discount buying, social facilities ☐
- Generous holiday/sick pay allowance ☐
- Shorter hours of work ☐
- Opportunities for overtime ☐   C66–67
- Good union representation ☐
- Healthy and safe working environment ☐
- Extra payment for effort ☐
- Job status/prestige ☐
- Opportunity for leadership or responsibility ☐
- Opportunity to learn and develop skills ☐
- Participation in decision making ☐   C68–69
- Recognition and praise for a job well done ☐
- Good working relationship ☐
- Reputation of the company ☐
- Fair allocation of work load ☐
- Management attitudes ☐

25. Have you worked with an incentive scheme before?   C70
    - Yes ☐
    - No ☐

    25a. If 'YES', what type of scheme was this?   C71
    - Individual ☐
    - Group ☐
    - Plant wide ☐
    - ....Other (SPECIFY) ☐

    25b. And what did you think of this type of scheme?   C72
    - Very good ☐
    - Acceptable ☐
    - Not good ☐

26. Are you male or female?   C73
    - Male ☐
    - Female ☐

27. What age are you?   C74
    - Under 21 years ☐
    - 21–29 years ☐
    - 30–44 years ☐
    - 45–60 years ☐
    - Over 60 ☐

Appendix II

HAVE YOU ANY FURTHER COMMENTS WHICH YOU WOULD LIKE TO ADD?	C75–79
	C80
	2
THANK YOU FOR YOUR HELP. PLEASE RETURN THE QUESTIONNAIRE IN THE STAMPED ADDRESSED ENVELOPE AS SOON AS POSSIBLE.	

Appendix II

QUESTIONNAIRE AS DISTRIBUTED TO SENIOR MANAGEMENT

List No.
Serial No.

UNIVERSITY OF STRATHCLYDE

QUESTIONNAIRE ON INCENTIVE SCHEMES

DO NOT PUT YOUR NAME ON THIS QUESTIONNAIRE

This questionnaire is part of a large scale study of productivity schemes and incentives being carried out by the Pay and Rewards Research Centre at the Strathclyde Business School, University of Strathclyde.

The study in your company is concerned with the .... scheme introduced on..................... in the .... section.

This questionnaire is *strictly confidential:* its results will only be used in such a way as to ensure the anonymity of yourself and your company.

We would greatly appreciate your help.

Instructions:
    Please tick the appropriate boxes and return the questionnaire *within a week* in the stamped addressed envelope.

For office use
C1–3
339
C4–6
C7–8
C9
C10
C11–13
C14–16
C17

Appendix II

QUESTIONNAIRE ON INCENTIVES

DECK I

1. How long have you worked for this company? [C18]

    - Under 6 months ☐
    - 6 months–1 year ☐
    - 1–3 years ☐
    - Over 3 years ☐

2. How long have you worked for this company in your present managerial capacity? [C19]

    - Less than 5 years ☐
    - 1–5 years ☐
    - Over 5 years ☐

> IN ALL QUESTIONS ON THE RELEVANT INCENTIVE SCHEME PLEASE READ 'PLANT' OR 'GROUP' IN PLACE OF 'SECTION' IF IT IS MORE APPROPRIATE

3. Please describe briefly the payment system used in the section where the new incentive scheme is in operation, *before* it was introduced. [C20–21]

    ....
    ....
    ....

4. Have incentive schemes operated in this section before? [C22]

    - Yes ☐
    - No ☐

    4a. If 'YES', what kind of a scheme was it? [C23]

    - Individual ☐
    - Group ☐
    - Plant wide ☐
    - Other (SPECIFY) .... ☐
    - Not applicable ☐

    4b. If 'YES', how long did it last? .... [C24–25]

5. What sort of incentive scheme has been introduced in the section? Please tick the relevant box. [C26–27]

    1. Piece-work bonus—employees paid entirely according to performance with no basic pay ☐
    2. Basic rate plus bonus which can vary ☐
    3. Basic rate plus fixed bonus ☐
    4. Basic rate plus bonus which is fixed under certain conditions ☐
    5. Higher basic rate(s) for maintaining specific performance level(s) ☐
    6. Higher basic rate(s) for some other reason (SPECIFY)............................... ☐

Appendix II

6. Is the new incentive scheme based on individual, group or plant performance? Individual ☐ Group ☐ Plant ☐		C28
6a. *If NOT plant wide*, how keen are the white-collar staff to have their pay related to productivity? Keen ☐ Indifferent ☐ Opposed ☐ Not applicable ☐		C29
7. How many trades unions, of representative groups of workers, do you negotiate with on this site? Number ☐		C30–31
8. How often does a shop steward/workers' representative from the section with the new incentive scheme raise a pay issue with someone in management? Frequently ☐ Occasionally ☐ Never ☐		C32
9. Were claims about differentials a source of difficulty *between groups in the company* before the new scheme was introduced? Yes ☐ No ☐ Not applicable ☐		C33
9a. If 'YES', do you think that this scheme will help to overcome them? Yes ☐ No ☐ Not applicable ☐		C34
10. Were claims about differentials a source of difficulty *compared with employees in other companies* before the new scheme was introduced? Yes ☐ No ☐ Not applicable ☐		C35
10a. If 'YES', do you think that this scheme will help to overcome them? Yes ☐ No ☐ Not applicable ☐		C36
11. When did negotiations on the new incentive scheme start and finish? Starting date .... Finishing date		C37–38

Appendix II

12. Which groups were involved in the initial design of the scheme? Please tick all relevant boxes.	C39–40
Senior management ☐	
Outside consultants ☐	C41–42
Management services ☐	
Supervisors ☐	
Union representatives/ workers' representatives ☐	C43–44
...............Some other (SPECIFY) ☐	
13. Which unions were involved in the discussions? Please list.	C45–46
1	
2	C47–48
3	
	C49–50
5	C51–52
None ☐	C53–54
14. What kind of labour is required to carry out the work in this section?	C55
Highly skilled ☐	
Moderately skilled ☐	
Unskilled ☐	
14a. How long does it take to gain the necessary skills?	C56
....	C57–58
Not applicable ☐	C59
15. How effectively can changes in employee effort be measured in this section?	C60
Very precisely ☐	
Fairly effectively ☐	
Not at all ☐	
15a. Is this true of all categories of employees in this section?	C61
Yes ☐	
No ☐	
16. How important are quality and material usage standards for the work performed in the section with the new incentive scheme?	C62
Critical ☐	
Important ☐	
Unimportant ☐	
Not applicable ☐	
17. Are most of the supervisors in this section	C63
Satisfactory ☐	
Unsatisfactory ☐	
Not applicable ☐	

Appendix II

18. Do you think that the company's rate of introducing new machinery or technology is | C64
    - Slow ☐
    - Moderate ☐
    - Rapid ☐
    - Not applicable ☐

19. How do you think that the introduction of this incentive scheme will effect prices to the customer? | C65
    - Increase ☐
    - No change ☐
    - Decrease ☐
    - Not applicable ☐

20. What do you think accounts for hold-ups in the present work flow? Please tick a *maximum of three* of the following. | C66–67
    - 01 Shortages of work ☐
    - 02 Equipment/machine breakdown/faults ☐
    - 03 Special work ☐
    - 04 Supply problems ☐
    - 05 Poor planning of work ☐ | C68–69
    - 06 Low employee performance ☐
    - 07 Poor timekeeping ☐
    - 08 Labour shortages ☐
    - 09 Inadequacies of supervision ☐
    - 10 Inability to adapt to market demand changes quickly ☐ | C70–71
    - 11 Poor training—low skill ☐
    - ....Some other (SPECIFY)

21. How is the bonus or higher rate earned? Please tick all relevant boxes. | C72–73
    - Volume of output ☐
    - Work measured performance ☐
    - Machine or equipment running efficiency ☐ | C74–74
    - Sales volume or value ☐
    - Quality improvement or standards ☐
    - Waste reduction or control ☐
    - Good attendance ☐
    - Tied to performance of some other group ☐ | C76–77
    - Accident record ☐
    - Merit or co-operation judged subjectively ☐
    - Share of profit ☐
    - Relation of total wages bill to added value ☐ | C78–79
    - Relation of total wages bill to sales value ☐
    - Improvements in added value ☐
    - ....Some other (SPECIFY)

Appendix II 279

C80
1
DECK II
C1–3
339
C4–8

22. How often is the bonus or higher rate paid? Please tick the relevant box. — C9

    Same week ☐
    One week in arrears ☐
    Two weeks in arrears ☐
    Two–four weeks in arrears ☐
    Four–six weeks in arrears ☐
    Over six months in arrears ☐
    ....Some other (SPECIFY)

23. Is the basis for payment of the bonus — C10

    A percentage of basic pay on all rates ☐
    A flat sum for all employees, on all rates ☐
    A sum varying from job to job ☐
    ....Some other (SPECIFY) ☐

23a. If *bonus is a percentage of basic pay*, what percentage is it? — C11–12

    Percentage ☐
    Not applicable ☐

23b. If *sum varies from job to job*, does it vary according to — C13

    Length of service ☐
    Age ☐
    Seniority ☐
    Grade ☐
    ....Some other (SPECIFY)
    Not applicable ☐

24. What effect do you think that the new scheme will have on each of the following? Please tick each line.

	Increase	No change	Decrease	
1 Skill/proficiency				C14–16
2 Quality/worth				C17–18
3 Safety				
4 Output				C19–20
5 Take home pay				
6 Differentials				
7 Morale				
8 Co-operation with management				C21–22
9 Co-operation between employees				

Appendix II

25. Do you think that the new incentive scheme will lead to a fall in manpower?
    - Yes—now ☐
    - Yes—later ☐   23
    - Never ☐

    25a If *new scheme will lead to a reduction in manpower* how do you think management will achieve this?
    (Please tick more than one box if necessary)   24 / 25
    - 01 Voluntary severance ☐
    - 02 Redundancy   26   27
    - 03 Natural wastage ☐
    - 04 Transfer to other work ☐   28
    - 05 Early retirement ☐
    - .... Some other (SPECIFY) ☐
    - Not applicable

26. Which departments will provide control data for the scheme?
    Please tick all relevant boxes.   29   30
    - Finance ☐
    - Supervision ☐   31   32
    - Personnel/industrial relations ☐
    - Management services ☐   33   34
    - .... Some other (SPECIFY) ☐   35
    - Not applicable ☐

27. Does this scheme require more information to be collected by management?   36
    - Yes ☐
    - No ☐

28. Has control by senior management been affected as a result of this scheme?
    - Yes ☐   37
    - No ☐
    - Not applicable ☐

LEAVE BLANK

29. Which of the following factors do you consider most necessary for the successful operation of your economy? Please tick ONE OR TWO boxes ONLY.
    - 01 Maintenance of quality ☐
    - 02 Meeting delivery dates ☐
    - 03 Keeping prices low ☐
    - 04 Production throughput ☐
    - 05 Balance of work or operation between sections ☐
    - 06 Elimination of waste ☐
    - 07 Retention of labour ☐
    - 08 Continuous running of plant ☐
    - 09 Flexibility to respond to customer specifications ☐
    - 10 Keeping up to date with technology ☐
    - 11 Development of new products/services ☐
    - 12 Bringing the company to the customer/consumer's attention ☐
    - 13 Bringing the product/service to the customer/consumer's attention ☐
    - 14 Personal relationship of sales staff with customers ☐

Appendix II

30. What were the company's aims and objectives in introducing this scheme? Please tick a MAXIMUM OF FIVE from the following list. 1 To increase earnings for employees ☐ 2 To increase output ☐ 3 To reduce wastage ☐ 4 To improve quality of product/service ☐ 5 To improve labour mobility or flexibility ☐ 6 To reduce stoppages or industrial action ☐ 7 To reduce absenteeism ☐ 8 To reduce labour turnover ☐ 9 To reduce overtime working ☐ 10 To reduce manpower ☐ 11 To decrease lead time on order deliveries ☐ 12 To improve recruitment ☐ 13 To adjust differentials between groups in this plant ☐ 14 To motivate and provide more employee commitment ☐ 15 To increase company profits ☐	LEAVE BLANK
30a. Which of the items listed in question 30 are you confident the scheme is achieving? Please tick boxes for all relevant numbers. 1 ☐ 6 ☐ 11 ☐ 2 ☐ 7 ☐ 12 ☐ 3 ☐ 8 ☐ 13 ☐ 4 ☐ 9 ☐ 14 ☐ 5 ☐ 10 ☐ 15 ☐	

31. Have you worked with incentive schemes before?
                                                   Yes ☐
                                                   No ☐
 	
31a If 'YES', please describe the type of scheme.
 	
                                    Individual ☐
                                    Group ☐
                                    Plant wide ☐
.... Other (SPECIFY) ☐
                                    Not applicable ☐	

32. Please give brief details of any training that you have done.	

33. What age are you?
                                        Under 21 years ☐
                                        21–29 years ☐
                                        30–44 years ☐
                                        45–60 years ☐
                                        Over 60 ☐	

Appendix III Construction of Composite Performance Indices

This appendix lists the variables from the questionnaire responses (managers) and interview comments (all respondents) which were used in the construction of composite indices of achievement. Each variable was scored, and the result was taken as warranting either the addition or subtraction of one unit from the cumulative performance index concerned.

Composite performance indices	Component variables	Data method Q = questionnaire I = interview	Number of Valid firms (N = 63)
Manning reduction	Manpower reductions Labour savings Cost	Q	60
	Changes in number of employees	I	52
Output increase	Changes in output volume Changes and effects on output (from several perspectives)	Q	58
	Productivity changes Output changes State of productivity Work flow	I	52
Financial improvements	Effects on costs Effects on profits	Q	55

Appendix III

Composite performance indices	Component variables	Data method Q = questionnaire I = interview	Number of Valid firms ($N = 63$)
	Effects on added value Effects on sales Expectations of cost reduction	I	52
	Profit changes Production cost changes	I	52
Quality improvements	Quality change Quality improvement expectations Effects on quality (several points of view)	Q	61
	Changes in quality of work Shop floor work changes	I	52
Other specific improvements	Effect on prices Effect on stockholding Effect on materials usage Effect on waste Reactions to change	Q	58
	Effects on wastage Effects on output rejects	I	52
Improved industrial relations	Reduced stoppages Reduced absenteeism Reduced labour turnover Improved recruitment Reduced overtime	Q	58
	Employee stability Absenteeism changes Overtime Labour turnover	I	52

Composite performance indices	Component variables	Data method Q = questionnaire I = interview	Number of Valid firms (N = 63)
	Timekeeping Recruitment Current levels of absence, labour turnover, and timekeeping		
Improved work attitudes	Employee motivation Employee – Management co-operation (several perspectives) Inter-employee co-operation (several perspectives) Morale (several views) Safety (several views)	Q	59
	Industrial relations changes Employee loyalty changes Employee identification with company changes Effort changes Safety changes Current level of employee identification with company	I	52
Better standards of management and work	Effects on skill (several views) Labour flexibility changes Productive capacity change Standards of management change	Q	62
	Communication within firm Labour flexibility changes	I	52

Appendix III

Composite performance indices	Component variables	Data method Q = question- naire I = interview	Number of Valid firms (N = 63)
	Current level of labour flexibility		
Improved pay relationships	Improved relativities Differentials adjusted Effect on differentials (several views)	Q	61
	Changes on differentials Changes on relativities Current state of differentials and relativities	I	52
Improved customer service	Product development Products brought to customer attention Flexibility to customer specifications Personal consumer relation development Improved delivery schedules Improved order lead times Reductions in delay	Q	30
Improved internal relations	Effects on shopfloor – management relations Effects on shopfloor – supervisor relations Effects on inter-employee relations	I	52

Composite performance indices	Component variables	Data method Q = questionnaire I = interview	Number of Valid firms (N = 63)
Generally improved company state	General state of company Future prospects of the company Economic condition of the company	I	52

Appendix IV Construction of Payment Scheme Implementation Indices

This appendix lists the variables from the questionnaire responses (all management and shop stewards) and interview comments (all respondents) which were used in the construction of composite indices of scheme implementation. Each component variable was scored and the result was taken as warranting either the addition or subtraction of one unit from the cumulative implementation index concerned.

Composite implementation indices	Component variables	Data method (Q = Questionnaire) (I = Interview)	Number of firms* (N = 63)
Extent of consultation and negotiation	Involvement in negotiation by: finance management marketing management supervisors Level of consultation of: top management plant management Shop steward consultation Marketing dept. awareness of Scheme's mechanics	Q	59

Appendix IV

Composite implementation indices	Component variables	Data method (Q = Questionnaire) (I = Interview)	Number of firms* (N = 63)
	Groups involved in initial design: senior management consultants management services supervisors union representatives		
	Extent of negotiation	I	52
	Extent of consultation		
	Adequacy of information about negotiation and consultation		
	Satisfactory explanation of scheme		
	Time spent explaining the scheme		
Information collection before scheme	Methods study updated and used	Q	49
	Work measurement used		
	Financial data used: cost budget wages added value		
	Increase in staff to implement the scheme		

Appendix IV

Composite implementation indices	Component variables	Data method (Q = Questionnaire) (I = Interview)	Number of firms* (N = 63)
Staffing changes to maintain scheme	Monitoring staff Staff increases in following departments to monitor scheme: finance personnel quality control supervision management services	Q	52
Extra monitoring information (other than financial)	Management required to collect more information More information prepared by: personnel management services supervisors marketing Department providing extra information: supervision quality control personnel management services New scheme based on time standards	Q	58
	Amount of information available to management	I	52

NOTE:
* Firms with sufficient scores from which to construct this index.

Appendix V Sample Pages of Diaries

Peter Gosnold, Wednesday, 19 April 1980

Back to work again after the Easter break also am now on afternoon shifts as face is now only producing on one shift and might as well follow this shift round. A bad turn up today, only 15 men, some of the team are taking their rest days making them a full week off so I can't see any improvement this week. We start off very well with machine but soon run into trouble. Floor lift over holidays has caused face conveyor to lift on face side. This causes the cutter to foul front legs on face supports a common fault after any holiday period. This type of delay will not be paid for under incentive agreement although we are cutting slow we are not stopped. After the first stop things are back to normal. We have 2 more big stoppages in shift with face conveyor stalled, a stoppage that will be paid for. This has been happening quite a lot these last few weeks. This I believe is caused by coal not being taken away from face delivery causing fines to be taken back into 13th race of face conveyor. All these problems are being caused by faulting on face and conveyor having to be graded to the dip. All this will be solved when we get back onto the right grade but this is a long slow process. We are getting away from the last fault at maingate end very nicely. We are now into full seam and caught all tops things are moving and improving but it's a very slow process and one we will have to put up with.

David McCormack, Monday, 24 March 1980

I went underground at 12.30 p.m. checked up on my supplies which were at the pit bottom. Travelled in on the manrider with the men. I recorded each man entering the district and closely recorded his attendance. I deployed the men off to their work. The dayshift chargeman arrived at the meeting station and I told him of last weeks delays which had not been authorised, one being an insertion of an 0.1 electric cable in the maingate and one which was for a delay which started at 10.25 a.m. and finished at 11.10 a.m. for extending the maingate and he said he would make inquiries into this matter. He then said that we had our £6 bonus to draw this week but we would only have a small one next week, because one of the coalface's went home after a dispute with the deputy manager thus causing output to be low.

I started my mid-shift inspection and travelled to the face. The cutter was doing quite well. I got to the cutter at 12 o'clock and proceeded to the top of the face, checking that everything had been done to receive the cutter, as it was 4.40 p.m. I stayed here and assisted with the face men in doing two cuts and setting the supports and got the cutter ready for cutting down after snap time. I then proceeded to do my pre-shift inspection and checking my supplies for the face. Everything was under control and we completed 2 cuts for the shift. A good start for the week as we had got four push-outs at the top end of the face and the bottom.

As I had been off work last Wednesday, Thursday and Friday with a torn muscle in my right shoulder I learned today that the face norm had been revised by the manager, and that he had given them two more men which altered their standard task by 1.6 mts. per lineal metre to 17.28 mts. per lineal metre which did not appeal to me at all, because the manager has been giving them shifts by reducing the amount of man-shifts on the face installation, thus raising their bonus. By giving them these two more men he has said that he will not give them any shifts at the end of the week.

Ed Howson, Wednesday, 20 February 1980

Went to work today sick to the teeth. Worked all the morning on the car, all to no avail. Plenty of men turned up today, they must all be skint. 27 turned up and only wanted 25. This suited me fine as it gave me 2 men which I could put on work outbye, which is miles behind. Put the 2 spare men dinting in the return gate, (dinting means getting floor up) in preparation for installing a man riding system. All the mechanical equipment is available for the manriding installation, all I require is manpower. The object of the manrider is in order to get the men to the coalface faster, thus giving more time at the face.

The coal face did a steady 2 cuts, $\frac{1}{2}$ cut down on the norm. It looks impossible to get the norm. Delays timbering had ground, a damaged ramp tray had to be taken off and several stoppages with the bunkers full. This is the bunkering problem I brought up at Ross Priory at weekend. 2 arches set at the return rip this shift, another good performance. The men complain that it's always our shift that gets 2 arches, and that the other shift have never once got 2 up. I agree with them entirely and have asked the officials on the other shift why. All I get are lame brained excuses and the truth is, the other team of rippers are too old. Not one of the other team is under 55 while the team on my shift are all young men in their twenties, just out of their coal face training. Or is it that with treating the men with the respect I do they are prepared to give you that little bit extra, I like to think so.

Bill McFarlane, Friday, 14 March 1980

Request for a meeting from Craftsmen's Representatives on overtime. Spoke to Mr ——— at the morning meeting on same and he re-iterated the need to keep control of overtime. Confided in me that certain sections of the Branch Committee were watching 'with interest, the outcome of the meeting stressing the need for overtime to be shared out equally amongst the pit. At the meeting with Craftsmen's Representatives I pointed out that overtime was at the discretion of management and had to be used for the benefit of the pit as a whole and not for individual departments. Mr ——— presented figures showing that his department had the highest percentage of O/T shifts. In spite of our pleas, the Mid-Area mechanics decided to ban all weekend work this coming Saturday and Sunday.

I cannot understand the mentality of people who can afford to throw away overtime to the value of £25 – 30 in spite of instructions to the contrary from their own officials.

Dispute with face men – When I was returning to the lamproom from the shaft at 12.50 p.m. a number of the oncoming shift were lingering on the corridor having a smoke before going to the shaft. Start to move the men to the shaft, when I spoke to —'s men in an attempt to get them moving they refused to go. I pointed out that the winding time for the aft. shift was 12.45 to 1.00 p.m. when all the men should be down the pit. Then came in conflict with ———, the chargehand and the argument became heated. Eventually he took the men home.

I could not understand the men's reluctance to move. This delay at man-riding time is a long standing problem at most pits and it is a regular occurrence for me and other members of management to 'push' the men to the shaft at this time. ——— informed me afterwards that the men were upset at the result of their particular incentive earnings for the previous week. They could not, or would not, accept that the extra overtime shifts incurred when on Day Shift should make a difference to the incentive earnings when compared to the previous week.

Probably this caused the men to be stubborn when being pushed to the shaft.

Chris Young, Monday, 18 February 1980

Today was the kind of day one only has bad dreams about. Everything we did went wrong. Firstly we had to pack round the arches for about 2 hours. We accept this as part of the job but today's excess packing was caused by a mixture of bad management and bad workmanship. Firstly the official in charge of the coal face should not have told the men to drill the holes so deep, causing too much ground to be exposed and when he did, well then, the men should have refused to do so. The men knew and the management knew that too much exposed ground would cause rockfall and too much rockfall means more rock to remove and therefore more time and more packing.

When the packing was done we were about 3 hours behind time and time wasted is time lost. This time cannot be booked in for bonus payments, because the only time that time can be booked in is when the actual coal cutter is stopped. All the time we were packing unnecessarily, the coal cutter was going, so no time can be booked, plus the fact that me and my two mates were working under dangerous uncovered ground. I was seriously injured a few years ago and this was in the back of my mind all the time. I was off work on crutches for 8 months and all the bonus in the world is not worth being injured again for.

We had our lunch break and straight away after someone on the coal face damaged the main electric cable by moving some supports in and not watching what he was doing. The cutter was stopped for about $2\frac{1}{2}$ hours. There will be discussions on this stopped time. The management will say it was negligence on the workers' part and I must confess they are right in this case, plus the fact that we had to manhandle a 180 yards of cable which is as thick as a man's arm, off the coal face and a new cable of equal dimensions onto the coal face. All in all, we worked harder today than normal, worked in dangerous conditions and hardly any actual progress was made. I wish I had stayed in bed this morning. We have had all this hassle today through sheer stupidity.

John Cameron, Wednesday, 26 March 1980

Firstly in answer to your question about the bonus being less of an incentive, personally I don't think that it did make any difference because you still think of your wage at the basic rate when you negotiate a rise and then any other things, e.g. bonus pay, bathing pay etc. are secondary. Once the rise has been sorted out you just carry on week for week trying to make the best bonus that you can.

We are having trouble today on the face with large lumps of stone falling out of the roof and getting fast on the panzer. The face panzer stalled and came off the sprocket at the other end of the face. Whilst my mate was repairing this I rested the bottom drive to make sure it was pulling at full force. It was so I knew that my end was o.k. The face men had found a big lump stuck under the cutter so they were removing this also at the same time. When we tried to run the panzer after about 1 hours stop it still wouldn't start and the fluid coupling the top drive blew. My mate was having no luck and as expected he was cursing. There is no need for me to go and help him through because the face men were helping him. He repaired the coupling and face men have removed some of the coal off the panzer. This time we are lucky and the panzer starts up and runs. The face overman now has to tell his men to keep an eye open for these lumps and stop the panzer when they come out.

Mr ——— has been round the district today and with any luck he will drop our target so that it will be easier for us to make money.

When conditions are very bad like this a face can be temporarily brought out of the pool of faces so that it doesn't bring everybody's bonus down. I think this should be done in our case.

Jim Hill, Tuesday, 18 March 1980

Sorry there is no proper diary today as face team is on strike and I will attempt to put you in the picture as to how it came about. On following the usual pattern of getting changed and drawing of lamps we were having a quiet smoke outside the lamp room which we always do when along came Mr McFarlane the manager who stopped talking to the face Bummer, about what went on yesterday when he had asked about half the team going onto dayturn. This was done so that he could get as much coal off as possible but as we were on a go slow the team said that we would not be split up, told him this and he said he would put some men on tomorrow. When walking away from ——— he then started to tell the men off our face to get down pit. He then went to some more men and told them to do the same but none of the men moved as at this time which was 12.45 p.m. we were all having a smoke in our own time as we do not start till 1.00 p.m. He then came over to me and said you get down pit. I said I would go as soon as I had finished my smoke he left me then and went and got hold of some men who were sitting down and pulled them up from the floor and told them to get down pit also. Again he came over to me and said you either get down pit or you go the other way, meaning home. I told him he was out of order as we were in our own time as we do not start till 1.00 p.m. He said that it was 12.50 p.m. on looking at his watch and that he wanted us through the deployment centre for 1.00 p.m. I said we would be and asked why he was picking on us as we were getting more coal than anybody else. He said that we were not. I said that the bonus board proved that we were. He then said that the board sometimes tells lies. He then turned round and told us all to get down the pit or go the other way again. ——— came over then and said that he was only picking on us because we would not come on day turn today to get him more coal. He then again said you 'bloody get' down pit or go the other way. It's an old threat and the men did not like it so they said we should see the union about it so ——— and ——— and I went towards the union cabin. He again stopped us and asked where we were going. ——— said that we were going to see the union about the way he had treated us. He said that we could do as we wanted adding a few 'Bloodies' in between. He also asked what the other men from off our own face were doing and we said they were staying on top until we got back from the union cabin. By the time we got to the cabin he had been on the phone to the union man and told a pack of lies about the time this had supposedly happened. We told the union man that we wanted an apology from him before we would go down pit. ——— the union man said that he would come with us and see him, so ——— and ——— and I went to tell the men what was happening but were stopped by ——— the undermanager for our district who asked us what was going on, we told him and he said the Mr McFarlane had been to him in his office at 7 minutes to 1 and told him to go and get the men down pit also. ——— in the meantime had been to see Mr McFarlane about seeing us but he told him that he would not see us till the men had gone down pit. We then went and told the men this and they said that they would not go down pit till they had an apology for the way he had behaved, so we all decided to go home. When getting dressed ——— came and said that Mr McFarlane had said that we had refused to go down pit when he has asked to do so. This is another lie as we told him that we would be through the deployment centre for 1.00 p.m. which is within our rights. As I have said in previous diaries we have no grumble with the management but if he wants to take this attitude it's alright with us. After a meeting outside the canteen it was decided to come to work tomorrow and see what happens.

Appendix VI Coalbridge Engineering: Calculation of Proposed Company Performance Related Payment Scheme

The Performance Payment was calculated by a formula derived from the following factors:

		Factor range %
(a)	Turnover performance factor	−10 to +10
(b)	Employment cost factor	−10 to +10
(c)	Sum of the turnover and employment cost factors, i.e. the company performance factor	0 to +10

Taking each separately they are made up and calculated in the following way.

TURNOVER PERFORMANCE FACTOR

This is made up of the number of targeted units produced and the remainder of the output valued at fixed prices or prices estimated by the company where fixed prices were not agreed. Other financial figures used are those declared in the accounts of the company.

Its calculation is based on cumulative turnovers for the company's financial year in the following manner.

	Turnover performance factor
	%
If actual turnover is:	
100% or more than planned turnover	+10
99% to 99.9% of " "	+ 9
98% to 98.9% " " "	+ 8
97% to 97.9% " " "	+ 7
96% to 96.9% " " "	+ 6
95% to 95.9% " " "	+ 5
94% to 94.9% " " "	+ 4
93% to 93.9% " " "	+ 3
92% to 92.9% " " "	+ 2
91% to 90.9% " " "	+ 1
If actual turnover is between:	
89.1% and 90.9% of planned turnover	0
If actual turnover is:	
88.1% to 89% of planned turnover	− 1
87.1% to 88% " " "	− 2
86.1% to 87% " " "	− 3
85.1% to 86% " " "	− 4
84.1% to 85% " " "	− 5
83.1% to 84% " " "	− 6
82.1% to 83% " " "	− 7
81.1% to 82% " " "	− 8
80.1% to 81% " " "	− 9
80% or below planned turnover	−10

EMPLOYMENT COST FACTOR

The basic employment costs are made up of the numbers employed in the company multiplied by their base rates. Added to this are any overtime and shift payments, company payments for national insurance and pensions and any other costs of employment excluding the performance payment.

Appendix VI

The planned basic employment costs are only altered should there be an increase in the labour force following an unexpected increase in orders or if the planned order intake is not achieved and there appears a surplus of labour. In either case the basic employment cost would be adjusted accordingly.

The following table shows the calculation of the employment cost factor cumulative for the company's financial year.

	Employment cost factor
If actual basic employment costs are	
10% or more below plan	+ 10%
9% to 9.9% ,, ,,	+ 9%
8% to 8.9% ,, ,,	+ 8%
7% to 7.9% ,, ,,	+ 7%
6% to 6.9% ,, ,,	+ 6%
5% to 5.9% ,, ,,	+ 5%
4% to 4.9% ,, ,,	+ 4%
3% to 3.9% ,, ,,	+ 3%
2% to 2.9% ,, ,,	+ 2%
1% to 1.9% ,, ,,	+ 1%
If actual basic employment costs are between:	
0.9% below and 0.9% above plan	0
1% to 1.9% above plan	− 1%
2% to 2.9% ,, ,,	− 2%
3% to 3.9% ,, ,,	− 3%
4% to 4.9% ,, ,,	− 4%
5% to 5.9% ,, ,,	− 5%
6% to 6.9% ,, ,,	− 6%
7% to 7.9% ,, ,,	− 7%
8% to 8.9% ,, ,,	− 8%
9% to 9.9% ,, ,,	− 9%
10% or more above plan	−10%

Both turnover and employment cost factors were designed to be calculated monthly and relate to cumulative actual performance, compared with cumulative planned performance in each financial year ending 30 September.

Appendix VI

Sum of the Turnover and Employment Cost Factors, i.e.
COMPANY PERFORMANCE FACTOR OR PERFORMANCE PAYMENT

To illustrate the calculation of the Company Performance Factor and performance payment two worked examples are presented below:

Example 1

Turnover achieved	99% of plan Factor +9%
Basic employment costs	102% of plan Factor −2%
Turnover performance factor	+9%
Employment cost factor	−2%
Company performance factor	+7%

The sum of money paid would be 7% of one-twelfth of the base rate existing at the time of the payment grossed up to an annual rate. On a base rate of £80 per week –

Payment for 7% would be $\frac{7}{100} \times \frac{80 \times 52}{12} = £24.27$

Example 2

Turnover achieved	102% of plan Factor + 20% (LIMIT)
Basic employment costs	98% of plan Factor + 2%
Turnover performance factor	+ 10%
Employment cost factor	+ 2%
Company performance factor	12%

But company performance factor is limited to a maximum of 10%. The sum of money paid would be 10% of one-twelfth the base rate existing at the time of the payment grossed up to an annual rate. On a base rate of £80 per week –

Payment for 10% would be $\frac{10}{100} \times \frac{80 \times 52}{12} = £34.66$

References

CHAPTER 1: INTRODUCTION

Lupton, T. (1963), *On The Shop Floor*, London: Pergamon Press.
Lupton, T. and Bowey, A. M. (1974), *Wages and Salaries*, London: Penguin Books. 2nd edn (1983) London: Gower Press.
Lupton, T. and Gowler, D. (1969), *Selecting a Wage Payment System*, Engineering Employers Federation, Research Paper No. 111. London: Engineering Employers' Federation.
Mayo, E. (1949), 'Hawthorne and the Western Electric Company' in *The Social Problems of an Industrial Civilisation*, Boston, Mass.: Routledge.
Roy, D. (1952), 'Quota Restriction and Goldbricking in a Machine Shop', *American Journal of Sociology*, 57, pp. 427–42.

CHAPTER 2: PAYMENT SYSTEMS AND PERFORMANCE IMPROVEMENT

Bowey, A. M. (1976), 'Pay Systems in Perspective', *Personnel Management*, April.
Burns, T. and Stalker, G. (1961), *The Management of Innovation*, London: Tavistock Press.
Child, J. (1972), 'Organisation Structure, Environment and Performance: the Role of Strategic Choice', *Sociology*, vol. 6, pp. 1–22.
Department of Trade (1977), 'Report of the Committee of Inquiry on Industrial Democracy', Cmnd 6706 (Chairman: Lord A. Bullock) London: HMSO.
Ditton, J. (1979) 'Baking Time', *The Sociological Review*, vol. 27, no. 1, February.
Feidler, F. E. and Chemers, M. M. (1974), *Leadership and Effective Management* Glenview, Illinois: Scott Foresman.
Goldthorpe, J. et al. (1968), *The Affluent Worker: Industrial Attitudes and Behaviour*, Cambridge University Press.
Hill, P. (1972), *Towards a New Philosophy of Management*, London: Gower Press.
Landsberger, H. A. (1958), *Hawthorne Revisited*, New York: Ithaca.
Lawrence, P. W. and Lorsch, J. W. (1967), *Organisation and Environment: Managing Differentiation and Integration*, Homewood, Ill.: Irwin.
Lupton, T. and Bowey, A. M. (1983), *Wages and Salaries, 2nd edn*, London: Gower Press.
McCormick, B. J. (1977), 'Methods of Wage Payment, Wage Structures and

the Influence of Product Markets', *British Journal of Industrial Relations,* vol. 15, no. 2, July.
Marchington, M. (1977), 'Worker Participation and Plant-wide Incentive Schemes', *Personnel Review,* vol. 6, no. 3, Summer.
Morris, J. and Burgoyne, J. (1973), *Developing Resourceful Managers,* London: Institute of Personnel Management.
Millward, N. (1968), 'Family Status and Behaviour at Work', *Sociological Review,* vol. 16, no. 2, July, pp. 149 – 64.
Roethlisberger, F. J. and Dickson, W. J. (1939), *Management and The Worker,* Cambridge, Mass.: Harvard University Press.
Thorpe, R. (1980), 'The Relationship Between Payment Systems, Productivity and the Organisation of Work', Strathclyde University Business School unpublished thesis, MSc.
Vroom, V. and Yetton, P. (1973), *Leadership and Decision Making,* University of Pittsburgh Press.

CHAPTER 3: PRODUCTIVITY MEASUREMENT

Bahiri, S. and Martin, H. W. (1970), 'Productivity Costing and Management' *Management International Review,* 10,1, pp. 55 – 77.
Bailey, D. and Hubert, T. (1980), *Productivity Measurement,* London: Gower Press.
Cox, B. (1980), *Value Added,* London: Heinemann.
Cradall, F. N. and Wooton, L. M. (1978), 'Developmental Strategies o Organisational Productivity', *California Management Review,* vol. XXI, no 2.
Faraday, J. F. (1971), *The Management of Productivity,* London: BIM Publications.
Ferris, R. (1980), 'Added Value and Productivity Bonus Schemes', *Th Australian Accountant,* June.
Gold, B. (1971), *Explorations in Managerial Economics,* London: Macmillan
Greenborough, J. H. (1980), 'Introduction' in Bailey, D. and Hubert T. (eds) (1980) *Productivity Measurement,* London: Gower Press.
Greiner, L. E. (1972), 'Evolution and Revolution as Organisations Grow *Harvard Business Review,* July – August, pp. 37 – 46.
Haire, M. (1959) 'Biological Models and Empirical Histories of the Growth c Organisations', in Haire, M., *Modern Organisation Theory,* New York: Joh Wiley.
Hofer, C. (1975), 'Towards a Contingency Theory of Business Strategy *Academy of Management Journal,* December, pp. 748 – 810.
ILO (1980), *Introduction to Work Study,* Geneva: International Labour Office
Ingham, H. and Harrington, L. T. (1980), *Interfirm Comparison,* Londor William Heinemann.
Kendrick, J. W. and Creamer, P. (1965), *Productivity Measurement,* New Yorl National Industrial Conference Board.
Lupton, T. (1963), *On the Shop Floor,* London: Pergamon Press.
Majoney, T. A. and Weitzel, W. (1969), 'Managerial Models of Organisation Effectiveness', *Administrative Science Quarterly,* vol. 14, pp. 357 – 69.

Minzberg, H. (1982), 'A Note on that Dirty Word "Efficiency"', *Interfaces*, 12, October, pp. 101 – 5.
Norman, R. G. and Bahiri, S. (1972), *Productivity Measurement and Incentives*, London: Butterworth.
Roy, D. (1952), 'Quota Restriction and Goldbricking in a Machine Shop', *American Journal of Sociology*, vol. 67. no. 2. pp. 427 – 42.
Smith, E. and Beeching (1968), *Measurement of the Effectiveness of the Productive Unit*, Enfield; Institute of Work Study Practitioners Monograph.
Smith, G. (1978), 'The Fundamental Truth on Productivity', *Management Services*, January.
Teague, J. and Eilon, S. (1973), 'Productivity Measurement: a Brief Survey', London: Imperial College of Science and Technology.
Teague, J. and Eilon, S. (1973), 'On Measures of Productivity', *Omega*, vol. 1, no. 5, pp. 565 – 75.
Thorpe, R. (1982), 'Productivity Measurement', ch. 10, in Bowey A. M. (ed.), *Handbook of Salary and Wages Systems*, London: Gower Press.
Wabe, J. S. (ed.) (1974), *Problems in Manpower Forecasting*, Westmead: Saxon House.
Webster, F. A. (1976), 'A Model for New Venture Initiation: a Discourse on Rapacity and the Independent Entrepreneur', *Academy of Management Review*, January, pp. 21 – 37.
Wilson, B. (1979), 'Creating and Sharing Wealth: the Added Value Approach', *Employee Relations*, vol. 1. no. 1.
Zammuto, R. F. (1982), *Assessing Organisational Effectiveness*, State University of New York Press.

CHAPTER 4: PAYMENT SCHEME DECISION CHOICES

Bain, J. S. and Price, R. (1980), *Profiles of Union Growth: a Comparative Statistical Portrait of Eight Countries*, Oxford: Blackwell.
Barton Cunningham, J. (1977), 'Approaches to the Evaluation of Organisational Effectiveness', *Academy of Management Review*, 2, pp. 463 – 74.
Bass, B. M. (1952), 'Ultimate Criteria of Organisational Worth', *Personnel Psychology*, 5, pp. 157 – 73.
Bobbitt, Jr, H. R. and Ford, J. D. (1980), 'Decision Maker Choice as a Determinant of Organisational Structure', *Academy of Management Review*, 5, pp. 14 – 23.
Bowey, A. M., Thorpe, R., Mitchell, F., Nichols, G., Gosnold, D., Savery, L. and Hellier, P. (1982), *Effects of Incentive Payment Systems, United Kingdom, 1977 – 80*, UK Department of Employment Research Report no. 36, Department of Employment, London: HMSO.
Bowey, A. M. (1979), 'Incomes Policies and Payment Schemes', *Management Services*, 23, pp. 4 – 7.
Bowey, A. M. (1980) 'The Effects of Recently Introduced Incentive Payment Systems in Britain', *Management Decision*, 18, pp. 295 – 302.
Bowey, A. M. (1972), 'Approaches to Organisation Theory', *Social Science Information*, 11, pp. 109 – 28.

Burns, T. and Stalker, G. M. (1961), *The Management of Innovation*, London: Tavistock.

Campbell, J. P., Brownas, E. A., Peterson, N. G. and Dunnette, M. D. (1974), *The Measurement of Organisational Effectiveness: a Review of Relevant Research and Opinion*, San Diego: Naval Personnel Research Center.

Child, J. (1972), 'Organisational Structure, Environment and Performance: the Role of Strategic Choice', *Sociology*, 6, pp. 1–22.

Connolly, T. A., Conlon, E. J. and Deutsch, S. J. (1980), 'Organisational Effectiveness: a Multiple Constituency Approach', *Academy of Management Review*, 5, pp. 211–18.

Department of Employment, UK (1978), 'Q. and A. on New Pay Policy', *Employment News*, 57, p. 3.

Department of Employment, UK (1981), 'Membership of Trade Unions in 1979', *Employment Gazette*, 89, p. 22–4.

Dubin, R. (1976), 'Organisational Effectiveness: Some Dilemmas of Perspective', in S. L. Spray (ed.) *Organisational Effectiveness: Theory – Research – Utilization*, pp. 7–13, Ohio: Kent State University Press.

Duncan, R. B. (1973) 'Multiple Decision-Making Structures in Adapting to Environmental Uncertainty: the Impact on Organisational Effectiveness', *Human Relations*, 26, pp. 273–91.

Etzioni, A. (1960), 'Two Approaches to Organisational Analysis: a Critique and Suggestion', *Administrative Science Quarterly*, 5, pp. 267–78.

Evan, W. M. (1976), 'Organisational Theory and Organisational Effectiveness: an Exploratory Analysis' in S. L. Spray (ed.) *Organisational Effectiveness – Research – Utilization*, pp. 15–28, Ohio: Kent State University Press.

Fiedler, F. E. (1967), *A Theory of Leadership Effectiveness*, New York: McGraw-Hill.

Freidlander, F. and Pickle, H. (1967), 'Components of Effectiveness in Small Organisations', *Administrative Science Quarterly*, 13, pp. 289–304.

Galbraith, J. (1977), *Organisation Design*, Reading, Mass.: Addison-Wesley.

Georgopolous, B. S. and Matejko, A. (1967) 'The American General Hospital as a Complex Social System', *Health Services Research*, 2, pp. 76–111.

Goldthorpe, J. H., Lockwood, D., Bechhoffer F. and Platt, J. (1968), *The Affluent Worker: Industrial Attitudes and Behaviour*, Cambridge University Press.

Hrebiniak, L. G. (1978), *Complex Organisations*, Minnesota: West Publishing Company.

Gluckman, M. (ed.), (1964), *Closed Systems and Open Minds*, London: Oliver & Boyd.

Katz, D. and Kahn, R. L. (1966), *The Social Psychology of Organisations*, New York: John Wiley.

Keeley, M. (1978), 'A Social Justice Approach to Organisational Evaluation.', *Administrative Science Quarterly*, 23, pp. 272–92.

Lawler, E. E. (1971), *Pay and Organisational Effectiveness: a Psychological View*, New York: McGraw-Hill.

Legge, K. (1978), *Power, Innovation and Problem Solving in Personnel Management*, London: McGraw-Hill.

Lupton, T. and Bowey, A. M. (1974), *Wages and Salaries*, London: Penguin, 2nd edn (1983), London: Gower Press.

Lupton, T. and Gowler, D. (1969), *Selecting a Wage Payment System*, Engineering Employers Federation Research Paper No. 111, London: Engineering Employers' Federation.

Mahoney, T. A. and Frost, P. (1974), 'The Role of Technology in Models of Organisational Effectiveness', *Organisational Behaviour and Human Performance*, 11, pp. 127–38.

Parsons, T. (1956), 'A Sociological Approach to the Theory of Organisations', *Administrative Science Quarterly*, 1, pp. 63–85.

Pennings, J. M. (1975), 'The Relevance of the Structural–Contingency Model for Organisational Effectiveness', *Administrative Science Quarterly*, 20, pp. 393–410.

Perrow, C. (1961), 'The Analysis of Goals in Complex Organisations' in W. A. Hill and D. Egan (eds.), *Readings in Organisational Theory: a Behavioural Approach*, Boston, Mass.: Allyn & Bacon.

Pfeffer, J. and Salancik, G. R. (1978), *The External Control of Organisations: a Resource Dependence Perspective*, New York: Harper & Row.

Price, J. L. (1968), *Organisational Effectiveness: an Inventory of Propositions*, Illinois: Irwin Inc.

Rawls, J. (1971), *A Theory of Justice*, Cambridge, Mass.: Balknop Press.

Schreyögg, G. (1980), 'Contingency and Choice in Organisation Theory', *Organisation Studies*, 1, pp. 305–26.

Silverman, D. (1970), *The Theory of Organisations: a Sociological Framework*, London: Heinemann.

Sheriff, P. (1982), 'Towards a Macrosociological Analysis of Organizations', paper presented at Colloquium of Inter-University Centre for European Studies, Montreal, Canada.

Spray, S. L. (ed.), (1976), *Organisational Effectiveness*, Ohio: Kent State University Press.

Steers, R. N. (1975), 'Problems in the Measurement of Organisational Effectiveness', *Administrative Science Quarterly*, 20, pp. 546–58.

Strasser, S., Evelend, J. D., Cummins, G., Deniston, O. L., and Romani, J. H. (1981), 'Conceptualising the Goal and System Models of Organisational Effectiveness–Implications for Comparative Evaluation Research', *Journal of Management Studies*, 18, pp. 321–40.

Thompson, J. D. and McEwen, W. J. (1958), 'Organisational Goals and Environment', *American Sociological Review*, 23, pp. 23–30.

Thorpe, R. (1980), 'The Relationships Between Payment Systems, Productivity and the Organisation of Work', M.Sc. thesis, Strathclyde Business School, Strathclyde University, Glasgow.

Weiss, C. H. (1970), 'The Politicalisation of Evaluation Research', *Journal of Social Issues*, 26, pp. 57–68.

White, M. (1981), *Payment Systems in Britain*, London: Gower Press.

UK Government (1975), 'Attack on Inflation', White Paper Cmnd 6151, London: HMSO.

UK Government (1976), 'The Attack on Inflation–the Second Year', White Paper Cmnd 6507, London: HMSO.

UK Government (1977), 'The Attack on Inflation After 31st July 1977', White Paper Cmnd 6882, London: HMSO.

UK Government (1978), 'Winning the Battle Against Inflation' White Paper Cmnd 7293, London: HMSO.

Vroom, V. and Yetton, P. (1973), *Leadership and Decision-making*, University of Pittsburg Press.
Wood, S. (1979), 'A Reappraisal of the Contingency Approach to Organisation', The *Journal of Management Studies*, 16, pp. 334–54.
Yuchtmann, E. and Seashore, S. E. (1967), 'A System Resource Approach to Organisational Effectiveness' *American Sociological Review*, 32, pp. 891–903.
Woodward, J. (1959), *Management and Technology*, London: HMSO.
— — (1965), *Industrial Organisation*, Oxford University Press.
Zammuto, R. F. (1982), *Assessing Organizational Effectiveness*, State University of New York Press.

CHAPTER 5: PAYMENT SCHEME PERFORMANCE

Bowey, A. M., Thorpe, R., Mitchell, F. H. H., Nichols, G. Gosnold, D., Savery, L. and Hellier, P. K. (1982), *Effects of Incentive Payment Systems: United Kingdom 1977–80*, research paper no. 36, Department of Employment, September.
Brayfield, A. H. and Brockett, W. H. (1955), 'Employee Attitudes and Performance', *Psychological Bulletin*, vol. 52, no. 5, pp. 396–424.
Brown, W. (1962), *Piecework Abandoned*, London: Heinemann.
Burns, T. and Stalker, G. M. (1961), *The Management of Innovation*, London: Tavistock.
Dalton, M., Collins, D., Roy, D. (1946), 'Restrictions of Output and Social Cleavage in Industry', *Applied Anthropology*, 5, no. 3, pp. 1–14.
Department of Employment (1977), *Employment News*, June/July, no. 45.
Glasser, B. G. (1978), *Theoretical Sensitivity: Advances in Methodology of Grounded Theory*, Mill Valley, Calif. Sociology Press.
Grinyer, P. H. and Kessler, (1967), 'The Systematic Evaluation of Methods of Wage Payment', *Journal of Management Studies*, 4, no. 3, pp. 309–20.
HMSO (1975), *The Attack on Inflation*, Cmnd 6151, London: HMSO.
HMSO (1976), *The Attack on Inflation – the Second Year*, Cmnd 6507, London: HMSO.
HMSO (1977), *The Attack on Inflation After 31st July 1977*, Cmnd 6882, London: HMSO.
HMSO (1978), *Winning the Battle Against Inflation*, Cmnd 7293, London: HMSO.
International Labour Office (1951), *Payments by Results*, Geneva: ILO.
Loveridge, R. (1980), 'What Is Participation?: a Review of the Literature and Some Methodological Problems, *British Journal of Industrial Relations*, 18, 3 November, pp. 297–317.
Lupton, T. and Bowey, A. M. (1974), *Wages and Salaries*, London: Penguin, 2nd edn, (1983) London: Gower Press.
Lupton, T. and Gowler, D. (1969), *Selecting a Wage Payment System*, Engineering Employers Federation: Research Paper no. III, London.
Marchington, M. and Loveridge, R. (1979), 'Non-Participation: the Management View?', *Journal of Management Studies*, 16, no. 2, May, pp. 139–70.
Marriot, R. (1957), *Incentive Payment Systems: a Review of Research and Opinions*, London: Staples Press.

Milward, N. (1968), 'Family Status and Behaviour at Work', *Sociological Review,* 16, no. 2, July, pp. 147-64.
Opsahl, R. L. and Dunnette, M. D. (1966), 'The Role of Financial Compensation in Industrial Motivation', *Psychological Bulletin,* 66, no. 2, pp. 94-118.
Ramsay, H. (1977), 'Cycles of Control: Worker Participation in Sociological and Historical Perspective', *Sociology,* 11, no. 3, pp. 481-506.
Roethlisberger, F. J. and Dickson, W. J. (1936), *Management and the Worker,* Cambridge, Mass.: Harvard University Press.
Rohner, R. P. (1977), 'Advantages of the Comparative Method of Anthropology', *Behavioural Science Research,* 12, pp. 117-44.
Roy, D. (1952), 'Quota Restriction and Gold-bricking in a Machine Shop', *American Journal of Sociology,* 57, pp. 427-42.
Roy, D. (1954), 'Efficiency and the "Fix"', *American Journal of Sociology,* 64, pp. 255-66.
Smith, H. W. (1975), *Strategies for Social Research: the Methodological Imagination,* Englewood Cliffs, NJ: Prentice—Hall.
White, M. (1981), *Payments Systems in Britain,* London: Gower Press.
Yetton (1979), 'The Efficiency of a Piecework Incentive System', *Journal of Management Studies,* 16, October, no. 3, pp. 253-69.

CHAPTER 6: PAYMENT SCHEME PROCESSES

Bowey, A. M. (1978), 'Productivity Motivation and Reward', *Human Resources Management,* Autumn, Australia.
Bowey, A. M., Thorpe, R., Mitchell, H. H., Nichols, G., Gosnold, D., Savery, L. and Hellier, K. (1982), *Effects of Incentive Payment Systems: United Kingdom, 1977-80,* Department of Employment Research Paper, no. 36, September.
Bryant, D. (1979), 'The Psychology of Resistance to Change', *Management Services,* March.
Buchanan, D. A. (1979), *The Development of Job Design Theories and Techniques,* Farnborough: Saxon House.
Chequer, G. (1976), 'Maximising Returns for Compensation', *Personnel Journal,* vol. 55, no. 7, July.
Child, J. (1972), 'Organisation Structure, Environment and Performance: the Role of Strategic Choice', *Sociology,* 6, no. 1, January, pp. 1-22.
Cochrane, D. J. (1983), 'The Development of a Productivity Scheme for a High Variety Workload at British Waterways Board', Glasgow University, unpublished thesis, Master of Engineering Degree.
Ditton, J. (1979), 'Baking Time', *The Sociological Review,* vol. 27, no. 1, February.
D'Aprix, R. (1982), 'The Oldest (and Best) Way to Communicate with Employees', *Harvard Business Review,* September/October.
Feeney, E. J. (1979), 'Management in Action: Conventional Compensation Plans: a Hindrance to Productivity', *Cost and Management* (Canada), 53, no. 5, September/October.
Fox, A. (1974), *Man Mismanagement,* London: Hutchinson.

Galbraith, J. (1967), *The Goals of an Industrial System*, Boston, Mass.: Houghton Mifflin.
Gedge, R. (1979), *Works Management and Productivity*, London: Heinemann.
Handy, C. B. (1976), *Understanding Organisations*, London: Penguin.
Jessup, G. (1977), 'The Case for Shop Floor Participation', *Department of Employment Gazette*, June.
Judson, A. S. (1982), 'The Awkward Truth about Productivity', *Harvard Business Review*, September/October.
Katz, D. (1964), 'The Motivational Basis of Organisational Behaviour', *Behavioural Science*, 9, pp. 134–46.
Keenan, E. (1980), 'The Study of the impact of Financial Incentive Schemes on Management Styles and Employee Attitudes, Motivation and Performance in Local Government', Glasgow University, unpublished thesis, Master of Business Administration Degree.
Lawler, E. E. and Bullock, R. J. (1978), 'Pay and Organisational Change', *The Personnel Administrator*, May.
Lawrence, P. R. and Lorsch, J. W. (1969), *Organisation and Environment: Managing Differentiation and Integration*, Homewood, Illin.: Irwin.
Lewin, K. (1948), *Resolving Social Conflicts; Selected Papers on Group Dynamics*, New York: Harper.
Lupton, T. and Bowey, A. M. (1974), *Wages and Salaries*, London: Penguin, 2nd edn (1983), London: Gower Press.
Lupton, T. and Gowler, D. (1969), *Selecting a Wage Payment System*, Engineering Employers' Federation, Research Paper no. 111, London.
Lupton, T. (1966), *Management and Social Sciences*, Harmondsworth: Penguin.
Mayo, E. (1949), 'Hawthorne and the Western Electric Co' in *The Social Problems of an Industrial Civilisation*, Boston, Mass.: Routledge.
Morse, N. C. and Reiner, E. (1956), 'The Experimental Change of Major Organisational Variable', *Journal of Abnormal and Social Psychology*, 52, pp. 120–29.
Parris, J. (1979), 'Diagnosing your Organisation's Problems,' *Management Services*, September.
Parris, J. (1979), 'Is There a Future for Work Study, Organisation and Methods', *Management Services*, November.
Peters, T. J. and Waterman, R. H. (1982), *In Search of Excellence: Lessons from America's best run companies*. New York: Harper & Row.
Roy, D. (1952), 'Quota Restriction and Goldbricking in a Machine Shop', *American Journal of Sociology*, vol. 57, pp. 427–42.
Roy, D. (1953), 'Efficiency and "The Fix": Informal Intergroup Relations in a Piecework Machine Shop', *American Journal of Sociology*, vol. 67, pp. 225–60.
Roy, D. (1953), 'Work Satisfaction and Social Reward in Quota Achievement: an Analysis of piecework incentives', *American Sociological Review*, vol. 18, no. 4.
Thorpe, R. (1982), 'New Incentive Schemes: Failures of Design and Some Pointers for Improvements', *Management Services*, no. 4, April.
Vroom, V. H. and Yetton, P. W. (1973), *Leadership and Decision Making*, University of Pittsburgh Press.

White, M. (1978), 'Pay Methods: Attitude Surveys, Diagnosis and Change', *Personnel Review*, vol. 7, no. 4, Autumn.
Whyte, A. (1978), Environment and Social Behaviour ch. 14, in Tajfel and Frazer (eds.), *Introducing Social Psychology*, Harmondsworth: Penguin.
Whyte, W. F. (1955), *Money and Motivation: an Analysis of Incentives in Industry*, New York: Harper & Row.
Work Research Unit (1982), 'Meeting the Challenge of Change: Guidelines for the Successful Implementation of Changes in Organisations', Department of Employment, London: HMSO.

CHAPTER 7: DEGENERATION OF PAYMENT SYSTEMS

Bowey, A. M., Thorpe, R., Mitchell, F. H. H., Nichols, G., Gosnold, D., Savery, L. and Hellier, P. K. (1982), *Effects of Incentive Payment Systems, United Kingdom, 1977–80*, Research Paper no. 36, Department of Employment, September.
Ditton, J. (1979), 'Baking Time', *The Sociological Review*, vol. 27, no. 1, February.
Lupton, T. (1963), On the Shop Floor, London: Pergamon Press.
Marchington, M. (1977), 'Worker Participation and Plant Wide Incentive Schemes', *Personnel Review*, vol. 6, no. 3, Summer.
National Board of Prices and Incomes (1968), *Payment by Results Systems*, Cmnd 3627, London: HMSO.
Roy, D. (1952), 'Quota Restriction and Goldbricking in a Machine Shop', *American Journal of Sociology*, vol. 57, pp. 427–42.
Roy, D. (1954), 'Efficiency and "The Fix": Informal Intergroup Relations in a Piecework Machine Shop', *American Journal of Sociology*, vol. 63, pp. 255–66.
Sowden, G. (1979), 'An Industrial Relations Case Study', BA in Business Studies, final year dissertation: Kingston Polytechnic, School of Business.
Thorpe, R. (1980), 'The Relationship Between Payment Systems, Productivity and the Organisation of Work', unpublished MSc thesis, Strathclyde Business School
Turner, B. and Leach, D. (1982), 'Payment for No Results', *Management Today*, May, pp. 58–61.
Wilson, S. (1953), Unpublished PhD. thesis, University of Manchester Department of Economics and Social Science.
Yetton, P. (1979), 'The Efficiency of a Piecework Incentive System', *Journal of Management Studies*, 16, October, no. 3. pp. 253–69.

Subject Index

Added value schemes, 25–31
adjustments, in productivity measurements, 57–8
aggregation, and errors in productivity measurement, 57
allowances, and payment scheme degeneration, 217–23

bonus payments, see incentive bonus schemes
boredom, 162–3, 188–90
Bullock Report (1976), 142
Bullock Report (1977), 21, 180

cluster analysis, in payment schemes classification, 120–2
Coalbridge Engineering Ltd., 225–37, 256
Complex Productivity Ratios, 40–2
composite implementation indices, 138–48
consultation, and incentive payment schemes, 136–44; extent, 152–4; importance of, 155–60; role, 160–73
context, and payment scheme results, 122–31; and variables, 150–60; see also perspective
contingency theories, 66–72, 126, 133, 152

data, in productivity measurement, 61–5
Department of Employment, 76, 88, 91n, 101–2, 234
detraction of effort, and productivity measurement, 57
discretionary decisions, in productivity measurement, 59
Domestic Appliances Ltd., 242–4

dynamism, and productivity measurement, 49–50

effectiveness, in productivity measurement, 47–9, 73–8
efficiency, in productivity measurement, 47
employees, perception of payment schemes, 165–9; see also employees, female; employees, male
employees, female, and incentive payments, 5–6; and fatigue, 8; see also workers, manual; workers, non-manual
employees, male, and incentive payments, 5–6; see also workers, manual; workers, non-manual

fatigue, and low productivity, 7–8
fixed collective bonus schemes, 117
flat-rate payment schemes, 177–8; see also PBR

'Hawthorne Effect', 8
Hillend Colliery, see National Coal Board
Human Relations Management, 8–9

incentive bonus schemes, and productivity, 8–16; 59–60; success of, 100–22; see also individual schemes
individual performance, and productivity measurement, 58
Industrial Fatigue Research Board, 254
Integrated Systems Productivity Model, 45

Subject Index

Jaguar cars, 256
job enrichment, 17–22
John G. Kincaid Ltd., 207–14, 256

Latex Fabricators, 247–9
'Law of Variable Proportions', 40–1
Longshore Dock Company, 241–2

management, pay and, 31–4; perspective of, 55, 164–5; and market conditions, 133–5; theory, 150; and Social Science, 159
Manchester Business School, 11, 15, 42
methodology, used in study, 93–9
motivation, analysed, 5–35; and payment system design, 35–9; and consultation, 160–3
multiple incentive payment schemes, 136
multivariate analysis, in payment scheme classification, 130–1

National Agreement of the Engineering Industry, 227
National Association of Colliery Overmen, Deputies and Shotfirers, 197–8, 210
National Board for Prices and Incomes (1968), 236
National Coal Board, 193–207, 244–7
National Power Loading Agreement, 193
National Union of Mineworkers, 193–4, 198, 200
negotiation, and incentive payment schemes, 139–43; see also consultation
New Earnings Survey (1977), 25, 93
normative contingency theory, 69–72, 152

objectives, in payment schemes, 79–85
organisational performance, evaluation of, 73–8

PBR (Payment by Results), 13–16, 178

PF consultation and negotiation, 152–5
participation, 21–2
Pay and Reward Research Centre, 90
payment scheme performance, 91–148
payment systems, analysed, 5–35; degeneration of, 215–53; see also incentive bonus schemes
performance, improvement analysed, 5–35; and productivity, 53; and incentive payment schemes, 91–148, see also productivity
performance related payment schemes, 178–80
'personal average' payment schemes, 229–30
perspective, and productivity measurements, 53–6; see also context
Positive Descriptive Contingency Theory, 66–9
processes, in payment system design, 149–214; see also individual processes
productivity, analysed, 5–35; measurement, 36–65; see also performance
Productivity Circles, in Kincaids, 209–14
proxy measures, in productivity measurement, 59

Rolls-Royce, 42

Scanlon Plan, 30–31
Shell Oil Company, 21
shortage of work, and productivity measurement, 58–9
Simple Productivity Ratios, 39–40
situation, and performance, 131–3; see also context
skill, and payment scheme performance, 135–6
Social Science Research Council, 76, 91n
strategy, and productive measurement, 50–3
Strathclyde Survey of Incentive Payment Systems, 225–6

Structure-Contingency Models, 66–9
System Productivity Measures, 42–7

Tavistock Institute of Human Relations, 164
technology, and change, 128
Total Productivity Measure, 36–7
transfer pricing, in productivity measurement, 60–1

unions, and participative payment schemes, 185

variable bonus schemes, 114–17, 119

Wage Payment Systems Research Team, 11
Western Electric Company, 8
Work Research Unit, 168
workers, manual, and incentive payments, 5–6; and productivity, 56–7
workers, non-manual, and incentive payments, 5–6

Name Index

Bahiri, S., and H. W. Martin, on productivity measurement, 45; see also Norma, R. G., and S. Bahiri
Bain, J. S., and R. Price, and white collar women, 88
Beeching, see Smith, E. and Lord Beeching
Bentley Associates, 26
Bobbitt, Jr., H. R., and J. D. Ford, and contingency theories, 67, 89
Bowey, Angela M., and system models, 75; and payment scheme performance, 91n; and 'scientific management', 165; and consultation, 168; on Kincaids, 207n, 208; et al., and incentive schemes, 104–5, 157, 225
Boyle, William, 213
Bryfield, A. H., and W. H. Crockett, and incentive schemes, 106
Brown, W., and incentive payment schemes, 106
Bryant, D., and consultation, 164
Buchanan, D. A., and management, 159
Bullock, R. J., see Lawler, E. E., and R. J. Bullock
Burgoyne, J., see Morris, J., and J. Burgoyne
Burns, T., and G. Stalker, on management systems, 9–10; and contingency theories, 67; and technological change, 128

Campbell, J. P., et al., and organisational effectiveness, 76
Child, J., and contingency theories, 16, 67, 89; and 'organisational goals', 150

Clarkson, J. P. E., and B. V. Elliot, on collapse of Rolls-Royce, 42
Cochrane, D. J., and management, 159
Collins, D., see Dalton, M., and D. Collins, and D. Roy
Connolly et al., and relativistic multiple constituency models, 75
Cox, B., on productivity measures, 45
Cradall, F. N., and L. M. Wooton, on productivity measurement, 53
Crockett, W. H., see Brayfield, A. H., and W. H. Crockett
Cunningham, Barton, and organisational effectiveness, 76

D'Aprix, R., and consultation, 153
Dalton, M., and D. Collins, and D. Roy, and incentive schemes, 106
Dickson, W. J., see Roethlisberger, F. J., and W. J. Dickson
Ditton, Jason, and saved time, 12; and consultation, 161; and payment systems, 217
Dorrian, Jim, 213
Dubin, R., and organisational performance, 74, 76
Duncan, R. B., and system models, 75
Dunnette, M. D., see Opsahl, R. L., and M. D. Dunnette

Eilon, S., see Teague, J., and S. Eilon
Elliot, B. V., see Clarkson, J. P. E., and B. V. Elliot
Etzioni, A., and organisational performance, 74
Evan, W. M., and system models, 75

Faraday, J. F., on productivity measurement, 36

Name Index

Fayol, H., and contingency theories, 67
Feidler, F. E., on managerial style, 55; and contingency theories, 67
Ferris, Bob, on productivity measures, 45; and payment scheme performance, 91n
Ford, J. D., *see* Bobbitt, Jr., H. R., and J. D. Ford
Fox, A., and consultation, 167
Frost, P., *see* Mahoney, T. A., and P. Frost

Galbraith, J., and contingency theories, 67; and 'organisational goals', 153
Gedge, R., and consultation, 160
Georgopolous, B. S., and A. Matjeko, and organisational effectiveness, 75
Glaser, B. G., and 'grounded theory', 137
Gluckman, M., and contingency theories, 67
Gold, B., on productivity measures, 43
Goldthorpe, J. H., and motivation patterns, 17
Gosnold, David, and payment scheme performance, 91n
Gowler, D., *see under* Lupton, T., and D. Gowler
Greiner, L. E., and productivity measurement, 52
Grinyer, P. H., and S. Kessler, and incentive payment schemes, 106

Haire, M., and productivity measurement, 52
Handy, C. B., and consultation, 167
Harrington, L. T., *see* Ingham, H., and L. T. Harrington
Hellier, Phil, and payment scheme performance, 91n
Herzberg, F., and motivation, 17
Hofer, C., and productivity measurement, 52
Hrebiniak, L. G., and power-oriented multiple constituency models, 75

Ingham, H., and L. T. Harrington, on productivity measures, 42

Jackson, Robert, 213
Jessop, G., *The Case for Shop Floor Participation*, 168
Judson, A. S., and consultation, 155

Katz, D., and consultation, 160; and R. L. Khan, and organisational performance, 73–5
Keeley, M., and social justice criteria, 76
Keenan, E., and management, 159
Kessler, S., *see* Grinyer, P. H., and S. Kessler
Khan, R. L., *see* Katz, D., and R. L. Khan

Lawler, E. E., and payment systems, 85; and consultation, 168; and Bullock, 155–6, 170
Lawrence, P. W., and J. W. Lorsch, on organisation design, 15; and management theory, 150
Leech, D., *see* Turner, B., and D. Leech
Legge, K., and contingency theories, 66, 69; *see also* Millward, N., and K. Legge
Lewin, K., and consultation, 157
Lorsch, J. W., *see* Lawrence, P. R., and J. W. Lorsch
Loveridge, R., *see* Marchington, M., and R. Loveridge
Lupton, Tom, and PBR, 11; and bonus payments, 59; and incentive schemes, 106, 217; and consultation, 157; and D. Gowler, 67, 69, 89, 107, 109, 113, 157; and A. M. Bowey, 89, 109, 157

McCann, Bob, 213
McCready, Bill, 214
Mahoney, T. A., and P. Frost, and system models, 75
Marchington, M., and participation, 21, 31, 142; and industrial relations, 224; and R. Loveridge, 142

Name Index

Martin, H. W., *see* Bahiri, S., and H. W. Martin
Marriott, R., and incentive schemes, 106
Maslow, A. H., and needs, 17
Matjeko, A., *see* Georgopolous, B. S., and A. Matjeko
Mayo, Elton, and worker fatigue, 7-8; and consulation, 161; and productivity and motivation, 254
Millward, N., and incentive schemes, 106; and K. Legge, 10
Minzberg, H., on productivity measurement, 48
Mitchell, Fanny, and payment scheme performance, 91n
Morris, J., and J. Burgoyne, on management development, 15
Morse, N. C., and E. Reimer, on consultation, 155

Nichols, Geoffrey, and payment scheme performance, 91n
Norman, R. G., and S. Bahiri, on financial ratios, 43; and Integrated Systems Productivity Model, 45

Opsahl, R. L., and M. D. Dunnette, and incentive payment schemes, 106

Parris, J., and management, 159
Pennings, J. M., on contingency theories, 66
Peters, T. J., and R. H. Waterman, and consultation, 168
Pfeffer, J., and G. R. Salancik, and power-oriented multiple constituency models, 75
Price, J. L., and organisational performance, 74
Price, R., *see* Bain, J. S., and R. Price

Ramsay, H., and worker participation, 142
Rawls, J., and social justice criteria, 76
Reimer, E., *see* Morse, N. C., and E. Reimer

Roethlisberger, F. J., and W. J. Dickson, on incentive schemes, 106
Rohner, R. D., and data bias, 95
Roy, Donald, and PBR, 11-12; and bonus payments, 59; and incentive schemes, 106, 217, 219-20, 239; and consultation, 161, 167; *see also* Dalton, M., and D. Collins, and D. Roy
Rucker, A. W., 26

Salancik, G. R., *see* Pfeffer, J., and G. R. Salancik
Savery, Lawson, and payment scheme objectives, 80n; and payment scheme performance, 91n
Scott, Bill, 208, 214
Seashore, S. E., *see* Yuchtman, E., and S. E. Seashore
Sheriff, P., and contingency theories, 67
Shreyögg, G., and contingency theories, 67
Silverman, D., and contingency theories, 68; and system models, 75
Smith, Sir Ewart on added value in productivity measures, 45; and 'triangulation', 95; and Lord Beeching, on productivity measures, 43-5
Sowden, G., and incentive bonus schemes, 228
Spray, S. L., and system models, 75
Stalker, G., *see* Burns, T., and G. Stalker
Steers, R. N., and organisational effectiveness, 76
Strasser, S., and goal-based models, 73-4, 76; and system models, 75

Taylor, John, 207n, 208
Teague, J., and S. Ellon, on productivity measurement, 37, 45
Thorpe, Richard, and 'skiving', 12; and productivity measurement, 37; and payment schemes, 83, 91n, 157, 217; and hierarchy, 153; and research, 174

Turner, B., and D. Leech, and manipulation of allowances, 239

Urwick, L., and contingency theories, 67

Vroom, V., and P. Yetton, and leadership, 15; and contingency theories, 67; and consultation, 155

Wabe, J. S., *et al.*, on productivity ratios, 42
Waterman, R. H., *see* Peters, T. J., and R. H. Waterman
Webster, F. A., and productivity measurement, 52–3
Weiss, C. H., and organisational performance, 74–6
White, M., and motivation, 17; and incentive payment schemes, 107, 119, 136

Whyte, W. F., and consultation, 156, 161
Wilson, S., on productivity measures, 45; and payment systems, 217
Wood, S., and contingency theories, 67
Woodward, Joan, and motivation, 9–10; and contingency theories, 67
Wooton, L. M., *see* Cradall, F. N., and L. M. Wooton

Yetton, P., and incentive payment schemes, 106, 219; *see also* Vroom, V., and P. Yetton
Yuchtman, E., and S. E. Seashore, and organisational effectiveness, 75

Zammuto, R. F., and productivity measurement, 36; and effectiveness, 73; and system models, 75–6

GPSR Compliance

The European Union's (EU) General Product Safety Regulation (GPSR) is a set of rules that requires consumer products to be safe and our obligations to ensure this.

If you have any concerns about our products, you can contact us on

ProductSafety@springernature.com

In case Publisher is established outside the EU, the EU authorized representative is:

Springer Nature Customer Service Center GmbH
Europaplatz 3
69115 Heidelberg, Germany

www.ingramcontent.com/pod-product-compliance
Lightning Source LLC
Chambersburg PA
CBHW031539230426
43749CB00025B/412